The Syntax of Sentential Stress

OXFORD STUDIES IN THEORETICAL LINGUISTICS

GENERAL EDITORS: David Adger, *Queen Mary College London*; Hagit Borer, *University of Southern California*

ADVISORY EDITORS: Stephen Anderson, *Yale University*; Daniel Büring, *University of California, Los Angeles*; Nomi Erteschik-Shir, *Ben-Gurion University*; Donka Farkas, *University of California, Santa Cruz*; Angelika Kratzer, *University of Massachusetts, Amherst*; Andrew Nevins, *Harvard University*; Christopher Potts, *University of Massachusetts, Amherst*; Barry Schein, *University of Southern California*; Peter Svenonius, *University of Tromsø*; Moira Yip, *University College London*

For a complete list of titles published and in preparation for the series, see pp 197–198.

The Syntax of
Sentential Stress

ARSALAN KAHNEMUYIPOUR

OXFORD
UNIVERSITY PRESS

OXFORD

UNIVERSITY PRESS

Great Clarendon Street, Oxford OX2 6DP

Oxford University Press is a department of the University of Oxford.
It furthers the University's objective of excellence in research, scholarship,
and education by publishing worldwide in

Oxford New York

Auckland Cape Town Dar es Salaam Hong Kong Karachi
Kuala Lumpur Madrid Melbourne Mexico City Nairobi
New Delhi Shanghai Taipei Toronto

With offices in

Argentina Austria Brazil Chile Czech Republic France Greece
Guatemala Hungary Italy Japan Poland Portugal Singapore
South Korea Switzerland Thailand Turkey Ukraine Vietnam

Oxford is a registered trade mark of Oxford University Press
in the UK and in certain other countries

Published in the United States
by Oxford University Press Inc., New York

British Library Cataloguing in Publication Data

Data available

Library of Congress Cataloging in Publication Data

Data available

Typeset by SPI Publisher Services, Pondicherry, India
Printed in Great Britain
on acid-free paper by
the MPG Books Group, Bodmin and King's Lynn

ISBN 978–0–19–921923–0 (Hbk.)
ISBN 978–0–19–921924–7 (Pbk.)

1 3 5 7 9 10 8 6 4 2

To Kamnoosh, Sabah and Soroosh

Contents

General Preface

The theoretical focus of this series is on the interfaces between subcomponents of the human grammatical system and the closely related area of the interfaces between the different subdisciplines of linguistics. The notion of "interface" has become central in grammatical theory (for instance, in Chomsky's recent Minimalist Program) and in linguistic practice: work on the interfaces between syntax and semantics, syntax and morphology, phonology and phonetics etc. has led to a deeper understanding of particular linguistic phenomena and of the architecture of the linguistic component of the mind/brain.

The series covers interfaces between core components of grammar, including syntax/morphology, syntax/semantics, syntax/phonology, syntax/pragmatics, morphology/phonology, phonology/phonetics, phonetics/speech processing, semantics/pragmatics, and intonation/discourse structure as well as issues in the way that the systems of grammar involving these interface areas are acquired and deployed in use (including language acquisition, language dysfunction, and language processing). It demonstrates, we hope, that proper understandings of particular linguistic phenomena, languages, language groups, or inter-language variations all require reference to interfaces.

The series is open to work by linguists of all theoretical persuasions and schools of thought. A main requirement is that authors should write so as to be understood by colleagues in related subfields of linguistics and by scholars in cognate disciplines.

In this monograph, Arsalan Kahnemuyipour explores the consequences of a particular architecture for the phonology/syntax interface: a multiple spell-out system where each spell-out point is sensitive to local "chunks" of syntactic structure. These chunks are identified as phases of the syntactic derivation, and the book argues that sentence stress can be predicted partly on the basis of these. The book also argues for a particular view of how the information-structure/syntax interface is organized, and builds a theory of the interaction of the two interfaces.

David Adger
Hagit Borer

Acknowledgements

This monograph is a revised version of my 2004 University of Toronto doctoral dissertation. As such, it owes immensely to the people who guided me through the writing of the thesis. In particular, I am most indebted to my supervisor Diane Massam and the other core members of my thesis committee, Elizabeth Cowper and Keren Rice, for their constant support and constructive feedback. The external examiner of my defense, Juan Uriagereka, encouraged me to get the thesis published and has been a source of support and inspiration ever since.

In addition to the individuals whose works are cited throughout the book, many others have helped me in shaping and reshaping the ideas that have led to this monograph in a more informal manner. First and foremost, I am grateful to Lisa Selkirk for reading my thesis shortly after it was completed and for engaging in an instructive (and ongoing) dialogue about many aspects of this work and its implications in other areas. Many thanks also to the following individuals who have influenced the present monograph, directly or indirectly, through comments and discussions: Gabriela Alboiu, Peter Cole, Rose-Marie Dechaine, Marcel den Dikken, Anna Maria Di Sciullo, Elan Dresher, Jila Ghomeshi, Shin Ishihara, Jaklin Kornfilt, Angelika Kratzer, Victor Manfredi, Martha McGinnis, Karine Megerdoomian, Ana Teresa Perez-Leroux, David Pesetsky, Milan Rezac, Norvin Richards, Yves Roberge, Simin Karimi, Lisa Travis, Michael Wagner, and many others at different conferences, workshops, and invited lectures. I am also grateful to the following individuals for their help with data: Karine Megerdoomian for Eastern Armenian, Bettina Spreng and Michael Wagner for German, Michael Barrie for English, Ana Teresa Perez-Leroux for Spanish, and Nick Pendar for Persian.

I would like to thank the following individuals at Oxford University Press: the two anonymous reviewers for their very valuable comments, the series editors David Adger and Hagit Borer for their support of the project, the linguistics editor John Davey for his patience and understanding, the copy-editor Peter Kahrel and the proofreader Francis Eaves-Walton for their careful work, and the production editor Elmandi du Toit for her help in the intense final stages of production.

On the personal side, I want to thank Sabah and Soroosh for bringing sheer joy to my life, for keeping me on the ground and for helping me maintain my sanity while challenging it everyday. Finally, I am forever grateful to Kamnoosh Shahabi for her unfailing love and support over the years and for helping me survive all the (often conflicting) demands of (academic) life. Without her, this book (and most other things) would not have been possible.

Arsalan Kahnemuyipour
Syracuse, May 2009

Abbreviations

1	first person
2	second person
3	third person
ABS	absolutive
ACC	accusative
AdjP	adjective phrase
AOR	aorist
BND	bounded
CLASSIF	classifier
CP	complementizer phrase
CSR	Contrastive Stress Rule
DP	determiner phrase
DUR	durative
D	determiner
ERG	ergative
Ez	Ezafe
FPA	Focus Projection Algorithm
FPR	Focus Prominence Rule
FS	focus stress
FUT	future
HT	head-terminal
IMPERF	imperfective
INSTR	instrumental
LA	lexical array
Lex	lexicon
LF	Logical Form
LOC	locative
NOM	nominative
NSR	Nuclear Stress Rule
PERF	perfective

PF	Phonological Form
PL	plural
PP	prepositional phrase
PRES	present
QR	Quantifier Raising
SEC	Strees Equalization Convention
SG	singular
Spec	specifier
SS	sentential stress
TP	tense phrase
VP	verb phrase

1

Setting the stage

1.1 Introduction

This monograph explores the nature of sentential stress (also known as nuclear stress), its manner of assignment, and its interaction with information structure. As such, it explores two independent yet interacting areas. On the one hand, it seeks a rule which determines the position of sentential stress in informationally neutral sentences. On the other hand, it attempts to capture the deviation from the default stress pattern and the complications that arise once the context of the uttered sentence is not informationally neutral.

The quest for a rule to determine the position of sentential stress, the most prominent word in a sentence, goes back at least to Newman's (1946) work on English stress. This rule, however, found its definitive expression in the generative literature in Chomsky and Halle's (1968) Nuclear Stress Rule. In the following two and a half decades, while problems with Chomsky and Halle's original proposal were noted and (slight) modifications were suggested, the proposed systems all shared one crucial property: they all involved a language-specific phonological rule applying to domains derived from syntactic structure (see ch. 2 for an overview of these phonological accounts). The need for a phonological rule to determine sentence stress was first challenged seriously by Cinque (1993). Cinque proposed that nuclear stress can be determined on purely syntactic grounds based on hierarchical structure, with cross-linguistic differences following from syntactic variations. Cinque's bold proposal had far-reaching empirical coverage but was later challenged by certain cross-linguistic stress facts (see ch. 3). In response to these problems and building on ideas by Schmerling (1976), Zubizarreta (1998) proposed a system for the calculation of nuclear stress which, like Cinque (1993), was purely syntactic but involved selectional considerations (to be elaborated in ch. 3) in addition to hierarchical structure. In doing this, Zubizarreta added another variable to the debate on sentential stress, namely, selectional considerations. With respect to the phonology–syntax debate, the present monograph sides with Cinque and Zubizarreta in suggesting that sentential stress is determined on purely syntactic grounds. Unlike Zubizarreta, however, I will provide several arguments against involving selectional considerations in the calculation of sentential stress and will show that stress can be read directly from hierarchical syntactic structure. I will show that with the correct formulation of the sentential stress rule, the problems raised for Cinque's system are overcome.

The relevance of information structure for sentence stress (or accent[1])— that the informationally most prominent word in a sentence (with non-neutral focus) receives primary stress—has been noted in various schools of linguistics, such as the Prague School (Daneš 1967) and Functionalism (Halliday 1967). This interaction was first formulated in the generative tradition in works by Chomsky (1971) and Jackendoff (1972), who argued that a provision beyond the Nuclear Stress Rule is required to ensure that nuclear stress falls on an element within a focused constituent if there is one. The interaction between information structure and sentential stress, however, led some scholars to reject a default sentential stress rule altogether. Bolinger (1958, 1972), for instance, argues adamantly against the need for a rule to determine sentential stress in neutral contexts. According to Bolinger, what speakers decide to highlight is not a matter of grammar but a matter of what they are trying to say in a specific context. Other scholars have taken the sentential stress/accent as the input to an algorithm which derives the focus structure of a sentence (Selkirk 1984, 1995; Rochemont 1986, 1998). The present monograph argues in favour of the existence of a default sentential stress rule (following, in spirit, Chomsky 1971, 1976; Jackendoff 1972). According to the system developed here, sentential stress is determined as a result of an interplay between two rules, one that is responsible for default stress and one that handles the interaction between focus structure and sentential stress.

The remainder of this chapter is organized as follows. In the second section, I discuss the theoretical framework in which this monograph is placed. I will then provide a summary of the proposals made in this book. The fourth section deals with the empirical scope of the present work. I end the chapter with an outline of the monograph.

1.2 Theoretical framework

This section lays out the syntactic framework adopted in this monograph. The present book is positioned within the general framework known as Minimalism (Chomsky 1995 and subsequent work), but within a particular

---

[1] A terminological distinction is sometimes made between "stress" and "accent", with the former being used for word stress and the latter for phrasal-level prominence (see e.g. Bolinger 1961). In this monograph the two terms are used interchangeably.

instantiation of it which is based on the idea of phases and multiple spell-out. Let us start with a brief and simplified review of this particular view of syntax.

1.2.1 *Minimalism*

The Minimalist Program (Chomsky 1993, 1995 and subsequent work) is a theory of grammar framed within the familiar approach in the generative tradition known as Principles and Parameters. The Minimalist Program is based on the working hypothesis that the faculty of language is an optimal (i.e. simple and economical) solution to design specifications. Every linguistic expression necessarily contains instructions to the performance systems which fall into two general types: articulatory—perceptual, and conceptual—intentional. Language, therefore, has to have at least one interface level for each performance system. The interface level providing instructions for the articulatory—perceptual system is commonly referred to as Phonological Form (PF) and the one providing instructions for the conceptual—intentional system as Logical Form (LF). No additional levels are necessary. Thus, optimal design would require that the levels of D-Structure and S-Structure from the Government and Binding theory (Chomsky 1981 and later) be dispensed with (see Chomsky 1995 and much of the Minimalist literature for the implications of this elimination of D- and S-Structure). The computational system or syntax accesses the lexicon (Lex) and generates linguistic expressions Exp = ⟨PF, LF⟩, which are shipped off to the PF and LF interface levels for phonological and semantic interpretation, respectively. This model is represented schematically in (1), with spell-out representing the point where Exp is shipped off to PF and LF.

(1)

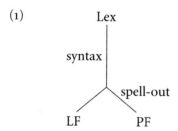

A property of the diagram in (1) which is crucial to the discussion in this monograph is that the paths to the two interface levels are separated—that is, LF and PF are connected via the only generative engine, the syntax. This is known as the Y-model of grammar, which is adopted in one way or another in the generative tradition.[2] One of the features of this model is that it disallows

---

[2] The Y-model is sometimes referred to as the inverted Y-model or the T-model.

the triggering of syntactic operations by purely phonological considerations. Nor does this model allow the PF and LF components to feed each other directly.

This is how a sentence is generated by the computational component or syntax in this framework. To reduce computational complexity, Chomsky suggests that the derivation does not access Lex at every point. Instead, the computational component makes a one-time selection of lexical items from Lex and puts it in a lexical array (LA). The computational component accesses the LA and has three operations available to generate a sentence. The first operation, indispensable for any language-like system, is Merge, which takes two syntactic objects (α, β) and puts them together to form K (α, β). The second operation is called Agree, an operation which establishes a relation (agreement, case checking, etc.) between a lexical item α and a feature F in some restricted domain. The third operation Move combines Merge and Agree in that in addition to establishing an Agree relation between α and F, it takes a phrase determined by F, P(F), and merges it in the specifier of α. Move is therefore more complex than its subcomponents Merge and Agree or even a combination of both because it also involves determining which phrase needs to be merged. Therefore, optimal design leads us to expect that Merge or Agree pre-empts Move.[3] These operations continue on the lexical items until the lexical array is exhausted and the sentence is shipped off to LF and PF for semantic and phonological interpretation, respectively.

In his later work, Chomsky (2000, 2001) makes a modification to the above system by introducing the notion of phases and multiple spell-out (see also Uriagereka 1999).[4] According to this view, the lexical array LA is selected in a phase-by-phase manner.[5] The same operations of Merge, Agree, and Move apply. Syntactic structure, however, is sent off to PF and LF in chunks in a phase-by-phase manner. In a derivation involving a phase-defining head, the complement of the phasal head is sent to PF and LF for interpretation. To illustrate this, consider the configuration [XP [H YP]] with H a phase-defining

---

[3] The preference of Merge over Move is used to account for certain empirical facts whose discussion would take us far afield from our purposes (see e.g. Chomsky 2000, 2001).

[4] While the idea of phase-by-phase spell-out reduces computational complexity, it was proposed for mainly empirical reasons. The details are beyond the scope of this monograph, but in short, in a sentence like *There is a possibility that proofs will be discovered*, given the preference of Merge over Move, if all the lexical items of the sentence were available in the LA, then we should never get the movement of *proofs* to the Spec-TP position in the lower clause but rather the merge of the expletive *there* in that position, rendering the given sentence ungrammatical. Under the multiple spell-out story, the expletive is not in the lexical array of the lower phase, thus making movement of *proofs* possible.

[5] To be more precise, the lexical array LA for the whole clause is taken from the Lex, and then a phase-worth of lexical items is taken from LA.

head. In this configuration, YP is the spelled-out constituent, referred to in this monograph as the SPELLEE. This system leads to the Phase Impenetrability Condition defined in (2).

(2) Phase Impenetrability Condition   (Chomsky 2000: 108)
    In phase a with head H, the domain of H is not accessible to operations outside a; only H and its edge are accessible to such operations.

If we apply (2) to our configuration [XP [H YP]], given that H is a phasal head, only XP and H should be accessible to operations outside the domain. In particular, YP is inaccessible to such operations.

A question arises as to what constitutes a phase. Chomsky (2000) suggests that phases are propositional, "either a verb phrase in which all theta roles are assigned or a full clause including tense and force" (p. 106). He concludes that only CP and transitive vP are phases. In particular, neither TP nor unaccusative/passive VP is a phase (p. 107). The latter assumption about unaccusative/passive verbs, as opposed to transitive or unergative ones, not inducing phasal boundaries will be crucial to the system of stress assignment developed in this monograph.[6]

This brief review of the minimalist program and the notion of phases and multiple spell-out should be sufficient for our purposes here. In this monograph, this particular conceptualization of how syntactic derivation proceeds will be used to account for the way sentential stress is assigned, in a manner to be summarized in section 1.4 and elaborated in the following chapters. To end this section, however, we need to look briefly at another syntactic framework employed in this monograph, namely, Kayne's (1994) antisymmetry. It is worth noting that while the Minimalist Program and Kayne's antisymmetry are probably ultimately compatible, they are independent frameworks and assuming one by no means necessitates assuming the other.[7]

---

[6] Sometimes the crucial distinction is described in terms of strength: CPs and transitive vPs are called strong phases, while unaccusative/passive vPs are called weak phases. The important point is that syntactic structure is transferred to PF and LF only at the point of a strong phase. For the sake of simplicity, I will avoid the terms strong and weak and use "phase" to refer to what is known as "strong" phase in the other classification. Weak phases, which by definition do not induce transfer to PF/LF, will be considered non-phases.

[7] While the question of the compatibility of Minimalism and Kayne's antisymmetry is open for further investigations, the aspects of the two frameworks adopted in this monograph are compatible. The one modification to Kayne's system that seems to be crucial for the Minimalist Program is to allow multiple specifiers. (For a suggestion as to how Kayne's system can be modified minimally to allow multiple specifiers, see Cinque 1996.)

1.2.2 *Antisymmetry*[8]

Kayne (1994) develops a theory which derives the linear ordering of elements from hierarchical structure. In particular, he suggests that asymmetric c-command invariably maps onto linear precedence. This particular proposal leads to a very specific theory of word order: complements must always follow their associated head and specifiers and adjoined elements must always precede the head; in other words, right adjunction is disallowed.[9] One consequence of Kayne's theory of antisymmetry is that the head parameter is dispensed with. Traditionally, the difference between the word order in an SVO language such as English and an SOV language such as Persian was accounted for by attributing different settings for the head parameter in the two languages. Thus, English would be a head-initial language, while Persian, for example, would be a head-final language. In Kayne's system, the difference can no longer be stated in these terms, except for descriptive purposes. Both language types start off as SVO and the surface order difference is the result of syntactic movement.

Building on Kayne (1994), other scholars (notably Cinque 1996, 1999, 2000, 2002, 2004 and others working in his framework) have extended the idea that the merge order of elements, from arguments to adjuncts, is identical across languages. Under this view, all elements are merged according to a universal hierarchy and any cross-linguistic variation in word order must be explained via applications of the operation Move. In this monograph, I will adhere to a weaker version of this view, according to which the relative order of elements in different languages is predetermined, but parametric variation across languages for the exact merge position of a particular element is allowed (see the discussion of manner adverbs in ch. 4).

After this overview of the theoretical framework adopted here, we are now ready to consider a summary of the main proposals made in this monograph.[10]

1.3 Summary of main proposals

With respect to the assignment of sentential stress, the central thesis of the present work is that the position of sentential stress is determined syntactically

---

[8] In this brief review of Kayne's (1994) theory of antisymmetry as it pertains to this monograph, I abstract away from technical details.

[9] In fact, under Kayne's view, the distinction between specifiers and adjuncts is lost. This characteristic of his system is not crucial to the present monograph.

[10] It is worth noting that while the system developed in this monograph for the assignment of sentential stress crucially depends on the above assumptions, most of the arguments made against previous accounts of sentential stress are made in their own terms and do not rely on these assumptions.

and that cross-linguistic differences in this respect follow from syntactic variations. In particular, I propose that the sentential stress rule is a rule that applies
in a phase-based manner. Following Chomsky, I take CPs and (transitive) vPs
to constitute phases. In particular, passive/unaccusative vPs are crucially taken
not to induce phasal boundaries. Recall that according to the theory of phases
and multiple spell-out, when the derivation reaches a phase, the (syntactic)
complement of the phase head is shipped off for phonological interpretation. I
called this syntactic chunk the SPELLEE (see 1.2.1). According to my proposal,
stress is assigned to the highest element (the phonological border) of the
SPELLEE; details to be elaborated in chapter 4. The phase-based system of
stress assignment is shown schematically in (3).[11]

(3)

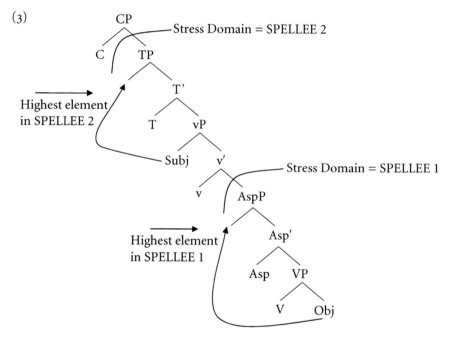

Let us briefly review some consequences of my proposal with respect to
the assignment of sentential stress, to be discussed in detail throughout the
monograph. The claim that the position of sentential stress is determined in
a purely syntactic manner allows us to account for certain contrasts within

---

[11] In addition to the present monograph, the incorporation of the notion of phases and multiple
spell-out in the computation of sentential stress has recently been explored in differing but interesting
ways by several other scholars (see e.g. Adger 2003; Wagner 2005; Kratzer and Selkirk 2007). For
practical reasons, in this monograph, I will not attempt to provide a comprehensive review of these
recent additions to the literature on the topic, and leave an evaluation of these competing approaches
to sentential stress for future research.

a language and cross-linguistically based on the syntactic properties of the corresponding constructions. For instance, a crucial property of the system proposed here is that sentential stress is not sensitive to the underlying syntactic position of a constituent, thus elements which move out of the stress domain for independent syntactic reasons may escape sentential stress. This property will be used to explain the difference in stress behaviour of specific and non-specific objects in some languages (see ch. 4) and the difference in the stress behaviour of wh-words across languages (see ch. 5).

The particular phase-based theory of sentential stress presented in this monograph enables us to provide a straightforward account for a wide range of cross-linguistic stress facts as well as for the apparently peculiar behaviour of unaccusative/passive sentences with respect to sentential stress (see 4.8). This proposal will also offer a straightforward account of the iterative nature of sentential stress (see 4.10). To the extent that the present monograph is successful in providing an account of these facts, it offers further support for the notion of phases and multiple spell-out, originally proposed on independent grounds. Another interesting consequence of the thesis that sentential stress is assigned in a purely syntactic manner is that it can then be used as a yardstick to evaluate different proposed accounts for syntactic constructions across languages. These implications are discussed further in the concluding chapter of the book.

In addition to the sentential stress rule which determines sentential stress in focus-neutral sentences, another rule—the focus stress rule—is proposed in this book to account for the interactions between information structure and sentential stress in languages with prosodic manifestations of focus. Sentential stress is thus a result of an interplay between the default sentential stress rule and the focus stress rule (in the spirit of proposals by Chomsky 1971 and Jackendoff 1972). Both the focus stress rule and the sentential stress rule apply to a sentence involving a focused constituent marking (different) elements to receive the corresponding stresses, with the element marked by the focus stress rule receiving higher prominence. Thus, if there is a conflict between the two rules, the constituent determined by the focus rule receives primary stress, with the one determined by the default sentential stress rule receiving secondary stress (see ch. 5 for details).

According to this view of the interaction between information structure and sentential stress, it is focus structure that feeds sentential stress, rather than the other way around. In other words, focus is seen as a syntactic property with semantic and phonological implications. In taking this view, I argue against proposals which have either attempted to dispense with the sentential stress rule altogether or have used sentential stress as input to an algorithm which derives the focus structure of a sentence, namely, the focus projection algorithm (Selkirk 1984, 1995; Rochemont 1986, 1998).

In the theory proposed in this monograph, in line with the Y-model of grammar presented above, the relation between syntax and phonology is unidirectional, always from syntax to phonology. I therefore argue against syntactic operations being triggered by prosodic considerations, as proposed, for instance, by Zubizarreta's (1998) p-movement for Romance languages. Such movements, which bear some syntactic–semantic effects, are purely syntactic and the stress facts follow from the same general principles proposed for other languages. PF-movement (if any) is restricted to those operations that have no bearing for syntax/semantics (see also Wurmbrand 2003), and based on the system of stress assignment proposed here, should have no interaction with sentential stress.

With this brief review of the main proposals made in this book, we are almost ready to delve into the details. Before doing that, however, a few comments are in order with respect to the empirical scope of this monograph.

1.4 Empirical scope

This monograph differs in an important way from previous (syntactic) accounts of sentential stress as regards the database it attempts to account for. Previous accounts set off their investigation with the assumption that sentential stress is essentially the application of the phrasal stress rule to the highest possible level, that is, the clause. As a result, they considered data from different syntactic phrases—the noun phrase (DP), the verb phrase (VP), the prepositional phrase (PP), the adjective phrase (AdjP), and the adverb phrase (AdvP)—and attempted to provide the one generalization that would correctly predict stress in all these phrases. Thus, for instance, Cinque (1993) proposed a rule to account for stress in sentences as well as other phrases and even compounds. This is by no means a necessary assumption. In fact, there is reason to believe that this may be the wrong assumption. While in dealing with stress at the sentence level (as compared to stress within the word), it has been observed that there is little variation from a cross-linguistic perspective, the same does not appear to hold true of lower phrasal levels.

Let us start by looking at variation at the clause level, where cross-linguistic variation appears to be very limited. It has been observed, for instance, that in simple transitive sentences, it is the object that receives stress in SVO, SOV and VSO languages, as exemplified in (4) by English and Spanish for SVO, Persian and Ondarroa Basque for SOV, and Scottish Gaelic for VSO (see also

Cinque 1993; Zubizarreta 1998; Arregi 2003, among others).[12] Throughout this monograph, stress is marked by underlining. Degrees of stress, if shown, are marked by numbers below the underlining.

(4) a. SVO languages
      English: John read a book.
      Spanish: Juan leyó un libro.   (Zubizarreta 1998)
      'Juan read a book.'

   b. SOV languages
      Persian: Ali ye ketaab xarid.
                Ali a book   bought
      'Ali bought a book.'

      Ondarroa Basque: Jonek   liburu   irakurri ban. (Arregi 2003)
                       Jon-ERG book-ABS read   had
      'Jon read the book.'

   c. VSO languages
      Scottish Gaelic: chuala Seònag Calum.   (Adger 2002)
                       heard   Seonag Calum
      'Seonag heard Calum.'

Once we turn to the lower phrasal levels, there appears to be much more variation. This is indicated in the stress pattern of the DP in Persian given in (5), as compared to its English counterpart (marked in the translations) (see also Nespor 1999; Kahnemuyipour 2003).

(5) a. in   do   ketaab
        this two book
        'these two books'

   b. ketaab-e Ali
      book-Ez   Ali
      'Ali's book'

---

[12] As pointed out by an anonymous reviewer, this generalization may be challenged by the behaviour of stress in a language such as Hungarian, which seems to place the main stress on the verb in a focus-neutral sentence (see Szendrői 2003). There seems to be disagreement on whether Hungarian neutral clauses are SVO (Kálmán 1985; Kenesei 1986; Marácz 1989; among others) or VSO (Kiss 2002). Nevertheless, if it is shown clearly that focus stress is not involved, stress on the verb poses a challenge to this generalization, which is a cornerstone of all syntactic accounts of sentential stress including the one developed in this monograph. I leave a closer examination of the Hungarian facts and the question of their ultimate compatibility with the theory developed here to future research. If syntactic theories of sentential stress are on the right track, then any deviation from the abovementioned generalization should also follow from the syntax of the particular language.

c. ketaab-e qermez
   book-Ez   red
   'red <u>book</u>'

d. gush-<u>dard</u>
   ear-ache
   '<u>ear</u>ache'

In (5a), we see an example of a DP involving a demonstrative and a numeral. Stress falls on the demonstrative in Persian rather than on the head noun, as it does in English (see also Lazard 1992).[13] Example (5b) shows that in a possessive construction, stress falls on the possessor DP in Persian, rather than on the head noun, the observed pattern in English. In (5c), we see that in a noun phrase containing an adjective, stress falls on the adjective in Persian, contrary to the English counterpart. Finally, (5d) illustrates that, unlike English, in Persian stress falls on the head noun in a compound.[14, 15]

The above examples indicate that there is more cross-linguistic variation in domains lower than the clause, which makes it difficult to maintain the generalizations made for these lower domains across languages (e.g. Cinque's 1993 proposal based on depth of embedding or Arregi's 2003 Comp and Spec generalizations based on branching). We will see in this monograph that the generalizations made in the literature, based on data from all the different phrasal levels, run into trouble at the clause level in the face of data from languages other than the ones they were originally proposed for. This monograph considers a different cross-section of the data. It only deals with stress facts at the sentence level. In doing so, it introduces the possibility that, contrary to traditional assumptions, the system governing sentential stress may be different from that of lower phrasal levels. The question this monograph addresses, therefore, is which position(s) in the sentence receive(s) stress. As briefly discussed above, it is proposed that the highest element in the SPELLEE receives stress. This element can be an X^0 head or an XP phrase. If the XP contains a single lexical word, it receives stress. If, on the other hand, the

---

[13] Some speakers report equal stress on the demonstrative and the head noun. The stress on the demonstrative, which is at least equally strong, is the issue here.

[14] Kahnemuyipour (2003) provides an account of the Persian facts in a phrasal phonology framework which covers the lower phrasal levels as well as the clause. See chapter 2 for arguments against a phrasal phonology account of sentential stress.

[15] Similarly to Persian, Scottish Gaelic has post-nominal adjectives and possessors and stress falls on the adjective or possessor (see Adger 2003). Eastern Armenian appears to provide an even more robust contrast to English in this respect. According to Megerdoomian (2007), in Eastern Armenian the adjective is pre-nominal as in English, but main stress is on the adjective, unlike English, where the head noun receives main stress. This lack of correspondence between word order and prosody in the noun phrase poses a challenge to any syntactic account of these facts, once more highlighting the difference between stress at the clause level as opposed to lower levels.

XP has a complex structure (e.g. a possessive DP), this monograph makes no claim as to which word in this phrase receives stress. Similarly, it makes no claims as to which part of a compound receives stress. This difference in approaching the data, I believe, is a crucial first step in arriving at the right generalizations with respect to sentential stress.[16]

In this section, we established that this monograph will only deal with clausal-level stress facts by providing some justification for this methodological choice. As for the empirical coverage of stress facts at the sentence level, it will consider the core database discussed in the literature for Germanic (English and German) and Romance (French, Spanish, and Italian) and will complement it with facts from Persian as well as some unexplained facts in the previously studied languages. There is also a brief discussion of (Eastern) Armenian in chapter 4.

1.5 Outline

The following chapters are organized as follows. Chapter 2 deals with phonological accounts of sentential stress—that is, those accounts which employ a language-specific phonological rule that applies to the syntactic structure of a phrase or clause to determine stress. It will be shown that these accounts suffer from an overgeneration problem and also run into trouble in the face of certain stress facts, in particular the behaviour of stress in passive/unaccusative sentences.

Chapter 3 discusses the previous syntactic accounts of sentential stress, focussing on Cinque (1993), the first influential analysis of this type, and Zubizarreta's (1998) revision of Cinque's system. While Cinque's system relies solely on the hierarchical structure of the clause, Zubizarreta employs an additional module which is sensitive to selectional constraints (to be elaborated in ch. 3). Several empirical and conceptual arguments against these systems will be provided.

In chapter 4, the main proposal of this monograph with respect to the assignment of sentential stress in focus-neutral sentences is laid out. The phase-based system of stress assignment is introduced and its application is illustrated through several examples. It will be shown that this proposal for the assignment of sentential stress has wider empirical coverage than the

---

[16] I am not ruling out the possibility of the system proposed here for the clause level being extended to cover lower-level phrases. Any such extension, however, would require an expansion of the notion of phases to include levels other than vP and CP and positing complex (independently motivated) syntactic structures which would derive the desired results in a wide range of languages. I am not pursuing this option in this monograph (see also the discussion in ch. 6).

previous accounts, as it can handle stress facts accounted for in the other accounts, and in addition certain stress facts which pose problems for the previous accounts. The new proposal does not run into the empirical and conceptual problems of the previous syntactic accounts.

Chapters 2 to 4 deal with the assignment of stress in focus-neutral sentences, that is, sentences in which no constituent is informationally more prominent than any other. Chapter 5 deals with the interaction between information structure and sentential stress. An additional component, namely the focus stress rule, will be introduced to handle such interactions. It will be shown that sentential stress is determined in an interplay between the default sentential stress rule and the focus stress rule. The proposed system conforms to the Y-model of grammar. Thus, the direction of the syntax/prosody interactions are expected to be always from syntax to prosody and not the other way around. In Chapter 5, arguments against Zubizarreta's prosodically motivated movement will be provided and an alternative way of handling the facts will be proposed. Moreover, as noted above, some linguists have attempted to dispense with the Nuclear Stress Rule in favour of a system which takes sentential stress/accent as input and derives the focus structure of a sentence from it. A critical review of Selkirk's (1995) influential focus projection algorithm concludes chapter 5. It will be shown that a system like the one proposed in this monograph, which employs two independent rules, one for the assignment of default sentential stress and another one for the interaction between information structure and sentential stress, fares better with the stress facts.

Chapter 6, the concluding chapter, summarizes our findings and discusses some implications, remaining questions, and possible directions for future research.

2

Sentential stress:
phonological accounts

2.1 Introduction

In this chapter we will consider phonological accounts[1] of sentential stress,
according to which some language-specific phonological rule determines
which word receives the highest prominence in the sentence.[2] We limit our
scope here and in chapters 3 and 4 to sentences with neutral focus, in other
words, sentences in which no constituent is informationally more prominent
than any other.[3] Chomsky and Halle (1968), for instance, develop a system
which assigns the main stress to the last word in an English phrase/sentence.
This, as we will see below, correctly accounts for sentence-final stress in (most)
English sentences. Taking Chomsky and Halle's Nuclear Stress Rule (NSR) as
a starting point, Halle and Vergnaud (1987) extend their metrical grid theory
to build a system within the Principles and Parameters framework which not
only accounts for English sentential stress, but also allows for the observed
cross-linguistic variation in this respect. Works within the general framework
of Phrasal (Prosodic) Phonology fall under the same type of approach. While
this framework has mostly been used to account for certain segmental phonological phenomena sensitive to syntactic structure, some scholars have used
it to account for phrasal or sentential stress (see e.g. Nespor and Vogel 1986,
1989; Hayes and Lahiri 1991; Nespor 1999; Hsiao 2002; Kahnemuyipour 2003).

---

[1] "Phonological" may be a bit of a misnomer. As we will see below, all these accounts rely on
syntactic structure in their mechanism for calculating phrasal/sentential stress. The crucial point,
however, is that all of them involve an additional language-specific phonological rule which comes
in at the end and assigns stress to a specific element.

[2] Most of the analyses discussed in this and the following chapter attempt to account for stress
in phrases in general. What we are interested in, however, is their extension to account for stress at
the sentence level. The goal of this monograph, as stated in chapter 1, is to develop a system that
correctly predicts which position(s) in a sentence receive(s) stress. (See ch. 1 and the discussion in 1.4
for justification of this position.)

[3] We will see in chapter 5 that the context in which such a sentence is uttered is known as the out-
of-the-blue context. This type of context if often identified by the context question *What happened?*
(but see 5.3 for some intricacies).

According to this approach, by allowing different choices of stress assignment for different prosodic domains, one can account for sentential stress in different languages.

We will see that these phonological approaches fail to account for certain empirical data which seem to beg for a structural analysis. In addition, they suffer from the problem of overgeneration: they allow stress patterns that have not been attested cross-linguistically. As noted in chapter 1, for instance, it has been observed that in simple transitive sentences, it is the object that receives stress in SVO, SOV, and VSO languages (see also Cinque 1993; Zubizarreta 1998; Arregi 2003, among others).[4] The universality of the claim about stress on the object is based on work on sentence stress mostly in SVO and SOV languages, but also on typological work pointing in the same direction. Based on data from Uralic, Altaic, and some Indo-European languages, Dezsö (1974, 1977, 1982) suggests that in SOV languages the usual place of sentence stress is the position preceding the verb, whereas in SVO languages it is after the verb. Kim (1988) confirms and extends Dezsö's findings by looking at a much wider range of languages. (See also Donegan and Stampe 1983, who confirm this correspondence between language type and sentence stress by comparing the SOV Munda family with the SVO Mon-Khmer family.) There is no report in the literature, on the other hand, of an SVO, SOV, or VSO language with stress on the subject in a transitive sentence uttered in a neutral context.[5]

Some examples of sentential stress in simple transitive sentences in SVO, SOV and VSO languages are given in (1), repeated from chapter 1.

(1)   a. SVO languages
        English: John   read   a book.
        Spanish: Juan   leyó   un libro.   (Zubizarreta 1998)
              'Juan read a book.'

      b. SOV languages
        Persian: Ali   ye ketaab   xarid.
                 Ali   a book   bought
                 'Ali bought a book.'

---

[4] As we will see in chapter 4, when more elements such as adverbials are introduced in the sentence, some variation is observed with respect to which element receives stress. This variation will be used in chapter 4 as an argument for a structural account of sentential stress. In other words, it will be argued that the object receives stress by virtue of its syntactic position and not its objecthood per se. Otherwise we would expect the stress to fall on the object invariably, that is, irrespective of the presence or absence of an adverbial.

[5] See n. 12 in chapter 1 for a possible challenge to these generalizations.

Ondarroa Basque:	Jonek	liburu	irakurri	ban.	
	Jon-ERG	book-ABS	read	had	
	'Jon read the book.'				(Arregi 2003)

c. VSO languages

Scottish Gaelic:	chuala	Seònag	Calum.	(Adger 2002)
	heard	Seonag	Calum	
	'Seonag heard Calum.'			

These examples reveal two important characteristics of sentential stress. On the one hand, they show variation across languages from a directional perspective. That is to say, while in the SVO and VSO languages stress is on the final constituent in the sentence, in an SOV language it is not. More importantly for our purposes, they show that regardless of word order, stress falls on the same element, namely, the object.[6] We will see in this chapter that nothing in the phonological accounts predicts such restrictions on the position of sentential stress.

This chapter is organized as follows. I start with a brief overview of Chomsky and Halle's (1968) Nuclear Stress Rule and Halle and Vergnaud's (1987) incorporation of this rule in their metrical grid theory. I then discuss Kahnemuyipour (2003) as an illustrative example of a Phrasal (Prosodic) Phonology account of sentential stress. I will show that these approaches are too powerful in that they allow for certain stress patterns that are not attested cross-linguistically. I end the chapter by providing additional data which pose a problem for any phonological account of sentential stress.[7]

2.2 The Nuclear Stress Rule: Chomsky and Halle (1968)

To account for stress on the last word in an English phrase, Chomsky and Halle (1968) propose a rule known as the Nuclear Stress Rule (NSR) given in (2).[8]

---

[6] This is an overly simplified statement solely used for descriptive purposes in this chapter. The correct characterization of the position of stress assignment will be refined throughout the book (see also n. 4).

[7] The purpose of this chapter is not to provide a comprehensive review of all phonological accounts of sentential/phrasal stress, but rather to review briefly a representative sample of these works to highlight the problems they all encounter.

[8] This is the original formulation of the rule, which they later modify. This simpler formulation is sufficient for our purposes.

(2)   Chomsky   and   Halle's   NSR

$$\overset{1}{V} \rightarrow 1 \quad / \quad [_A \ X \ \overset{1}{V} \ Y \ — \ Z]$$

where Z contains no $\overset{1}{V}$ and A ranges over major categories such as NP, VP, S.

The effect of the NSR in (2) is to assign primary stress to the last stressed vowel in a phrase. The NSR is taken to be a cyclic rule. That is to say, assuming labelled brackets for the structure of phrases, the rule first applies within the innermost brackets and then these brackets are erased, then the rule applies within the innermost brackets of the remaining structure, and so on. Chomsky and Halle further assume that every application of the NSR within a cycle reduces all other stress values by 1. We are now ready to apply the rule to a simple English SVO sentence. An example is given in (3).

(3)   2   3   1   2nd cycle
                      2   1   1st cycle
           1   1   1   word stress
    [_S John [_VP saw   Mary]].

At the word level, each word is stressed. In the first cycle, the NSR applies to the VP, assigning 1-stress to the rightmost word, the object, and reducing the stress on the verb to 2. In the second or S cycle, the NSR assigns 1-stress to the rightmost stressed word, i.e. the object, and the other stresses are reduced one level. The result is shown in (3) which correctly predicts primary stress on the object and secondary stress on the subject.

The NSR, as formulated by Chomsky and Halle, is an English-specific rule. Thus, to account for the non-final stress on the object in an SOV language such as Persian, one would have to come up with a rule specific to that language. In fact, nothing in their system predicts a correlation between language type and nuclear stress. Therefore, one might expect to have different NSRs for English, German, Persian, French, Spanish, Scottish Gaelic, etc. The system is thus missing a generalization within and even across language types. We will return to this issue below.

We have seen that Chomsky and Halle's NSR can account for the sentence-final stress in English. Recall from the data in (1), on the other hand, that stress is not sentence-final across languages. Thus, if one wants to maintain a directional phonological rule to determine sentential stress and yet allow for cross-linguistic differences, one would need to incorporate some parameters into the system which would then allow different settings in different languages. This is essentially what Halle and Vergnaud (1987) do in their metrical grid theory (originally proposed by Liberman 1975). While the metrical grid theory was originally designed to account for the cross-linguistic variation in word stress, Halle and Vergnaud extend it to account for the Nuclear Stress Rule in English. Their proposal is the topic of the following section.

2.3 The metrical grid theory: Halle and Vergnaud (1987)

Halle and Vergnaud (1987) propose using the metrical grid theory and a set of parameters to account for the considerable cross-linguistic variation of stress patterns in words. Within metrical grid theory, stress is represented on a separate autosegmental plane by means of metrical constituent structure. Let us look at how the metrical constituent structure is formed.

The autosegmental line for stress is a sequence of potentially stress-bearing positions conventionally marked by asterisks on line 0. Constituents are formed on this line according to language-specific parameter settings, discussed below. Each constituent includes a head which is projected to line 1, representing stressed positions. The projected heads make up one or more constituents on line 1, with the head projecting to line 2. This stacking of constituent structures gives rise to columns of projection of various heights, with the height of the column reflecting the degree of the prominence of the corresponding position. By constructing constituents and marking their heads according to rules of constituent construction and language-specific parameter settings, one can account for the considerable variety of word-stress patterns in the languages of the world.

The parameters used by Halle and Vergnaud to account for the word stress patterns are the following:[9] ±BND (depending on whether a constituent on a certain line is bounded or unbounded), ±HT (depending on whether a constituent is head-terminal or not), left or right (depending on the direction of headedness for +HT constituents), left-to-right or right-to-left (depending on the direction the constituents are constructed). Thus, for instance, the word-stress pattern of Maranungku (a Daly language spoken in Australia), where the stress falls on odd syllables with the main stress on the leftmost one, is obtained by the parameter settings given in (4a). The resulting grid structure for a five-syllable word is shown in (4b), where constituents are marked on every line by brackets and the head of the constituent is marked by an asterisk on the line above it. On line 0, all the syllables which are potentially stress-bearing are marked by an asterisk. Given that the parameters

---

[9] This is a simplified representation of their theory. A few more parameters such as extrametricality are in fact introduced to account for the stress pattern in some languages. Such details are irrelevant to the point being made here and are thus left out.

are set to left-to-right and +BND on this line, constituents are constructed from left to right counting every two asterisks. The final remaining asterisk constitutes a constituent on its own. The head parameter on line o is set to left, hence the asterisks on line 1. On line 1, on the other hand, the constituent is unbounded, therefore the three asterisks constitute a single constituent, which is left-headed, marked accordingly on line 2. The grid structure in (4) correctly accounts for Maranungku word stress with stress on odd syllables and main stress on the leftmost one.

(4)　a. parameter settings for Maranungku
　　　　Line o: +HT, +BND, left, left-to-right
　　　　Line 1: +HT, −BND, left

　　　b. Grid structure for a five-syllable Maranungku word

```
    *                line 2
(*    *    *)         line 1
(*  *)(*  *)(*)       line o
CVCVCVCVCV           a five-syllable word
```

Different choices of the aforementioned parameters account for other word-level stress patterns observed cross-linguistically. The crucial point is that the above parameters, plus a few more not discussed in this overview, are all needed to cover all the attested word-stress patterns across languages (see Halle and Vergnaud 1987; Hayes 1995; and references cited therein).

　Halle and Vergnaud extend their word-stress theory to account for the stress pattern of phrases and sentences in English. Thus, they propose the following system for constructing the grid structure for lines 3 and above to incorporate into their theory Chomsky and Halle's (1968) Nuclear Stress Rule, which predicts stress on the rightmost element in English sentences (see section 2.2 for more details).

(5)　Halle and Vergnaud's Nuclear Stress Rule (1987: 264)

　　　a. Parameter settings on line N (N greater than or equal to 3) are [−BND, +HT, right]

　　　b. Interpret boundaries of syntactic constituents composed of two or more stressed words as metrical boundaries.

　　　c. Locate the heads of line N constituents on line N + 1.

　In applying the system in (5) to English phrases and sentences, one has to observe the principle of the cycle (thus starting from the innermost syntactic constituent working outwards). Consider the application of this system to

a simple English SVO sentence such as *John saw Mary*. The syntactic constituents have been marked by square brackets in (6). Each (stressed) word
on line 3 has received an asterisk. To observe the principle of the cycle, we have
to start with the innermost syntactic constituent, the VP. This constituent is
composed of two stressed words, thus according to (5b) its boundaries have
to be interpreted as metrical boundaries, yielding the metrical brackets on
line 3. Following (5c), the head of this metrical constituent is marked on line
4 according to the parameters in (5a). The same rules apply to line 4 resulting
in the grid structure in (6).

(6)   *   line 5
         (*)   line 4
         *   (*   *)   line 3
         S   V   O
      [John [saw <u>Mary</u>]]

The grid structure in (6) correctly predicts main stress on the object *Mary*,
but fails to account for the higher prominence of the subject *John* in comparison to the verb *saw*. To account for the relatively higher prominence of
the subject, Halle and Vergnaud propose the Stress Equalization Convention
in (7).

(7)   Stress Equalization Convention (Halle and Vergnaud 1987: 265)
      When two or more constituents are conjoined into a single higher-level
      constituent, the asterisk columns of the heads of the constituents are
      equalized by adding asterisks to the lesser column(s).

Applying the Stress Equalization Convention (SEC) in (7) to the sentence
in (6) would lead to the new grid structure given in (8). This is due to the fact
that when the VP and the subject are conjoined to form the whole sentence,
we need to equalize the asterisk columns before applying the NSR. The grid
structure in (8) correctly predicts main stress on the object and secondary
stress on the subject.

(8)   *   line 5
         (*   *)   line 4
         *   (*   *)   line 3
         S   V   O
      [<u>John</u> [saw <u>Mary</u>]]
         2   1

The parametric nature of Halle and Vergnaud's NSR has the benefit of
allowing us to account for sentential stress in other languages. Take the case of

Persian, an SOV language with main stress on the object. The relevant example is repeated from (1b).

(9)   Ali   <u>ye ketaab</u>   xarid.
      Ali   a book   bought
      'Ali bought a book.'

To account for the stress on the object in (9), we need to change the NSR proposed for English minimally. The only change we need to make to Halle and Vergnaud's NSR for English in (5) is to take the parameter setting on line N (N greater than or equal to 3) to be [−BND, +HT, left]. If we take the constituents to be left-headed in Persian, as opposed to the right-headed English, we get the grid structure in (10).

```
(10)                 *                line 5
          (          *        )       line 4
          *          (*      *)       line 3
          S          O       V
         [Ali   [ye ketaab   xarid]].
```

The grid structure in (10) correctly predicts main stress on the object. It is worth noting here that the SEC has been intentionally left out of the picture, as it would lead to a wrong prediction: main stress on the subject and secondary stress on the object. The resulting grid structure is shown in (11). In Persian, just like English, on the other hand, primary stress falls on the object and secondary stress on the subject.

```
*(11)     *                          line 5
         (*          *        )       line 4
          *          (*      *)       line 3
          S          O       V
         [Ali   [ye ketaab   xarid]].
          2           1
```

We are thus left with a conundrum. On the one hand, we would like to have something like the SEC to account for different degrees of stress in an SVO language like English. On the other hand, the SEC would result in the wrong prediction for even the main stress in an SOV language like Persian. What we appear to need is different parameter settings for different lines. This is not allowed in the Halle and Vergnaud system for lines 3 and above, but is essentially what is done in the Phrasal Phonology framework, to which we will turn in section 2.4. Let us put this problem aside for now and focus on Halle and Vergnaud's Nuclear Stress Rule.

The crucial problem with Halle and Vergnaud's Nuclear Stress Rule, as for any phonological account of sentential stress, is that in looking at the sentential stress pattern of different languages, we are not confronted with the same range of possibilities found at the word level. Take the case of a transitive sentence in an SOV language, setting aside secondary stress for now and focussing on main stress. Of the three logical possibilities shown in (12), only (12b) has been reported in the literature.[10] In (12), I have also shown how Halle and Vergnaud's system allows for all the three logical possibilities.

(12)   H&V's system and the logical possibilities for main stress in an SOV language

    a. *S̲ O V: unattested
       Parameter settings on line N (N ≥ 3) [−BND, +HT, left] +SEC

    b. ✓S O̲ V: attested
       Parameter settings on line N (N ≥ 3) [−BND, +HT, left] −SEC

    c. *S O V̲: unattested
       Parameter settings on line N (N ≥ 3) [−BND, +HT, right] ±SEC

The unattested pattern in (12a), with the main stress on subject, is achieved by assuming a left-headed constituent and the application of the SEC, in other words, the metrical grid structure given in (11) above. The attested pattern in (12b) is the Persian pattern, which can be captured by assuming left-headed constituents and no SEC.[11] Finally, the unattested pattern in (12c) is allowed for by assuming a parameter setting like English for an SOV language.[12] Whether we assume the SEC or not has no bearing on main stress in this case.

The illustration in (12) clearly demonstrates that Halle and Vergnaud's system fails to account for the limited sentential stress patterns found in SOV languages. Of the three possibilities in (12) allowed for by Halle and Vergnaud's system, only one is attested. This is unlike word stress for instance, where all the three logical possibilities of main stress in a three-syllable word are

[10] Recall that we are crucially dealing with focus-neutral sentences only, the only context the NSR is meant to account for. The effects of focus on sentence stress will not be discussed until chapter 5.

[11] As noted above, while this parameter setting captures the primary stress facts, it presents a problem with respect to secondary stress. We put this problem aside here.

[12] We will see in chapter 4 that the stress pattern in (12c) is found in (some) SOV languages (e.g. Persian) when the object is specific. We will provide a structural account for this fact. This has no bearing upon the argument here. If anything, it provides further support for a structural (as opposed to a phonological) account of sentential stress. To account for such instances under the phonological approach outlined above, one would need to allow for construction-specific parameter settings within a single language, an undesirable move.

attested across languages. The same case made for SOV languages in (12) can also be made for SVO languages. There is nothing in Halle and Vergnaud's system, for example, that would disallow an SVO language with the same constituent structure and direction of branching as English but with the following parameter settings on line N ≥ 3 : −BND, +HT, left. This would predict stress on S in a transitive SVO sentence as shown in (13). Line 3 is the same as the English example discussed above. The constituent is left-headed, thus the asterisk above V on line 4 with the Stress Equalization Convention adding an asterisk above the subject. The left-headed constituent is marked on line 5.

(13)   *   line 5
       (*   *   )   line 4
       *   (*   *)   line 3
       S   V   O

The grid structure in (13) would predict an SVO language with primary stress on the subject and secondary stress on the object in focus-neutral sentences. Such a language does not exist. The cases in (12c) and (13) are especially revealing. They point to a correlation between the direction of headedness and the direction of branching, such that a right-branching language like English has its head parameter set to 'right' (see Cinque 1993 for a discussion of this issue).[13] Such dependence on structure is unexpected in the phonological frameworks discussed in this chapter.

In applying Halle and Vergnaud's system to account for sentential stress in a Persian SOV sentence, where main stress is on the object and secondary stress on the subject, we faced a problem. On the one hand, if we left out the SEC, we would not be able to account for secondary stress at all. On the other hand, if we included it, primary stress would be wrongly predicted on the subject. It was noted that allowing different directional rules on different lines would resolve the problem. While such variability is not allowed in Halle and Vergnaud's system, it is perfectly legitimate in another phonological framework to which we turn below. There have been several attempts within the general framework known as Phrasal/Prosodic Phonology to account for stress at the phrasal and sentential levels. In the next section we look at Kahnemuyipour (2003) as a representative example of this type of approach to sentential stress.

---

[13] In the system developed in this monograph, we will dispense with such directional parametric variations with respect to the assignment of nuclear stress. Variations, if any, follow from syntactic differences among languages.

2.4 Phrasal phonology and sentential stress

In the previous sections we looked at two phonological approaches to sentential stress. The other major phonological treatments of sentential stress fall within the general framework known as Phrasal Phonology (e.g. Selkirk 1980a, b, 1981, 1984, 1986; Nespor and Vogel 1982, 1986). It has been long observed that some phonological rules appear to be sensitive to syntactic structure in one way or another. To account for such interactions between phonology and syntax, Phrasal Phonology adopts an indirect approach in which: (1) mapping rules derive phrasal domains from morphosyntactic constituents; (2) phonological rules then apply with reference to these phrasal domains. The hierarchically organized prosodic domains are the phonological word, the phonological phrase, the intonational phrase, and the utterance. These prosodic domains are derived from syntactic constituents via mapping rules that are schematically represented in (14).

(14)   *Syntax*   *Prosodic Hierarchy*
       Utterance   →   Prosodic Utterance
       (Root) clause   →   Intonational Phrase
       XP   →   Phonological Phrase
       X^0 →   Phonological Word

There is a vast body of literature on the relevance of these domains for segmental phonological phenomena. A few linguists have utilized them to serve as domains for the assignment of stress (for the level of prosodic word, see Dixon 1977a, b; Selkirk 1980a, b; McCarthy and Prince 1993; Peperkamp 1997, among others; for higher levels, see Nespor and Vogel 1986; Hayes and Lahiri 1991; Nespor 1999; Hsiao 2002; Kahnemuyipour 2003, among others). For illustration purposes, let us consider Kahnemuyipour (2003), a case where Phrasal Phonology has been used to account for stress as high as the sentence level.

In his account of stress in Persian, Kahnemuyipour (2003) uses the following settings for the assignment of stress in different prosodic domains defined by Phrasal Phonology: rightmost at the phonological word level, leftmost at the phonological phrase level, and rightmost at the intonational phrase level. In addition to these settings, an algorithm is required for the mapping of prosodic phrases from syntactic constituents. Kahnemuyipour (2003) follows Selkirk's (1986) end-based approach, assuming that in Persian the left edge of a syntactic constituent is aligned with the left edge of a prosodic domain (for details see Kahnemuyipour 2003).

We can see the application of Kahnemuyipour's (2003) system to a Persian SOV sentence in (15). At the phonological word level, prominence is right-most, thus an asterisk at the top of the final syllable/vowel of each (stressable) Persian word. Kahnemuyipour assumes left-edge alignment of a phonological phrase with a syntactic phrase in Persian. Therefore, a left bracket is placed to the left of each syntactic constituent, resulting in a bracket to the left of the DP object (where the left edge of the VP and the object DP coincide) and a bracket to the left of the DP subject. The right brackets are determined in a manner that would respect the exhaustivity and nonrecursivity principles, which ensure that all prosodic constituents are parsed while disallowing nested brackets.[14] The result is the phrasal constituents marked on the Phonological Word line. Prominence is leftmost at the phonological phrase level, hence the asterisks on the Phonological Phrase line. Finally, at the Intonational Phrase level, prominence is rightmost, leading to the asterisk on the highest line, the Intonational Phrase line in (15).

(15)
```
              *                    Intonational Phrase
     *        *                    Phonological Phrase
    (*)    (  *       *)           Phonological Word
     S        O       V
   [Ali   [ye ketaab  xarid]]
    Ali    a book     bought
```

The grid structure in (15) correctly predicts primary stress on the object in a simple SOV sentence in Persian. This analysis has the added benefit of correctly accounting for secondary stress on the subject, without facing the problem posed by Halle and Vergnaud's account in this respect. Recall from section 2.3 that in Halle and Vergnaud's system, we had to use the Stress Equal-ization Convention to account for secondary stress in English. Meanwhile, we noted that the same type of rule would make wrong predictions, even for primary stress, for an SOV language like Persian. Thus we had to leave out the SEC for Persian, which then left the secondary stress facts unaccounted for.

By parameterizing the direction of headedness as well as the direction of alignment of a phonological phrase with a syntactic phrase, one could account for the stress facts in a language like English. Let us assume, for instance, that in English, prominence is rightmost at both the phonological and intonational

---

[14] For a more detailed discussion of these constraints, see Kahnemuyipour (2003) and references cited therein.

phrase levels.[15] In addition, phonological phrases are aligned with the right edge of a syntactic XP. The result of this phrasing is illustrated for a simple SVO sentence in (16). The right brackets are placed to the right of the object DP (where the right edge of the VP and object DP coincide) and to the right of the subject DP. The left brackets are added while respecting exhaustivity and nonrecursivity. The asterisks are placed in accordance with the rightmost setting of prominence at both levels in English. The grid structure in (16) correctly predicts the primary and secondary stress facts in English.

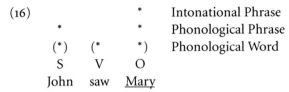

We have shown that the Phrasal Phonology account outlined in this section fares better than Halle and Vergnaud (1987) in the face of cross-linguistic data. However, as we will see below, it suffers from the same problem, namely, overgeneration.[16] The Phrasal Phonology approach allows for certain stress patterns not attested across languages. Nothing in the system, for instance, would disallow a language with the same settings for the levels of phonological word and phonological phrase as Persian but a leftmost stress at the intonational phrase level. This would be an SOV language that consistently puts sentential stress on the subject in focus-neutral sentences, an unattested case (see 15). Unlike variation at the word level, the cross-linguistic variation of sentential stress is much more restricted than any of the above phonological accounts would allow.

In addition to the overgeneration problem, certain stress facts seem to beg for a syntactic account. These facts have been a major motivation to try to find an analysis which is sensitive to syntactic structure. While these facts will be discussed in more detail in the following chapters, we will consider them briefly in the next section for the sake of completeness.

2.5 Empirical facts against phonological accounts

We have seen so far that the phonological accounts of sentential stress are too powerful in that they predict some stress patterns that are not attested

---

[15] Word-level stress in English, a much more complicated issue, is irrelevant to the point being made here.

[16] In fact, by allowing different settings on every line, it allows for far more possibilities, thus leading to a more severe case of overgeneration.

across languages. In this section we consider a different kind of problem for these phonological accounts. There are some empirical data, even within a single language, which defy any phonological approach to sentential stress. It has been observed, for instance, that in passive and unaccusative sentences uttered in out-of-the-blue contexts, primary stress falls on the subject (see Selkirk 1984, 1995; Rochemont 1998; Zubizarreta 1998; Legate 2003, among others). This is illustrated in the examples in (17). The example in (17a), which will be used throughout this book, is from Legate (2003), the rest being from Rochemont (1998).[17, 18]

(17)   a. <u>My bike</u> was stolen. (Context: What happened yesterday?)
       b. <u>A letter</u> arrived for you today.
       c. <u>A strange man</u> came into my office.
       d. <u>The bulb's</u> fused.
       e. <u>Your eyes</u> are red.
       f. <u>Some new legislation</u> was announced today.

To account for the facts in (17) in a phonological framework, we would need to have parameter settings which are construction dependent, an undesirable outcome. Take the Phrasal Phonology framework for instance. With both the phonological and intonational-phrase-level stresses set as rightmost in English, we were able to account for primary stress on the object. These settings would wrongly predict stress on the verb for the examples in (17). The grid structure for (17a) under these settings is given in (18).

(18)   *   Intonational Phrase
              *   *   Phonological Phrase
            (*)   (*)   Phonological Word
             S   V
         [My bike   [was stolen]].

The right edge of the VP and the right edge of the subject DP impose the right brackets shown on the Phonological Word level. Completing the bracketing and applying the rightmost stress rules at the different levels results in the grid

---

[17] Rochemont (1998) also provides some exceptional cases where the stress on the verb rather than the subject appears to be preferred in some passives or unaccusatives. He suggests that some additional pragmatic factors may be responsible for the behaviour of these problematic cases. The problem lies, it seems, in the correct characterization of an out-of-the-blue context. In other words, speakers tend to attribute contexts to certain utterances which makes the elicitation of the out-of-the-blue pattern difficult (see chapter 5).

[18] The example in (17e) exhibits stress on the subject under the more salient stage-level reading of *red*. There is difference in the behaviour of stress between sentences involving stage-level as opposed to individual-level predicates. This issue will be taken up in chapter 5.

structure in (18), with primary stress wrongly predicted on the verb. The same can be extended to the other examples in (17).

To account for primary stress on the subject, we would need to change the Intonational Phrase rule to leftmost solely for such constructions. Such a condition does not follow naturally in the Phrasal Phonology framework. In a system where the only relevant syntactic information is phrasehood (i.e. being XP as opposed to X^0), there is no principled reason why these as opposed to the other constructions require a different setting. The Nuclear Stress Rule, as originally proposed by Chomsky and Halle (1968) or as revised by Halle and Vergnaud (1987), faces the same type of problem. Essentially, it would predict stress on the last word in the sentence, contra the facts in (17). The facts in (17) strongly point to a syntactic account of sentential stress. We will return to these facts and syntactic approaches to account for them in chapters 3 and 4. We will note that the same pattern is observed in Persian unaccusatives, with the subject receiving the main stress of the sentence. Kahnemuyipour's (2003) Phrasal Phonology account of Persian stress, which had stress at the intonational-phrase level as rightmost, would face a problem accounting for stress on the subject in Persian unaccusative sentences. Once again, one would have to stipulate the intonational phrase level stress to be leftmost only in the case of unaccusative sentences: an undesirable result.

2.6 Conclusion

In this chapter we have looked at phonological approaches to sentential stress. All of these approaches have in common a language-specific phonological rule that determines sentential stress. We have seen that by parameterizing this rule, either along the lines of Halle and Vergnaud (1987) or within the Phrasal Phonology framework, we can account for some cross-linguistic variation. Meanwhile, all these approaches suffer from the overgeneration problem in that they allow certain stress patterns not attested across languages. The restriction on the cross-linguistic variation of sentential (as opposed to word) stress is a surprise in the phonological frameworks. Moreover, we discussed some facts within a language, namely, the behaviour of passive and unaccusative sentences, that are extremely hard to capture under the phonological approaches. We will see in chapters 3 and 4 that syntactic accounts of sentential stress do not suffer from the overgeneration problem and provide a natural way of accounting for the unaccusative/passive facts.

To conclude this chapter, it should be noted that providing a syntactic account of sentential stress does not entail that all other phonological phenomena accounted for within a Phrasal Phonology framework can be reworked in purely syntactic terms. In fact, there are some reasons to believe that stress is distinct from other phonological processes in terms of the way it interplays with syntax. These include phenomena such as the interaction between sentential stress and information structure and scope. The debate between an indirect approach to the phonology/syntax interaction à la Phrasal Phonology and a direct one in which phonological rules can refer to syntactic structures directly is not a new one (see e.g. Cooper and Paccia-Cooper 1980; Kaisse 1985; Odden 1987, 1990; Rizzi and Savoia 1992 for a direct approach; and Selkirk 1980a, 1981; Nespor and Vogel 1986; Hayes 1989; Truckenbrodt 1995 for arguments against a direct approach). With the recent advances in syntactic theory and the introduction of phases and multiple spell-out, the debate has taken a new perspective. In a theory in which syntactic structure is sent off to PF in chunks in a phase-by-phase manner, the question is now whether phases can replace the prosodic domains used in Phrasal Phonology (see e.g. McGinnis 2001; Seidl 2001; Collins 2002). This monograph makes a contribution to this debate by providing a syntactic account of an apparently phonological phenomenon—namely, sentential stress—framed within a multiple spell-out system (see also Wagner 2005; Adger, 2003; Kratzer and Selkirk, 2007). In this monograph, however, I limit my scope to sentential stress and leave the possibility of extending this approach to other phonological phenomena for future research (see also the discussion in ch. 6).

3

Sentential stress: syntactic accounts

3.1 Introduction

In the previous chapter we looked at some phonological accounts of sentential stress. It was shown that these analyses suffer from two main problems. The first problem was referred to as the overgeneration problem; these accounts fail to capture the restrictions on the variety of sentential stress patterns found across languages. Cinque (1993), the first linguist to tackle this problem, argues for a purely syntactic account of sentential stress which explains the limited cross-linguistic variation in this respect. We start our examination of syntactic approaches to sentential stress by looking at Cinque's influential work. We will see that Cinque's system fails to overcome the second set of problems with the phonological accounts in that it fails to explain the behaviour of passive and unaccusative sentences with respect to sentential stress. Further conceptual and empirical problems with Cinque's system will also be presented. We will then move on to another influential account of sentential stress, namely Zubizarreta (1998). Zubizarreta's monograph can be divided into two parts. One part of her work deals with the interaction between prosody and focus, and will be taken up in chapter 5, where we discuss such interactions. The part of Zubizarreta's work that will be discussed in some detail in this chapter is her account of nuclear stress in focus-neutral contexts. She proposes a modularized Nuclear Stress Rule, which consists of a component sensitive to hierarchical constituent structure (her C-NSR) and another component sensitive to selectional ordering of constituents (her S-NSR). Using this modular system of stress assignment, Zubizarreta accounts for the core facts in Germanic and Romance languages as well as those which Cinque's system failed to capture. Several conceptual and empirical arguments against her modular system will be presented here. Finally, we will consider Legate's (2003) proposed revision to Cinque's system to capture the passive/unaccusative facts which Cinque's system failed to account for. We will see that her proposal introduces some new empirical problems. Meanwhile, as it relies crucially on a Cinque-style system, it inherits many of the other conceptual and empirical problems with Cinque's original proposal. To sum up, while a syntactic approach to sentential stress is the right approach in that it attempts to capture the stress facts without facing the overgeneration problem, it will be shown that all the syntactic accounts proposed so far face some other conceptual and empirical problems. In chapter 4, I propose a new syntactic account of sentential stress based on the notion of phases and multiple spell-out, which does not suffer from these problems.

3.2 Nuclear stress, a syntactic account: Cinque (1993)

Cinque (1993) starts off with an observation about previous generative treatments of phrasal and sentential stress (e.g. Chomsky and Halle 1968; Halle and Vergnaud 1987). He correctly points out that while all these approaches generally assume (surface) constituent structure as a fundamental determinant, they either implicitly or explicitly opt for the need for an additional language-specific phonological rule to account for phrasal/sentential stress. These so-called phonological approaches and their problems were discussed in chapter 2. Cinque questions the need for an additional phonological rule by pointing out the restriction on the variety of phrasal/sentential (as opposed to word) stress patterns across languages. We referred to this problem as the overgeneration problem in the previous chapter. Cinque sets out to develop a theory of sentential/phrasal stress that dispenses with a language-specific (phonological) rule and determines phrasal/sentential stress solely on the basis of surface syntactic constituent structure and general principles of grid construction using a refined version of Halle and Vergnaud's (1987) metrical grid theory.[1] Let us consider Cinque's theory in more detail.

The system proposed by Cinque to account for phrasal/sentential stress is given in (1).

(1)   Cinque's Stress System (1993: 244)

   a.   Interpret boundaries of syntactic constituents as metrical boundaries.
   b.   Locate the heads of line N constituents on line N+1.

---

[1] In fact, Cinque's goal is broader than phrasal and sentence stress and includes compound stress as well. I will limit the discussion to the application of his theory to sentential stress, the topic of this monograph. For a discussion of why I have chosen to differentiate sentential stress from other lower level phrasal and compound stresses, see chapter 1, section 1.4.

  c. Each rule applies to a maximal string containing no internal boundaries.

  d. An asterisk on line N must correspond to an asterisk on line $N-1$.

Let us look at the system in (1) more closely. Clause (1a) is very similar to Halle and Vergnaud's (1987) mechanism for the mapping of syntactic constituents to metrical boundaries (see (5b) in chapter 2). This provision is different from Halle and Vergnaud's counterpart, however, in a small but important way. In Halle and Vergnaud's system, only syntactic constituents composed of "two or more stressed words" would translate into a metrical boundary. In Cinque's system, a syntactic constituent consisting only of a single stressed word is sufficient. This simplification, as we will see below, is crucial for Cinque to obtain the correct result. Clause (1b) is a basic principle in constructing metrical grid structure (compare Halle and Vergnaud's (5c) in chapter 2). Clause (1c) is essentially the principle of the cycle, thus ensuring that the rules apply starting from the innermost syntactic constituent working outwards (see chapter 2). Clause (1d) is the condition that there be no gap in an asterisk column.

  To illustrate how the system works, consider Cinque's application of (1) to two abstract cases, one representing a right-branching structure (2a) and the other a left-branching one (2b). Both bracketed and tree structures are provided for the sake of clarity. In this illustration, A, B, and C are arbitrary syntactic maximal projections and the asterisks indicate the main stress of the words that constitute these projections.

(2) a. Right-branching structure b. Left-branching structure

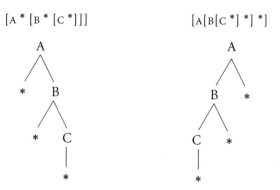

  Application of (1) to (2) gives rise to the grids in (3). Given the principle of the cycle (1c) we have to start with the innermost syntactic constituent (C), which is rightmost in (2a) and leftmost in (2b). The constituent consists

of only a single grid mark, a possibility crucial to Cinque's system but not allowed in Halle and Vergnaud's. This is how Cinque dispenses with the need for a right/left parameter to determine the head of the constituent. When (1b) applies to locate the head of this constituent, the asterisk on line 4 is placed right above the one on line 3, the only available position. On the next cycle (B), (1b) will again require that the head of this constituent be located on line 5. The innermost constituent of line 4, however, has two positions. Here is where (1d) comes into play and guarantees that the asterisk be placed in the same column as the asterisk on line 4. Re-application of the same procedure completes the grid structures as in (3).

```
(3)   a.              *       b.     *                line 6
          (.    .    *)          (*    .     .) line 5
          (.   (.    *))        ((*   .)      .) line 4
          (*   (*   (*)))      (((*)  *)     *) line 3
           A    B    C           C    B      A
```

At first glance, the procedure in (1) seems to suffer from the same deficiency as Halle and Vergnaud's Nuclear Stress Rule in that it seems not to be able to account for secondary stress on the subject in a simple SVO sentence such as *John saw Mary*. Recall that Halle and Vergnaud had to introduce a Stress Equalization Convention to address this problem. To resolve this problem, Cinque points out that a sentence consists of two non-intersecting constituents, the subject NP and the predicate VP. He then suggests that the subject NP and the predicate VP undergo two parallel cycles before joining at the sentence level. In other words, at the first cycle, there are two innermost constituents: one is the object NP (as part of the predicate) and the other one is the subject NP. By applying the stress system in this manner, the higher degree of stress on the subject as compared to the verb is correctly accounted for. This is shown for the simple sentence *John saw Mary* in (4).

```
(4)                       *        line 6
          (               *   )    line 5
          ( *      (      *   ))   line 4
         ((* )    ( *    ( *  )))  line 3
         [[John]  [saw  [Mary]]].
```

In the remaining discussion of Cinque's stress system, we put secondary stress aside and focus on the main stress in a sentence. Let us distance ourselves from the above technicalities and consider the gist of Cinque's proposal. The effect of his stress system is essentially to put the main stress on the "most deeply embedded" element in a phrase. Thus, if like Cinque, we assume that the relation between two constituents is always asymmetrical in the sense that one of them is always more deeply embedded than the other, reference to direction of stress assignment, as found in any previous forms of the Nuclear Stress Rule, can be dispensed with. In Cinque's system, the first constituent to receive an asterisk will attract all later asterisks. The first constituent to receive an asterisk, on the other hand, is always the most deeply embedded element, due to the principle of the cycle. In what follows, we will not return to the details of how stress is calculated in Cinque's system and will only use the simpler characterization of his system, namely, that an element which is embedded in more layers of structure will receive primary stress. In simple terms, the element with more syntactic brackets around it is the one which is predicted to receive primary stress. In both the right-branching and left-branching configurations in (5), for instance, x has more syntactic brackets around it, and is thus the element expected to receive stress in Cinque's system.

(5)   a. Right-branching   b. Left-branching
      $[_Z z [_Y y [_X x]]]$ $[_Z [_Y [_X x] y] z]$

We are now ready to consider the application of Cinque's system for the calculation of sentential stress in SVO and SOV languages. Cinque's stress system accounts for sentential stress on the object in both these language types. Examples from English and Persian are given in (6). Note that in both SVO and SOV the most deeply embedded element is the object, assuming, as Cinque does, that the head parameter is what accounts for the order difference between SVO and SOV. In other words, in both SVO and SOV, the object, being the complement of the verb in surface structure, is buried in more syntactic structure than any other element in the sentence. The bracketing in (6) shows this point more clearly.

(6)   a. $[[_{DP} John] [_{VP} bought [_{DP} \underline{a\ book}]]]$.
      b. $[[_{DP} Ali] [[_{VP} [_{DP} \underline{ye\ ketaab}]\ xarid]]]$.
          Ali   a book   bought

It is worth noting here that Cinque's system crucially relies on the head parameter. So, for example, the object is the complement of the verb and is thus considered "most deeply embedded" in both head-final SOV and head-initial SVO languages. If the head parameter is dispensed with (Kayne 1994 and subsequent work), with SOV being derived from SVO via movement, it is not clear how this system could be made to work.[2] Note that in Cinque's system, as we will see below, stress is crucially read off surface syntactic structure, making

---

[2] As we will see in chapter 4, in his more recent work on the syntax of adverbs, Cinque adopts Kayne's antisymmetric framework. The two bodies of work should be kept separate.

unavailable an account in which SOV starts off as SVO with the O receiving stress in its merge position where it is the "most deeply embedded" element. In short, in a system which derives SOV from SVO, the object cannot be the complement of the verb and thus the most deeply embedded element in its final surface position.[3]

An apparent problem arises with sentences containing adverbial phrases. As shown in (7), stress falls on the adverbial phrase in an English sentence uttered out of the blue.

(7) They are following the lecture <u>attentively</u>. (Cinque 1993: 263)

If we assume the traditional structure for (7) with the AdvP right-adjoined to the verb phrase, as illustrated in (8), the object NP rather than the adverb would be the most deeply embedded element and the stress on the adverb is unexpected under Cinque's system.

(8)

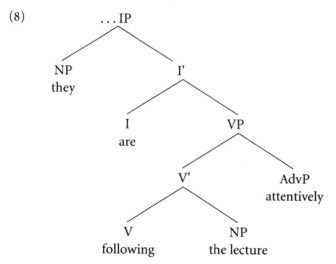

To solve this problem, Cinque adheres to a body of work in syntactic literature (see Barss and Lasnik 1986; Larson 1988; Stroik 1990, among others) which propose the right-branching structure for AdvPs shown in (9).

---

[3] Building on Kiparsky (1966), Cinque shows that in a language like German with some left-branching and some right-branching phrases, we see the mixed effect, with the left-branching phrases assigning stress on the right and right-branching phrases on the left. He argues that this follows naturally from his head parameter dependent stress system. Head-initial NPs and PPs have stress on the complement (which is to their right), while head-final VPs have stress on the complement (which is to their left).

(9)

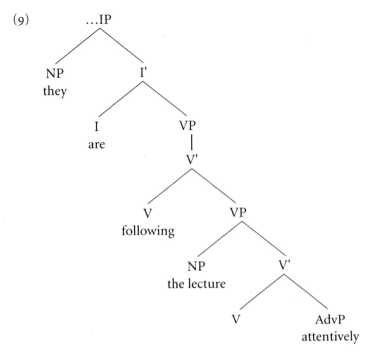

In this type of structure, the object asymmetrically c-commands the VP adverbial (at least) at surface structure. The adverbial is thus more deeply embedded, and as predicted by Cinque's system, it receives sentential stress. We will see in chapter 4 that in his work on the syntax of adverbials, Cinque (1999, 2002, 2004) provides a different syntactic analysis of adverbials. It is worth noting here that under his more recent analysis, the above account cannot be maintained. In chapter 4, I will provide a different account of the stress behaviour of adverbials, one that is compatible with Cinque's more recent analysis of their syntactic structure.

As noted by Cinque, however, his system faces a more serious problem in cases where the subject DP has more layers of embedding than the predicate. Given that Cinque's system predicts stress on the element buried in more layers of structure, in these cases one would expect an element within the subject to receive primary stress. This is contrary to fact, as shown in the example in (10) with primary stress on the object *Mary*.[4] The element buried in more

---

[4] Cinque uses the intransitive sentence in (i) to illustrate the problem. This is a poor choice. As mentioned previously and discussed in more detail later, in sentences such as (i), with unaccusative verbs, primary stress in fact falls on the subject in focus-neutral contexts. Once the example provided by Cinque is corrected by shifting the stress from the verb to the subject, the sentence is not a counterexample any longer to Cinque's "most deeply embedded" generalization. To avoid this problem,

layers of structure, on the other hand, is *senescence*. Note that *senescence* has five layers of syntactic brackets around it, whereas *Mary* has three.[5]

(10) [[The author of [many popular articles on [the effects of [senescence]]]] [kissed [<u>Mary</u>]]]

Cinque addresses this problem and provides the following solution. He suggests that such cases should be dealt with in the light of the interaction between prosody and information structure. He argues that depending on whether the subject or the predicate provides new information, the stress may fall on one or the other. Within each cycle, according to Cinque, stress obeys the "most deeply embedded" generalization. We will deal with the interaction between sentential stress and focus in chapter 5. We will see that the interaction arises with sentences which are not informationally neutral, in other words, sentences containing focussed constituents. In an out-of-the-blue context, the whole sentence is the focus of the sentence. The fact that a sentence like (10), uttered out of the blue, has its primary stress on the object strongly indicates that Cinque's system of stress assignment is not on the right track. By resorting to information structure to account for the stress pattern in (10), Cinque's theory loses its predictive power even in the more general cases. We noted above that his theory can account for the fact that stress falls on the object in transitive sentences in both SVO- and SOV-type languages. Under his explanation, that we should in fact treat the two cycles separately and decide whether the subject or the predicate receives stress according to focus structure, it remains a question why the subject never receives primary stress in transitive sentences uttered in an out-of-the-blue context. Why is it that the predicate receives stress not only in cases where the predicate is focussed but also when the whole sentence is focussed? A null theory of stress, as Cinque calls his theory, should be able to account for the out-of-the-blue stress in (10) without recourse to information structure. There seems to be a fundamental difference between the subject and the predicate regardless of the depth of embedding, something Cinque's system fails to capture.[6]

I have used a transitive sentence. Unaccusative and passive sentences will be dealt with later in this section and in chapter 4.
(i) [The author of [many popular articles on [the effects of [senescence]]]] [<u>died</u>]. (Cinque 1993: 246)

[5] A similar problem arises in sentences with a complex object DP and a sentence-final manner adverb such as the one in (i). Once again, Cinque's system wrongly predicts stress on the element buried in more layers of structure, thus an element within the DP object, whereas main stress is on the adverb.
(i) [They [are following [the lecture by [the author of [many popular articles on [the effects of [senescence]]]]]] <u>attentively</u>]].

[6] The case of the sentences containing a complex DP object and a manner adverb discussed in n. 5 is even more problematic because according to Cinque's system both the object and the adverb belong

Further empirical problems arise with Cinque's stress system when we look at the behaviour of unaccusative and passive sentences. Cinque's system fails to account for stress on the subject in passives and unaccusatives uttered in an out-of-the-blue context (see also Zubizarreta 1998; Legate 2003). Two examples are given in (11). The stress on the subject in the passive example in (11a) and the unaccusative example in (11b) is unexpected under Cinque's theory, as the subject does not qualify as the most deeply embedded element in the clause (for more examples of this kind, see ch. 2 and references cited therein).[7]

(11)   a.   (What happened yesterday?) My bike was stolen. (Legate 2003)
     b.   (What happened?) The mail arrived.

Given the standard assumption that in unaccusative and passive sentences the subject starts off as the internal argument of the verb, one may be tempted to attribute its primary stress to its being base-generated in the most deeply embedded position in the clause. This is in fact the line that Legate (2003) adopts. We will return to Legate's proposal in the next section and will show that it faces its own problems. What is important to note here is that Cinque's system, in which sentential stress is crucially derived from surface syntactic structure, is incapable of accounting for the facts in (11) with no further stipulation such as an undesirable recourse to information structure.

Another piece of evidence against Cinque's theory of stress comes from the behaviour of sentential stress in Persian. Cinque's stress system, laid out above, predicts sentential stress on the "most deeply embedded" element in the clause. In an SOV language, this translates into the element immediately preceding the verb (Cinque 1993: 250). The "immediately preceding the verb" generalization may hold true of the core cases in some SOV languages such as German V-final sentences, the only case of SOV discussed by Cinque in some detail. Later we will see that this generalization runs into trouble in the face of some other German stress facts. More importantly, however, the system faces serious problems in the face of data from Persian, another SOV language. We will see in chapter 4 that stress facts in Eastern Armenian, which are strikingly similar to Persian, create similar problems for this generalization. Consider the Persian data in (12) and (13) (see also Kahnemuyipour 2003).

(12)   a.   Ali   [xord].
        Ali   ate

---

to the same cycle and yet main stress does not fall within the object DP, i.e. on the element embedded in more layers of structure.

   [7] German examples will be discussed in section 3.4 and Persian examples in chapter 4.

b. Ali [mi - xord].
    Ali DUR-ate
    'Ali would (used to) eat.'

c. Ali [qazaa mi-xord].
    Ali food   DUR-ate
    'Ali would (used to) eat food.'

d. Ali [xub qazaa mi-xord].
    Ali well food   DUR-ate
    'Ali would (used to) eat well.'

(13) a. Maryam [did].
          Maryam saw

      b. Maryam [mi-did].
          Maryam DUR-saw
          'Maryam would (used to) see.'

      c. Maryam [film mi-did].
          Maryam film DUR-saw
          'Maryam would (used to) see films.'

      d. Maryam [xeyli film mi-did].
          Maryam a lot film DUR-saw
          'Maryam would (used to) see films a lot.'

The examples in (12a) and (13a) show simple sentences with a subject and a verb with the stress on the verb. The stress is expected under Cinque's system. The sentences in (12b) and (13b) show that if a mood marker is prefixed to the verb, stress falls on the mood marker (for the status of these mood markers and some similarly behaving adverbial prefixes, see Kahnemuyipour 2003). The stress behaviour of the Persian mood markers is similar to some German separable prefixes discussed by Cinque. To account for stress on these separable prefixes, he suggests that they are heads of intransitive PPs selected by the verb as its complement and thus, in his system, they would take stress as the "most deeply embedded" element. We will return to the German separable prefixes below, but if we assume a similar treatment of the Persian mood markers, the stress facts in (12b) and (13b) are not surprising under Cinque's system.[8] Sentences (12c) and (13c) illustrate examples of an SOV sentence with a non-specific object. Stress falls on the object, as expected, in compliance

---

[8] I am putting aside the question of whether extending Cinque's proposal for German separable prefixes to Persian is at all plausible. It is worth noting that in Persian these prefixes are not separable, which was one of the motivations for Cinque's analysis.

with Cinque's system.[9] Examples (12d) and (13d) are problematic for Cinque, however. They show that if other elements (for example, Left Edge Markers like some manner or measure adverbs) appear to the left of the object, they receive stress. These are clear counterexamples to Cinque's system, which predicts stress on the element to the immediate left of the verb. If, on the other hand, we define the stress rule in such a way that it would assign stress to the leftmost element within a stress domain, marked by brackets in (12) and (13), the facts could be accounted for straightforwardly. This is precisely what I will do in chapter 4. We will see that the system developed in this monograph will identify the stress domains in a unified manner and will correctly predict stress on the leftmost element in these domains, which ends up being the element immediately preceding the verb when there is only a single preverbal element in the stress domain. In chapter 4 we will return to the details of this proposal and how it will fare with data from other languages, particularly the German data discussed in Cinque (1993). The important point here is that Cinque's "most deeply embedded" stress system fails to account for the stress facts in Persian which clearly question the assignment of stress to the element to the immediate left of the verb, expected for an SOV language under Cinque's proposal.

Before we end this section, let us look at Cinque's proposal to account for the stress behaviour of German separable prefixes more closely. As mentioned above, in German, there are some separable verbal prefixes which receive stress, as shown in (14). Cinque suggests that the separable prefixes are heads of intransitive PPs selected by the verb as its complement and thus, in his system, they would receive stress as the "most deeply embedded" element.

(14) ...Wann   werden   wir   <u>an</u>+kommen?   (Cinque's footnote 20, (ia))
       when   will   we   arrive

Cinque's analysis breaks down as soon as we look at a sentence involving a non-specific object in addition to the separable prefix. Recall that Cinque's prediction would be that stress should remain on the separable prefix, the most deeply embedded element in the clause or the element immediately preceding the verb. This prediction is not borne out, as shown in the examples

---

[9] In fact, we cannot maintain a treatment of the mood markers similar to that of the German separable prefixes and at the same time account for the stress on the object when both a mood marker and an object are present. If the stress on the mood marker is due to its being the element immediately preceding the verb in a Cinque-style system, then the stress should remain on the mood marker when an object is added, contrary to the facts in (12c) and (13c). We will see below that this problem extends to the German separable prefixes as well. Let us assume for the moment that the stress on the mood marker has an independent explanation and the stress on the object is thus expected under Cinque's system.

in (15).[10] We will see in chapter 4 that the system developed in this monograph, with stress predicted on the leftmost element within the stress domain (to be made precise), fares better with these data.

(15) a. Karl wird <u>Kleider</u> um-arbeiten.
         *Karl wird Kleider <u>um</u>-arbeiten
          Karl will   dresses   alter
          'Karl will alter dresses.'

      b. Karl hat <u>ein Buch</u> ein-gekauft.
         *Karl hat ein Buch <u>ein</u>-gekauft
          Karl has a   book   shopped
          'Karl shopped for a book.'

      c. Ein Mädchen hat <u>einen Ballon</u>   auf-gepumpt.
         *Ein Mädchen hat einen Ballon   <u>auf</u>-gepumpt.
          a   girl   has a   balloon inflated
          'A girl inflated a balloon.'

In this section we have looked at Cinque (1993), the first and most influential purely syntactic account of phrasal/sentential stress. Several conceptual and empirical arguments against Cinque's stress system were provided. We noted that Cinque's system crucially depends on the head parameter and is thus incompatible with an antisymmetric view of syntax, as proposed by Kayne (1994) and subsequent authors. It was also shown that his account of adverbials involves a particular assumption about their syntax. This particular view of the syntax of adverbs runs into trouble in the face of certain other syntactic considerations. As a result, some scholars, in particular Cinque (1999, 2002, 2004), have proposed a different analysis of the syntax of adverbials which is incompatible with Cinque's stress system. We will return to the syntax and prosody of adverbials in chapter 4. In addition, to account for the stress on the predicate in cases where the subject involved more layers of embedding, even in out-of-the-blue contexts, Cinque had to resort to the interaction between prosody and information structure, an undesirable move for a null theory of sentence stress. We further showed that Persian poses a serious problem for Cinque's theory, which predicts stress on the element to the immediate left of the verb in SOV languages. In fact, German separable prefixes, which at first glance seemed to provide support for Cinque's theory, presented further counterexamples for the "stress on the element immediately preceding the verb" generalization. Finally, it was pointed out that Cinque's

[10] I am grateful to Bettina Spreng and Michael Wagner for their help with the German data throughout this monograph.

theory is incapable of accounting for stress on the subject in sentences with passive or unaccusative verbs. We noted that Legate (2003) attempts to modify Cinque's system slightly to account for the latter discrepancy. The next section deals with Legate's proposal.

3.3 Revisiting Cinque (1993): Legate (2003)

It was noted above that Cinque's (1993) stress system fails to account for the stress on the subject in the passive and unaccusative sentences repeated below.

(11)   a.   (What happened yesterday?) <u>My bike</u> was stolen. (Legate 2003)
       b.   (What happened?) <u>The mail</u> arrived.

Legate (2003) attempts to account for (11) by proposing that a Cinque-style sentence stress rule applies in a phase-based manner. The details of how a multiple spell-out system works were provided in chapter 1. Let us briefly review the main points.

According to the theory of phases and multiple spell-out, syntactic structure is sent off to PF and LF for interpretation in chunks. Derivation proceeds bottom-up in a phase-by-phase manner. When the derivation reaches a phase, the (syntactic) complement of the phase head is shipped off for phonological interpretation. I called this syntactic chunk the SPELLEE. This process is shown schematically in the diagram in (16).

(16) $H_{PHASE}P$

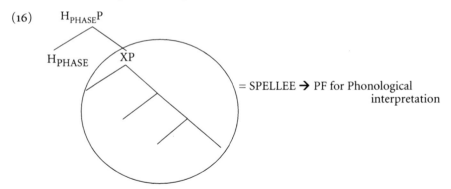

= SPELLEE → PF for Phonological
interpretation

What constitutes a phase is a matter of controversy. According to Chomsky (2000, 2001), CPs and (transitive) vPs constitute phases. Chomsky crucially takes unaccusative and passive verb phrases not to induce phasal boundaries.[11] The same assumption will play an important role in the analysis put forth

---

[11] I am abstracting away from the distinction between strong and weak phases (see ch. 1, n. 6).

in this monograph (see ch. 4). In Legate's system, on the other hand, unaccusative and passive (just like transitive) verb phrases constitute phases.

Legate also makes use of the copy theory of movement (Chomsky 1993, 1995, and subsequent authors). According to the copy theory of movement, every instance of movement involves two identical occurrences of the moved element, one in the position it has moved from and one where it has moved to. If there are intermediate landing sites, there will be more than two occurrences. These occurrences are called copies. Instructions to the LF and PF components determine which copy should be interpreted or pronounced, respectively.

Here is how Legate's proposal works in simple terms. She suggests that a Cinque-style stress rule applies in a phase-based manner. The application of this rule results in the assignment of stress to the lower copy of the subject in its base-generated sentence-final position. Instructions to PF later delete this lower copy. Meanwhile, stress is inherited by the higher copy from this lower (or lowest) copy. As a result, the subject in unaccusative and passive sentences receives primary stress.

By making the stress assignment system sensitive to the base-generated position of the subject in passive and unaccusative sentences, Legate (2003) is able to account for the stress on the subject in these cases. According to Legate's system, however, any element which moves from a stress-bearing position within a phase to a position outside the phase should receive stress. Topicalized objects and wh-objects, which, as standardly assumed, move from internal argument positions, provide counterexamples to this prediction. This is shown in (17).[12, 13]

(17) a. What did John <u>buy</u>? vs. John bought <u>books</u>.
          *<u>What</u> did John buy?

      b. Beans, I <u>like</u>. vs. I like <u>beans</u>.
          *<u>Beans</u>, I like. (under the topicalized reading)

---

[12] The fact that the wh-word in (17) does not receive stress cannot be attributed to some idiosyncracy of wh-elements. Note that wh-words receive stress in situ (Who bought <u>what</u>?) and in a focusfronting language such as Persian *Ali <u>chi</u> xarid?* 'Ali what bought?' (see Kahnemuyipour 2001). We will return to the issue of stress in wh-questions in chapter 5.

[13] Given that the passive and unaccusative examples in (11) involve A-movement as opposed to A′-movement in (17), one may be inclined to use this distinction to account for the observed contrast. Note, however, the difference cannot follow from the A-A′ distinction in any natural way. One can, of course, stipulate the difference by stating, for instance, that only A-copies inherit stress from their lower counterpart. Alternatively, if we give up the copy theory and try to account for the stress facts by ordering the stress rule with respect to A- and A′-movements in a way that it would only apply to the element that undergoes A-movement, we would have to allow A′-movement to be ordered before and A-movement after stress assignment, a conceptually implausible result.

In addition to the problematic examples in (17), as a system which adopts Cinque's account of phrasal/sentential stress to start with, Legate's system inherits all the problems raised for Cinque's theory in section 3.2, such as the problems with the adverbials, subjects with more layers of embedding and the Persian and German facts with stress on elements not immediately preceding the verb. Moreover, we noted that Legate's system relies on the sensitivity of the stress rule to the underlying position of elements. This monograph, on the other hand, takes stress to be a rule which applies to "surface structure". We will see in chapters 4 and 5 that this assumption will enable us to account for certain stress facts across languages, namely, the stress behaviour of specific (vs. non-specific) objects and wh-elements. In chapter 4 I propose a theory of sentential stress which accounts for all the above facts without facing the range of problems discussed so far. Before moving on to this proposal, we should consider another influential theory of sentential stress which attempts to address some of the problems raised in this chapter. In the following section, we look at Zubizarreta's (1998) account of sentential stress.

3.4 A modular theory of nuclear stress: Zubizarreta (1998)

Zubizarreta (1998) attempts to account for certain facts with respect to prosody, focus, and word order in Germanic (exemplified by English and German) and Romance languages (exemplified by French, Italian, and Spanish). To this end, she makes two major proposals. Her first proposal involves revising the Nuclear Stress Rule (as defined by Cinque 1993) from a monolithic rule solely sensitive to hierarchical constituent structure to a modular one which also relies on selectional properties. Her second proposal deals with the interaction among prosody, focus and word order in Romance. She suggests that certain movement operations, which she calls p-movement, can be motivated by prosodic requirements in these languages. p-movement will be addressed in chapter 5 in the context of the discussion of the interaction between information structure and sentential stress. In this section we focus on Zubizarreta's proposal with respect to the Nuclear Stress Rule. We will see that even though her system fares better than Cinque's with certain empirical data, it suffers from several empirical and conceptual problems.

Let us turn to Zubizarreta's (1998) conceptualization of the NSR. As mentioned above, Zubizarreta proposes that the NSR needs to be modularized into two rules, one solely sensitive to hierarchical constituent structure, or asymmetric c-command to be more precise (her C-NSR), and one which refers to selectional properties (her S-NSR). We start our discussion of Zubizarreta's theory with the more familiar C-NSR, which is essentially a slightly revised version of Cinque's stress rule. While abstracting away from many technical details of her theory, some basic definitions fundamental to her system will be reviewed.

Zubizarreta's formulation of the C-NSR crucially depends on asymmetric c-command and adopts the weaker version of Kayne's (1994) linear correspondence axiom given in (18) (see also Chomsky 1995).

(18)   Given two constituents A and B, if A asymmetrically c-commands B, then every terminal that A dominates precedes every terminal that B dominates.

According to (18), asymmetric c-command can be translated into linear ordering. Conversely, if a constituent precedes another constituent, the former also asymmetrically c-commands the latter. The C-NSR can now be formulated as in (19).

(19)   Zubizarreta's C-NSR (Zubizarreta 1998: 40)
        Given two nodes C_i and C_j that are metrical sisters, the one lower in the syntactic asymmetric c-command ordering is more prominent.

While (19) refers to asymmetric c-command, given the correlation between asymmetric c-command and linear ordering in (18), one does not need to worry about the exact syntactic structure of a sentence to determine which constituent is lower in the structure for the application of C-NSR. The surface word order is sufficient to determine which constituent wins out in the application of C-NSR. Essentially, the constituent closer to the end of the sentence is lower in the structure, thus the one assigned higher prominence based on the C-NSR. For example, in a sentence such as *They are following the lecture attentively*, discussed in section 3.2, the exact syntactic treatment of adverbials is beside the point for Zubizarreta. The fact that the adverbial appears at the end of the sentence is sufficient to show that it is the lowest constituent in the structure, thus receiving primary stress according to the C-NSR in a way to be elaborated below.

The formulation of the C-NSR in (19) refers to metrical sisterhood, a notion that has to be teased apart from the more familiar notion of syntactic sisterhood. Metrical sisterhood is in a sense a less restricted version of syntactic sisterhood in that it may ignore intervening syntactic constituents that are not metrically visible. In other words, all syntactic sisters are metrical sisters, but some constituents that are not syntactic sisters may qualify as metrical sisters if they involve metrically invisible intervening items. Metrically invisible items include functional categories such as determiners, light lexical categories such as auxiliaries, certain prepositions, and anaphoric constituents.[14] Crucially, phonologically null elements such as traces are also metrically invisible in her theory, leading to a system that is insensitive to deep structure and reads sentential stress solely off surface structure.

To illustrate the notion of metrical sisterhood, let us look at the hypothetical structure in (20), where each C_i, i = 1, 2, 3, 4, e is a head and C_e stands for a metrically invisible constituent (Zubizarreta 1998: 41–2).

(20) $[_{C_1} C_1 [_{C_e} C_e [_{C_e} [_{C_4} C_4 C_e] [_{C_e} C_e [_{C_2} C_2 [_{C_3} C_3 C_e]]]]]]$

The pairs of metrical sisters in (20) are listed in (21).

(21)   a. C_1 and $[_{C_e} C_e [_{C_e} [_{C_4} C_4 C_e] [_{C_e} C_e [_{C_2} C_2 [_{C_3} C_3 C_e]]]]]$
      b. C_1 and $[_{C_e} [_{C_4} C_4 C_e] [_{C_e} C_e [_{C_2} C_2 [_{C_3} C_3 C_e]]]]$
      c. C_e and $[_{C_e} [_{C_4} C_4 C_e] [_{C_e} C_e [_{C_2} C_2 [_{C_3} C_3 C_e]]]]$
      d. $[_{C_4} C_4 C_e]$ and $[_{C_e} C_e [_{C_2} C_2 [_{C_3} C_3 C_e]]]$
      e. $[_{C_4} C_4 C_e]$ and $[_{C_2} C_2 [_{C_3} C_3 C_e]]$
      f. C_2 and $[_{C_3} C_3 C_e]$
      g. C_2 and C_3
      h. C_3 and C_e

Of the metrical sister pairs in (21), only those in (21a, c, d, f, h) are sisters in the standard syntactic sense. The pairs in (21b, e, g) are metrical sisters by virtue of the fact that the elements in the pairs in (21a, d, f) are separated only by metrically invisible constituents marked as C_e. In other words, from the point of view of metrical sisterhood, two constituents will count as equivalent in case they differ only by metrically invisible heads.

The application of the C-NSR in (19) to some of the metrical sisters in (21) is straightforward. Take (21b) as an example. The constituents C_1 and $[_{C_e} [_{C_4} C_4 C_e] [_{C_e} C_e [_{C_2} C_2 [_{C_3} C_3 C_e]]]]$ are metrical sisters. On the other hand, given the intervening C_e in (20), C_1 asymmetrically c-commands $[_{C_e} [_{C_4} C_4 C_e] [_{C_e} C_e [_{C_2} C_2 [_{C_3} C_3 C_e]]]]$. As a result, the application of the C-NSR would assign more prominence to the metrical sister lower in the asymmetric c-command relation, namely $[_{C_e} [_{C_4} C_4 C_e][_{C_e} C_e [_{C_2} C_2 [_{C_3} C_3 C_e]]]]$. If we consider a more complicated case from (21), the importance of the above conventions with respect to metrical invisibility will become clear. Consider the two pairs of categories $(C_2, [_{C_3} C_3 C_e])$ and (C_2, C_3) in (21f) and (21g). The categories C_2 and $[_{C_3} C_e]$ are syntactic sisters (as well as metrical sisters) and thus, strictly speaking, no asymmetric c-command relation holds between them. A question therefore arises as to whether the C-NSR

[14] Zubizarreta (1998) suggests parametric variation among languages in this respect. Thus, for example, Romance languages do not all show the same range of metrical invisibility.

can apply to these metrical sisters. Here is where metrical invisibility becomes crucial. C_2 asymmetrically c-commands C_3 and since C_3 and $[C_3\ C_e]$ are metrically indistinct, C_2 asymmetrically c-commands $[C_3\ C_e]$ derivatively. Therefore, the C-NSR can apply to C_2 and $[C_3\ C_e]$ (as much as to C_2 and C_3), assigning more prominence to $[C_3\ C_e]$.

A somewhat similar situation arises in the real world if we consider the case of a head and its sister complement $[_{XP}$ X YP$]$. The (syntactic) sisterhood and asymmetric c-command requirements seem to be in contradiction in this case. The desired result is to have the C-NSR apply and assign more prominence to the complement YP. X and YP are (syntactic and metrical) sisters, satisfying one of the two requirements of the rule. The problem is that by virtue of being syntactic sisters, neither can asymmetrically c-command the other. Zubizarreta suggests that in these cases the syntactic structure will always include metrically invisible elements that allow both requirements of metrical sisterhood and asymmetric c-command to be met at the same time. That is to say, we would always be dealing with a configuration like $[_{XP}$ X $[_{ZP}$ e YP$]]$. In this configuration, YP is asymmetrically c-commanded by X and it also a metrical sister of X, by virtue of the intervening metrically invisible element. We can illustrate this by an actual case, a preposition and its NP complement. An example is given in (22), where e represents a null D(eterminer).

(22)   [John [talked near $[_{DP}\ [_{D}$ e $[_{NP}$ Mary$]]]]]$

In (22), the preposition *near* asymmetrically c-commands the NP *Mary*. Meanwhile, the NP is metrically indistinct from the DP, given the null D. Therefore, the NP will be both the metrical sister of the preposition and asymmetrically c-commanded by it. The C-NSR can therefore apply to the NP and the preposition with no problem. By assuming that there is always some metrically invisible element involved in such cases, Zubizarreta has avoided the conundrum.

Zubizarreta goes through several more definitions to formally incorporate the notions of metrical sisterhood/invisibility/indistinctness in her version of the NSR. Such details are irrelevant to the main point and will be kept out of our discussion. The crucial point is that in calculating sentential stress in Zubizarreta's system, we should take special note of the fact that sisterhood is defined in metrical terms as elaborated above. It is worth noting that the same provision is extended to the other component of the NSR, namely, the S-NSR, the component relying on selectional ordering. In what follows, any reference to "sister" should be interpreted as "metrical sister".

Let us now turn to the second component of Zubizarreta's NSR, her S-NSR. Zubizarreta points out that certain stress facts in German V-final sentences indicate that the C-NSR alone cannot be responsible for the assignment of nuclear stress and claims that selectional relations play a major role in determining the location of nuclear stress (in the spirit of suggestions by Schmerling 1976, Gussenhoven 1984, Selkirk 1984, 1995). We begin an investigation of the S-NSR by considering the core German cases as presented in Zubizarreta's work. I will later take issue with some of her German data based on my German consultants' judgements and some discussions in the literature, but at this point, the goal is to provide a clear presentation of her theory and as such, I remain loyal to her representation of the facts. Example (23) shows that in German V-final transitive structures, sentential stress falls on the direct object.[15]

(23)   Transitive
    Karl hat das/ein <u>Buch</u> gekauft.
    Karl has the/a   book bought
    'Karl bought a book.'

As shown in (24), in a sentence with a ditransitive verb, main stress falls on the indirect object.

(24)   Ditransitive
    Karl hat ein Buch ins   <u>Regal</u> gestellt.
    Karl has a   book on-the shelf put
    'Karl put a book on the shelf.'

Finally, similar to the English facts discussed in section 3.3, in passive or unaccusative sentences uttered out of the blue, it is the subject that receives primary stress. In contrast, in an unergative sentence, sentential stress falls on the verb. This contrast is illustrated in (25) and (26), with the former involving an unaccusative verb and the latter an unergative one.

(25)   Unaccusative
    Es heißt, daß der/ein <u>Junge</u> kommt.
    it is-said that the/a   boy   comes
    'It is said that a boy is coming.'

(26)   Unergative
    Es heißt, daß ein Junge <u>getanzt</u> hat.
    it is-said that a   boy   danced has
    'It is said that a boy danced.'

---

[15] The sentence in (23) can be uttered with stress on the verb rather than on the direct object. Zubizarreta suggests that in such cases the object is defocalized and, as a result, metrically invisible. We return to the variation in the realization of stress on direct objects in chapter 4.

Before proceeding with how Zubizarreta accounts for these facts, a point about the data is in order. The unaccusative and unergative facts in (25) and (26) and elsewhere in this monograph are somewhat different from what Zubizarreta reports. Zubizarreta claims that primary stress is ambiguously on the subject or the predicate in unergative sentences in both English and German and in unaccusative sentences in English. My consultants, on the other hand, report sentential stress on the subject in unaccusative sentences and on the predicate in unergative sentences as the focus-neutral one in German and English (as well as Persian, to be discussed in ch. 4). The contrast between the stress pattern in unergatives and unaccusatives has also been noted in the literature, where it is pointed out that unaccusatives exhibit single stress on the subject while unergatives pattern like transitives and show (primary) stress on the predicate and (secondary) stress on the subject (see e.g. Selkirk 1984, 1995; Rochemont 1998; Legate 2003). In fact, Zubizarreta makes some qualifying remarks about her data which point to the correctness of this contrast. As for unaccusatives in English, she points out that four out of her five consultants only accepted primary stress on the subject. In the case of unergatives, she points to a communicative difference between the two possibilities with the sentence with stress on the subject, indicating that the subject is "informationally more relevant".[16] While Zubizarreta finds such differences grammatically irrelevant, I argue that such considerations should be taken into account in deciphering the real out-of-the-blue context (see section 5.3). The crucial point is what happens when neither the subject nor the predicate can be said to be "informationally more relevant" than the other. Given the aforementioned considerations, one can safely assume, as I will in what follows, that, under these conditions, primary stress is unambiguously on the subject in unaccusative sentences and on the predicate in unergative sentences (see Winkler and Göbbel 2002 for a similar objection to Zubizarreta's data).[17]

Let us return to the facts in (23) to (26). Given that sentential stress is not on the last constituent in the sentence (i.e. the lowest constituent in terms of asymmetric c-command relations), Zubizarreta correctly points out that her C-NSR alone is incapable of accounting for these facts. To capture these facts, she proposes a second module to the NSR, one reflecting a different kind of

---

[16] Interestingly, she does not make the same claim explicitly about stress on the predicate. If stress on the subject and the predicate is truly ambiguous in unergatives, one would expect stress on the predicate to render the predicate as "informationally more relevant".

[17] In fairness, it should be pointed out that Zubizarreta does not report the unaccusative/unergative data as she does to simplify her task. In fact, her system is considerably complicated given her interpretation of the data.

ordering established by the ordered sequence of selected heads. The partial selectional ordering in (27), represented as a tree for convenience, will suffice for the general cases considered in this monograph.

(27)   Selectional ordering (Zubizarreta 1998: 53)

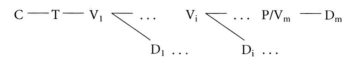

C selects T, which in turn selects a verbal projection. The selectional ordering within the verbal projection is given by the syntactic structure of the predicate, where the lexical verb is analysed into elementary verbs or prepositions $V_1, \ldots, V_i, \ldots, P/V_m$ (see Hale and Keyser 1993). D_m is the nominal argument of the last (possibly only) element P/V_m and D_i, $i = 1, 2, \ldots, m - 1$ is the nominal argument of V_i, when there is more than one element. A category C_r to the right of a category C_q is said to be "lower than" C_q in the selectional ordering. Note that ordering is defined strictly between selector heads and selected constituents and thus no ordering holds between co-arguments. Meanwhile, in order to make the system work, Zubizarreta further assumes that the ordering can be extended from the selected heads to their projections. This leads to a crucial asymmetry in the system: while a selector is necessarily a head, a selected constituent may be a head or some projection of it. Thus, for instance, while the V head selects the D head of the object, one can conclude that the object DP is selectionally lower than the verb. This asymmetry is employed extensively in her system.

We are now ready to encounter Zubizarreta's S-NSR, the part of the nuclear stress rule that relies on the selectional ordering of constituents. This is given in (28), with the selectional ordering given in (27).[18]

(28)   Zubizarreta's S-NSR
Given two nodes C_i and C_j that are metrical sisters, the one lower in the selectional ordering is more prominent.

Zubizarreta has thus modularised the NSR into two rules, the S-NSR in (28) and the C-NSR in (19), repeated below. The two rules in (19) and (28) work together to determine sentential stress in the German examples discussed above. These rules, however, may have conflicting results in some cases. Zubizarreta suggests that the two rules are ranked in German in a way that the S-NSR has primacy over the C-NSR. The details will be illustrated below.

---

[18] I have modified Zubizarreta's definition to make it completely parallel to the C-NSR in (19). Zubizarreta incorporates the S-NSR into the C-NSR and provides the NSR as a single bipartite rule.

(19)   Zubizarreta's C-NSR (Zubizarreta 1998: 40)
Given two nodes C_i and C_j that are metrical sisters, the one lower in the syntactic asymmetric c-command ordering is more prominent.

In order to apply Zubizarreta's stress rules in (19) and (28) to the German verb-final sentences in (23)–(26), we need to consider the structures Zubizarreta attributes to these sentences. Following Hale and Keyser (1993), Zubizarreta assumes the syntactic structures in (29)–(32) for transitives, unergatives, unaccusatives, and ditransitives.[19] The transitive structure (29) contains two verbal heads, each selecting an argument. The unergative structure is analysed as a type of covert transitive, with the argument of the lower verbal head being incorporated into its selecting head, as shown in (30). The unaccusative structure (31) is different from the transitive/unergative structure in that it only has a single verbal head. Finally, in the ditransitive structure, the lower verbal head V_2 selects the prepositional predicate P_3, which is turn selects a nominal argument D_3, the lowest constituent in the selectional chain. This is shown in (32).

(29)   Transitive structure (example 23)

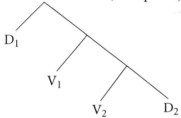

(30)   Unergative structure (example 26)

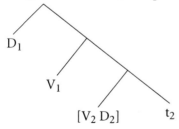

(31)   Uaccusative structure (example 25)

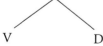

[19] One can replace V_1 with the now more standard little v and V_2 with V. Keeping Zubizarreta's numbering system, however, makes the application of the S-NSR easier to follow.

(32)   Ditransitive structure (example 24)

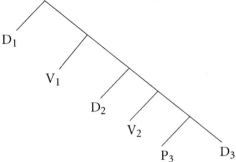

The realization of the structures in (29)–(32) for the German V-final sentences is shown in (33)–(36). Following Kayne's (1994) antisymmetric system, Zubizarreta works under the assumption that SOV is derived from SVO with the leftward movement of the object, as indicated in these examples.[20] I have marked primary stress by underlining in these structures to make the ensuing discussions easier to follow.

(33)   Transitive
[$_{CP}$ Karl$_1$ [hat [t$_1$ [v$_1$ [ein Buch$_2$ [v$_2$ gekauft [t$_2$]]]]]]].
       Karl   has   a   book   bought

(34)   Ditransitive
[$_{CP}$ Karl$_1$ [hat [t$_1$ [v$_1$ [ein Buch$_2$ [t$_2$ [ins [Regal]$_3$]]$_4$
       Karl   has   a   book   on-the shelf
[v$_2$ gestellt [t$_4$]]]]]]]].
       put

(35)   Unaccusative
[$_{CP}$ daβ [ein Junge$_1$ [v kommt [t$_1$]]]].
       that a   boy   comes

(36)   Unergative
[$_{CP}$ daβ [ein Junge$_1$ [t$_1$ [v$_1$ [v$_2$ getanzt hat]]]]]].
       that a   boy   danced has

We can now apply the rules in (28) and (19) to these structures. Consider the transitive structure in (33) first. Recall that, according to Zubizarreta, the S-NSR has primacy over the C-NSR in German. In (33), the metrical sisters D$_1$ (= Karl) and [D$_2$ V$_2$] (= [ein Buch$_2$ [v$_2$ gekauft [t$_2$]]]), metrically non-distinct from [ein Buch$_2$ [v$_2$ gekauft]] are not selectionally ordered

---

[20] Following suggestions by Travis (1991) and Borer (1994), Zubizarreta assumes that the object moves to the specifier of AspP, a projection between V$_1$ and V$_2$, perhaps for case assignment. A similar assumption will be made in chapter 4, where the stress system proposed in this monograph is developed.

according to the selectional ordering in (25).[21] Thus, the S-NSR cannot apply. The C-NSR applies and assigns prominence to the lower constituent, namely $[D_2 \; V_2]$. The algorithm reapplies to the metrical sisters D_2 (= ein Buch) and V_2 (= $[_{V2}$ gekauft $[t_2]$]), metrically non-distinct from $[_{V2}$ gekauft]. The S-NSR applies in this case as D_2 is lower than V_2 (derivatively) in the selectional ordering, thus receiving more prominence. Given that the determiner *ein* is metrically invisible, primary stress on *Buch* is correctly predicted.

Let us turn to the ditransitive example in (34). The metrical sisters D_1 (= Karl) and $[D_2 \; [[P \; D_3]_4 \; V_2]]$ (= ein Buch$_2$ ins Regal gestellt) are not selectionally ordered. S-NSR cannot apply. C-NSR applies and assigns prominence to the lower constituent $[D_2 \; [[P \; D_3]_4 \; V_2]]$. The algorithm applies to the latter constituent. D_2 (= ein Buch) and $[[P \; D_3]_4 \; V_2]$ (= ins Regal gestellt) are not selectionally ordered, thus S-NSR fails to apply. C-NSR applies and assigns prominence to $[[P \; D_3]_4 \; V_2]$, which is asymmetrically c-commanded by D_2. This time, V_2 (= [gestellt t_4], metrically non-distinct from [gestellt]) is higher in the selectional ordering than its metrical sister $[P \; D_3]_4$. The S-NSR applies and assigns more prominence to $[P \; D_3]_4$ (= ins Regal). Finally, P is selectionally higher than D_3. The S-NSR applies and correctly predicts stress on D_3, or the nominal *Regal*.

In the unaccusative example in (35), the metrical sisters D (= ein Junge) and V (= [kommt t_1]), metrically non-distinct from *kommt*, are selectionally ordered. The S-NSR applies and correctly predicts sentential stress on the selectionally lower constituent D or *Junge*.

Finally, we can apply the now familiar algorithm to the unergative example in (36). The metrical sisters D_1 (= ein Junge) and V_1 (= $[_{V1} \; [_{V2}$ getanzt hat]]), metrically non-distinct from $[_{V2}$ getanzt]) are not selectionally ordered. The crucial point here is that D_1 is selected by V_1 and thus selectionally ordered with respect to this verbal head. However, D_1 and $[_{V1}$ e] are not metrical sisters, so the S-NSR cannot apply to them. On the other hand, even though D_1 and V_2 are metrical sisters, there is no selectional ordering between them, and the S-NSR fails to apply in this case as well. The C-NSR applies instead, assigning more prominence to the lower constituent V_1, correctly predicting stress on the verb *getanzt*.

So far, we have considered only V-final German sentences. Since German SVO sentences (or more precisely sentences in which the verb is not in the final position) behave very much like English sentences with respect to sentential stress, I will skip Zubizarreta's discussion of these cases and move on to her discussion of English. In this discussion, we will also see cases in which the presence of an adjunct will block the application of the S-NSR, leading to

---

[21] Note that *hat*, an auxiliary verb, is metrically invisible and thus ignored in the calculation.

sentence-final stress predicted by the C-NSR. This mechanism will play an important role in the ensuing discussion.

We are already familiar with the English facts from the discussions in the previous chapter and the beginning of this chapter. In the core cases, sentential stress falls on the final constituent in the sentence. Zubizarreta's (1998: 67) examples in (37) reaffirm this generalization.

(37)   a.   Karl lost <u>his book</u>.
       b.   Karl lost his book in the <u>living room</u>.
       c.   Karl worked in <u>his office</u>.
       d.   Karl worked on <u>his manuscript</u>.
       e.   Karl worked on his manuscript in <u>his office</u>.

Zubizarreta's C-NSR (which is in fact a revised syntactic version of Chomsky and Halle's original NSR) can account for the facts in (37). However, the same facts that raised a problem for Chomsky and Halle's theory, namely unaccusative and passive sentences, prove the inadequacy of the C-NSR for English. Some English examples are provided in (38) (for more examples, see ch. 2).

(38)   a.   <u>The sun</u> came out.
       b.   <u>The mail</u> has arrived.
       c.   <u>My bike</u> was stolen.

The stress pattern in (38) indicates to Zubizarreta that the S-NSR is at work in English as well.

In applying Zubizarreta's system to the English examples, let us assume that both the S-NSR and the C-NSR are active and that, like German, the S-NSR takes precedence over the C-NSR in English.[22] In (37a), the S-NSR fails to apply to the subject and the predicate as they are not selectionally ordered, the C-NSR assigns more prominence to the predicate, the S-NSR then applies and assigns stress to the object, which is selectionally lower than the verb. Thus, it is the application of the S-NSR that is responsible for primary stress on the object. It is worth noting here that there was no need for the S-NSR to correctly predict stress on the object. The C-NSR alone could have predicted stress on the object. We will return to this issue later.

Turning to (37b), the only difference between this example and (37a) is an extra PP adjunct. As a result of the existence of this adjunct, the S-NSR fails to apply to [lost his book in the living room], in other words, *lost* and *his book in the living room* are not selectionally ordered. The stress on the adjunct is

---

[22] For Zubizarreta, who takes stress both on the subject and on the predicate to be possible in the unaccusative/passive sentences, the S-NSR and C-NSR are not ranked in English, allowing either to apply first. This difference does not have a significant bearing on our discussion.

therefore the result of the successive application of the C-NSR. We can now extend this logic to the other cases. In the cases in which the verb phrase contains an adjunct, namely (37c) and (37e), the C-NSR alone is responsible for stress on the final constituent. In (37d) with no adjunct, on the other hand, the S-NSR assigns more prominence to the object as compared to the verb.

Turning to the unaccusative/passive sentences in (38), in a manner very similar to the identical German facts, the S-NSR applies and assigns prominence to the subject.

In the case of the transitive sentences in (37), we observed that the addition of an adjunct blocks the application of the S-NSR and as a result the stress is decided by the C-NSR, putting stress on the last phrase in the clause. One would expect the same thing to happen in the case of the unaccusative/passive sentences. This prediction is borne out, as illustrated in the unaccusative pair in (39) (provided by Zubizarreta) or the passive pair in (40).[23]

(39) a. <u>Our dog</u>'s disappeared.
       b. Our dog's mysteriously <u>disappeared</u>.

(40) a. <u>My bike</u> was stolen.
       b. My bike was mysteriously <u>stolen</u>.

Consider (39). While [Our dog] is selectionally ordered with respect to [disappear], it is not so with respect to [mysteriously disappeared]. As a result, while the S-NSR applies to (39a) and assigns prominence to the subject, it fails to apply to (39b) and stress is determined solely on the basis of C-NSR, thus assigning stress to the sentence-final verb. The same can be said about (40). To sum up, the examples in (39) and (40) show that passive and unaccusative sentences exhibit stress on the subject only when there is no additional adjunct in the sentence. Zubizarreta uses her modular NSR and the idea of additional adjuncts blocking the application of the S-NSR to account for these facts. A different account of these facts will be provided in chapter 4, section 4.8.

Zubizarreta finally turns to Romance languages, using examples from French and Spanish. She points out that in these languages nuclear stress is always rightmost. In other words, these SVO languages behave like the core cases in English, the other SVO language we have looked at, with the only difference that, in these languages, the rightmost generalization applies even to unaccusative/passive sentences. The relevant French examples, taken from Zubizarreta (1998), are given in (41).

---

[23] Note that these facts provide additional evidence against Legate's (2003) idea that it is the base-generated sentence-final position of the subject that is responsible for its stress. If so, we would not expect the addition of the adverb to make a difference.

(41)   French

    a. Marie a   mangé <u>le gâteau.</u>
        Marie has eaten   the cake
        'Marie ate the cake.'

    b. Pierre a   mis ton   livre dans <u>sa poche.</u>
        Pierre has put your book in   his pocket.
        'Pierre put your book in his pocket.'

    c. Le   courier est <u>arrivé.</u>
        the   mail   is   arrived
        'The mail has arrived.'

    d. Le bébé <u>rit.</u>
        the baby laugh
        'The baby is laughing.'

Example (41a) shows that stress falls on the object in a simple SVO sentence in French. In the ditransitive sentence in (41b), the stress falls on the sentence-final object of the preposition. So far, the data replicate English facts. By contrast, (41c) and (41d) with an unaccusative and an unergative verb, respectively, show that the distinction found in English and German between the two verb types is not extended to French. In French, regardless of whether the verb is unaccusative or unergative, stress falls on the predicate. The Spanish facts parallel to the French facts in (41) are provided in (42).[24]

(42)   Spanish

    a. María se comió <u>el   pastel.</u>
        Maria   ate   the cake
        'Maria ate the cake.'

    b. Pedro puso tu   libro en <u>su bolsillo.</u>
        Pedro put   your book in his pocket
        'Pedro put your book in his pocket.'

    c. El   correo <u>llegó.</u>
        the mail   arrived
        'The mail arrived.'

    d. El bebé <u>ríe.</u>
        the baby laugh
        'The baby's laughing.'

---

[24] Example (42b) is not from Zubizarreta. I have added it by consulting a native speaker of Spanish to keep the parallelism with (41).

To account for the facts in (41) and (42), or essentially the fact that stress is rightmost even in unaccusative/passive sentences in Romance, Zubizarreta suggests that these languages lack the S-NSR and that the nuclear stress rule is monolithic in these languages, only consisting of the structurally dependent C-NSR.

To sum up, Zubizarreta (1998) proposes a modularized version of the Nuclear Stress Rule. According to her system, one module, the C-NSR, is sensitive to hierarchical syntactic structure, while the other one, the S-NSR, relies on the selectional ordering of the constituents. Using her modular theory of nuclear stress, she attempts to account for stress facts in German, English, French, and Spanish. In German V-final sentences—the only SOV language type she considers—sentential stress falls on the object, or rather, according to her, on the constituent immediately preceding the verb, which is the lowest constituent in the selectional ordering. Moreover, in unaccusative sentences, stress falls on the subject. These are the cases which the C-NSR fails to account for. To capture these facts, Zubizarreta suggests that the S-NSR has precedence over the C-NSR in German. Thus, in a simple verb-final sentence, it is the S-NSR that is responsible for the stress on the object. The same holds true of unaccusative sentences with the S-NSR assigning stress to the subject. Note, however, that even in the case of a simple SVO sentence in German, where the C-NSR would have been able to capture the facts with no problem, it is the S-NSR that assigns more prominence to the object. This is due to the way Zubizarreta's system is set up with the S-NSR taking precedence over C-NSR. This is also seen in the case of English. While the passive/unaccusative facts are similar to German, thus necessitating the existence of the S-NSR, the other facts can in fact be captured solely on the basis of the C-NSR. In other words, the application of the S-NSR to account for the stress pattern in an English SVO sentence is unnecessary, something Zubizarreta's system cannot avoid. We will return to this problem below. As for Romance—or French and Spanish in particular—the unaccusative facts do not parallel English and German. Zubizarreta suggests therefore that these languages lack the S-NSR and that the C-NSR is solely responsible for their sentence-final stress.

In what follows, I will first look at some conceptual problems with Zubizarreta's theory of stress and then provide some empirical arguments against her theory, mainly based on the behaviour of stress in Persian.[25] Let us take the summary in the above paragraph as a point of departure. A closer look at Zubizarreta's theory reveals a certain level of redundancy that

---

[25] As we will see in chapter 4, section 4.9, Eastern Armenian exhibits a sentential stress pattern similar to Persian, thus posing the same kind of problems for Zubizarreta's system.

should preferably be dispensed with. Take the case of a German (or English) SVO sentence. As noted above, both the S-NSR and the C-NSR can account for the stress on the object in these sentences.[26] According to the details of Zubizarreta's theory, with the S-NSR taking precedence over the C-NSR, the S-NSR is involved in assigning stress on the object. Given the facts, however, either of the two rules can capture stress on the object thus deeming the other one redundant. This problem can be seen from a different angle if we add the Romance facts to the picture. In Romance, there is no S-NSR, therefore it is the C-NSR that is responsible for the assignment of stress to the object in a simple SVO sentence. In other words, two different modules of the stress system are responsible for very similar facts in Germanic and Romance, an implausible outcome. Let us consider the whole picture once again. The only cases in the above data that necessitate the existence of the S-NSR are the stress facts in German V-final sentences and the unaccusative/passive facts in German and English. In all the other cases, the S-NSR is at best unnecessary.[27] In chapter 4, a theory will be developed which relies solely on hierarchical constituent structure, thus dispensing with the S-NSR. It will be shown that with a particular formulation of the sentential stress rule, we are able to account for the facts which seemed to necessitate the existence of the S-NSR in Zubizarreta's account. This theory will be shown to be descriptively stronger (in that it can account for a wider range of facts), while not suffering from the inherent redundancy of Zubizarreta's system.[28]

Before we turn to the Persian stress facts, it is worth noting that Zubizarreta's system also fails to account for secondary stress in a sentence. It has been observed, for instance, that in a simple transitive sentence, while the object receives the main prominence of the sentence, the subject is more prominent than the verb (see Halle and Vergnaud 1987, among others, as discussed in ch. 2). This is shown in the example in (43) with levels of stress marked by numbers.

(43)   <u>John</u>   saw   <u>Mary</u>.
        2   1

---

[26] Technically speaking, the S-NSR alone cannot account for the stress on the object. Given that these rules apply to metrical sisters, the C-NSR is required in the first stage of the application of the NSR to assign prominence to the predicate, as opposed to the subject. It is in the next stage of the application of the rule that either the C-NSR or the S-NSR could apply to give us the right result.

[27] We will see below that the S-NSR makes the wrong predictions in some cases, with evidence from German and Persian.

[28] One might also question Zubizarreta's crucial reliance on the ranking of the two modules of the NSR. While this type of ranking is very much in the spirit of a constraint-based Optimality Theory architecture (à la Prince and Smolensky 1993, and subsequent authors), its status is questionable in the type of derivational computational system Zubizarreta seems to work in. It is not clear where exactly this implied ranking is expressed in her adopted model.

Zubizarreta's theory fails to account for the secondary stress on the subject in (43). In fact, given the way the system is set up, her system would predict, if anything, the subject to be less prominent. Recall that in the application of Zubizarreta's NSR, first the C-NSR applies to the metrical sisters [John] and [saw Mary], assigning more prominence to the predicate. Then the S-NSR applies to [saw] and [Mary], assigning more prominence to the object. One way to interpret this mechanism of determining stress is to take the subject to be the least prominent element in the clause, given that the subject loses out to the predicate in the first application of the C-NSR. In reality, Zubizarreta's theory should not be seen in these terms, as the intermediate steps in calculating prominence have no status in her theory. Meanwhile, if a theory is proposed that can account for the secondary stress facts in addition to the primary stress facts, it should be seen as superior to Zubizarreta's system. We will see in chapter 4 that the iterative system of stress assignment developed in this monograph has the added benefit of being able to account for the secondary stress facts.[29]

The German V-final sentence type is the only case of SOV Zubizarreta considers. Below we turn to facts from another SOV language, namely, Persian. We will see that the Persian stress facts defy any attempt to determine sentential stress on the basis of the selectional ordering of heads and arguments in a manner detailed above.[30] We noted in section 3.1 that in Persian, when elements are added to the left of the verb within a certain domain (to be defined more precisely in chapter 4), stress falls on the leftmost constituent, regardless of whether it is an adjunct or an argument. The Persian data in (12) are repeated in (44).

---

[29] Zubizarreta (1998) provides two arguments to justify the assumption that the nuclear stress rule determines the position only of primary (as opposed to non-primary) stress. She claims that only the location of primary stress is intimately related to the focus structure of the sentence. We will see in chapter 5 that in a multiple focus environment, a focused constituent may receive secondary stress. She also points out that only non-primary stress is influenced by rhythmic considerations. It is not clear if such rhythmic considerations can be extended to the sentence level, and even if so, whether this would necessarily lead to Zubizarreta's conclusion.

[30] In fairness, one has to point out that Zubizarreta takes the empirical scope of her theory to be Germanic and Romance. In fact, she clearly suggests that different languages may have different mechanisms to determine nuclear stress (Zubizarreta 1998: 91–2). It is worth noting, however, that typological differences are accounted for, in the generative tradition, by allowing variation along a parametric axis. That is a fundamental principle of the Principles-and-Parameters framework, the framework adopted by both Zubizarreta (1998) and the present monograph. Suggesting that two completely different mechanisms are responsible for a linguistic phenomenon in two different languages goes against this very basic principle. The theory developed in this monograph, on the other hand, adheres to this principle. Needless to say, regardless of one's theoretical persuasion, a theory which can account for a wider range of facts without having to introduce a radically different system should be preferred.

(44)   a.   Ali   [xord].
             Ali   ate

       b.   Ali   [mi-xord].
             Ali   DUR-ate
             'Ali would (used to) eat.'

       c.   Ali   [qazaa   mi-xord].
             Ali   food   DUR-ate
             'Ali would (used to) eat food.'

       d.   Ali   [xub   qazaa   mi-xord].
             Ali   well   food   DUR-ate
             'Ali would (used to) eat well.'

In (44a), the predicate consists of a single verb and the stress falls on the verb. This would be correctly predicted by Zubizarreta's C-NSR, given that there is no selectional ordering between the verb and the external argument. Example (44b) shows that if a mood marker is prefixed to the verb, stress falls on the mood marker. Kahnemuyipour (2003) shows that the best way to handle examples such as (44b) is to take the verbal prefix to constitute a separate morphosyntactic word, thus letting the "leftmost" generalization apply regularly and put stress on the prefix. Any other approach leads to an unnecessary complication of the otherwise very simple Persian word-level stress rule which places stress on the final syllable of a word. Sentence (44b), therefore, emerges as a problem for Zubizarreta's system. One would have to treat the prefix-verb either as a single word, thus adopting the complications discussed in Kahnemuyipour (2003), or as a separate word, in which case Zubizarreta's system would wrongly predict stress on the verb stem. Note that there is no selectional ordering (in Zubizarreta's sense) between the verb and the prefix, so the S-NSR cannot apply.[31] Sentence (44c) is an example of an SOV sentence with a non-specific object. Stress falls on the object. This is expected under Zubizarreta's system if we assume that, in Persian as in German, the S-NSR takes precedence over the C-NSR. The object is selectionally lower than the verb. Zubizarreta's system, however, fails to account for the stress on the manner adverb in (44d). There is no selectional ordering between [*xub* well] and [*qazaa mi-xord* food DUR-ate]. The S-NSR fails to

---

[31] One could perhaps adopt Cinque's (1993) treatment of the German separable prefixes, where it is suggested that the verb selects a PP with a null preposition (see 3.2). If such an analysis is adopted, then Zubizarreta's S-NSR correctly predicts stress on the prefix. However, it will still run into trouble for (44c), where an object is added to the picture. The expectation based on her theory would be that the stress should remain on the selectionally lowest element, which is the prefix. This is essentially the same problem Cinque's system had in the face of these facts.

apply and thus Zubizarreta's system would predict stress to remain on the non-specific object. Such examples indicate that allowing sentential stress to be sensitive to selectional considerations to account for stress facts in SOV languages is misguided. While it appears to be able to capture some SOV facts in German, it fails to do so in the core cases in Persian, another SOV language.

Further evidence against Zubizarreta's system comes from the stress behaviour of Persian sentences with a ditransitive verb. An example is provided in (45), which shows stress on the direct object.

(45)   Ali   <u>ye ketaab</u>   ru   miz   gozaasht.
       Ali   a   book   on   table   put
       'Ali put a book on the table.'

The application of Zubizarreta's NSR would predict stress on the prepositional phrase. The S-NSR fails to apply to $[DP_{obj}]$ and [PP V] as there is no selectional ordering between the two metrical sisters. C-NSR applies and assigns more prominence to [PP V]. Then the application of the S-NSR assigns prominence to the selectionally lower PP. Recall that we had to assume the S-NSR is ranked higher than the C-NSR in Persian to get the basic SOV facts correct in Zubizarreta's system. Meanwhile, a different ranking of the rules would not solve the problem as the C-NSR alone would wrongly predict stress on the verb. The example in (45), therefore, proves once again that a nuclear stress rule sensitive to selectional ordering makes the wrong predictions about Persian. The structurally sensitive rules we have seen so far, on the other hand, make the wrong predictions about (45) as well. While the sole application of Zubizarreta's C-NSR predicts stress on the verb, Cinque's system predicts stress on the constituent immediately preceding the verb, namely the PP. In chapter 4 we will see that an appropriate formulation of a purely structural sentential stress rule will correctly predict stress in these and the other cases discussed so far.

We used the Persian ditransitive example in (45) as evidence against Zubizarreta's selectionally sensitive stress system. The reader may recall, however, that Zubizarreta used a German example with a ditransitive verb, very similar to the Persian (45), as a canonical case supporting her theory. Let us have a closer look at the German example, repeated in (46), with the stress marking intentionally left out.

(46)   Karl   hat   ein   Buch   ins   Regal   gestellt.
       Karl   has   a   book   on-the   shelf   put
       'Karl put a book on the shelf.'

According to Zubizarreta, in the focus-neutral context, stress falls on the indirect object *Regal* in (46), providing support for the existence of the S-NSR. In their review of Zubizarreta (1998), Winkler and Göbbel (2002) take issue with the judgement provided by Zubizarreta for (46). Contrary to Zubizarreta, they report primary stress on the direct object *Buch* as the focus-neutral stress pattern.[32] To support their claim they provide the examples in (47) (the translations and the notational conventions are mine). Example (47a) is their own example, (47b) is attributed to Jacobs (1991: 22) (who calls it 'a perfect neutral stress pattern') and (47c) to Stechow and Uhmann (1986: 315ff).

(47) a. weil   er   eine Pistole auf   den   Tisch gelegt   hat.
          because he   a   gun   onto the   table put   has
          'because he put a gun on the table.'

      b. weil   er   ein Loch   in   die   Wand   geschlagen hat.
          because he   a   hole   into the   wall   hit   has
          'because he punched a hole in the wall.'

      c. weil   Ede mit   der   Hacke dies Loch   ins   Eis
          since Ede with the   axe   this hole   into.the ice
          gehackt hat.
          cut   has
          'because Ede cut a hole in the ice with an axe.'

An example from Krifka (1984) with nuclear stress marked on the direct object confirms the above stress judgments.[33] This is given in (48) (see also ch. 4 for more discussion).

(48) Maria hat   das   auto   in   die   garage gefahren.
      Mary   has   the   car   into the   garage driven
      'Mary has driven the car into the garage.'

Given the above evidence, it is safe to assume that in the German ditransitive sentences too, stress falls on the direct object. We have already seen that stress on the direct object poses a serious problem for Zubizarreta's system which would predict stress on the indirect object given the selectionally sensitive S-NSR.[34] A question remains as to why Zubizarreta's consultants provided

---

[32] Both of my consultants, too, clearly prefer stress on the direct object *Buch*, in an out-of-the-blue context. For one consultant stress on the indirect object forces a narrow focus reading, while for the other, it does not. The latter consultant still clearly prefers stress on the direct object in an informationally neutral setting.

[33] Thanks to Michael Wagner for bringing this example to my attention.

[34] These examples are also problematic for Cinque's (1993) system which predicts stress on the element immediately preceding the verb (see 3.2).

the facts with stress on the indirect object. It is worth noting that the interaction between information structure and sentential stress can easily complicate matters and make the correct recognition of neutral stress very difficult. Thus, for instance, the Persian example with stress on the PP, shown in (49), would be a perfectly acceptable sentence, one with the direct object topicalized. Importantly however, (49) would not be appropriate in an out-of-the-blue context. We return to the discussion of the interactions between information structure and sentential stress in chapter 5. More examples involving ditransitive verbs and PP arguments will be considered in chapter 4.[35]

(49)   Context: What did Ali do to a book/the books?
       Ali ye ketab ru <u>miz</u> gozaasht.
       Ali a book on table put
       'Ali put a book on the table.'

To sum up, in this section we looked at Zubizarreta's theory of nuclear stress and provided some conceptual and empirical evidence against her theory. In particular, it was shown that her theory suffers from a level of redundancy, as a result of which certain facts can be accounted for by either of the two modules of her stress system. On the other hand, similar facts in two languages, for example the stress on the object in two SVO languages such as English and Spanish, are accounted for by a different module in each language. Moreover, it was argued that Zubizarreta's theory fails to account for secondary stress. In addition to these conceptual problems, several empirical arguments were made against Zubizarreta's theory. These arguments were mainly based on the behaviour of sentential stress in Persian, where stress is neither sentence-final (as expected by a language that only employs the C-NSR), nor is it on an element predicted by the selectionally sensitive S-NSR. Finally, a closer look at ditransitives in German revealed another problematic case for Zubizarreta's theory.

3.5 Conclusion

In this chapter, we have looked at several influential syntactic approaches to sentential stress. We showed that even though these approaches have an advantage over phonological approaches in that they do not suffer from the overgeneration problem, they face other conceptual and empirical difficulties.

---

[35] In Persian and German, specific objects can move to a higher position, thus not receiving nuclear stress (see Cinque 1993 and chapter 4). Therefore, to elicit neutral stress in a [DP$_{subj}$ DP$_{obj}$ PP V] situation, one has to ensure that the object is non-specific and thus not able to undergo such movement. In the case discussed above, one way to ensure this is to ask a question such as *What does Karl do?* (meaning 'What is his job?') to elicit *He puts books on shelves.*

We started the chapter by looking at the most influential syntactic approach to sentential stress, that of Cinque (1993). On the conceptual side, it was argued that his theory falls apart once the head parameter is dispensed with (à la Kayne 1994). Moreover, to account for stress on the subject when the subject is more complex than the predicate, he had to resort to information structure, an implausible move for a null theory of sentential stress. Several empirical problems with Cinque's theory were presented, mainly based on the behaviour of sentential stress in Persian, but also with respect to German ditransitives as well as sentences involving both a separable prefix and an object. In all these cases, stress falls on the leftmost element within a certain stress domain rather than the constituent to the immediate left of the verb, as predicted by Cinque's system. Unaccusative and passive sentences with stress on the subject pose further problems to Cinque's theory. To circumvent this latter problem, Legate (2003) suggested that a Cinque-style stress rule applies in a cyclic phase-based fashion. She further allowed stress to be sensitive to the base-generated position of a constituent. We showed that while this may explain stress on the subject in unaccusative and passive sentences with the subject starting off as the internal argument of the verb, it runs into trouble in the face of wh-sentences and topicalized sentences. Moreover, as it relies on a Cinque-style system, it inherits all the problems his theory has with the Persian and German cases.

We finally looked at Zubizarreta (1998) who modularizes the nuclear stress rule into a structurally sensitive component, the C-NSR, and a selectionally sensitive component, the S-NSR. Using different rankings of these rules for different languages, she was able to account for a wide range of facts in German, English, French, and Spanish. It was shown, however, that her theory suffers from several conceptual and empirical problems. On the conceptual side, her theory exhibits internal redundancy and also fails to account for secondary stress. On the empirical side, we presented a range of problems from Persian and German which take into question any attempt that relies on the selectional ordering of constituents in determining sentential stress.

In the following chapter, we will develop a new theory of sentential stress which can account for all the above facts without facing the problems discussed in this chapter. This system shares with the theories discussed in this chapter the property that it is purely syntactic in that it does not rely on an additional language-specific (phonological) rule which refers to the direction of stress assignment, but it differs from them in several respects. It differs from Zubizarreta's theory in that selectional ordering plays no role in the way sentential stress is calculated. Like the C-NSR component of her theory, it only relies on the hierarchical syntactic structure of a sentence. It differs from Cinque's theory in that it does not depend on the head parameter. Unlike Legate's theory, it is not sensitive to the merge position of the syntactic constituents, making it capable of accounting for a range of cross-linguistic facts pointing to sensitivity to "surface structure", while avoiding the problems raised with respect to sentences with wh-objects or topicalized objects which show insensitivity to "deep structure". We will see, however, that its biggest difference from all of these theories is in the way the sentential stress rule is formulated. It is this new formulation that will enable it to account for the wide range of facts discussed in this chapter and the next.

4

Sentential stress:
a phase-based account

4.1 Introduction

In the previous two chapters we reviewed several influential phonological and syntactic approaches to the computation of sentential stress. In chapter 2, it was shown that the phonological analyses suffer from the over-generation problem and also fail to account for the stress pattern of passives and unaccusatives in languages like English and German. The syntactic analyses discussed in chapter 3, on the other hand, avoid the overgeneration problem but suffer from several other conceptual and empirical problems. On the conceptual side, Cinque's (1993) theory has to resort to information structure to account for stress on a complex subject in an informationally neutral context, an implausible result. Zubizarreta's (1998) theory, on the other hand, is internally redundant in that in some cases it has more than one way of accounting for identical facts. On the empirical side, both accounts (as well as Legate's 2003 modified version of Cinque) run into trouble in the face of facts from Persian, and also from a wider range of data from languages including those they were originally developed to account for.

In this chapter, I propose a syntactic account of sentential stress, based on the notions of phases and multiple spell-out, that does not encounter these problems. I start with a brief review of the basic principles of a multiple spell-out system. I then propose a new formulation for the sentential-stress rule within the multiple spell-out framework. By applying the proposed system of sentential-stress assignment to the cases we have considered so far as well as to some new cases, I show how it can account for them without facing the problems discussed in the previous chapter for the other syntactic accounts. In what follows we continue to consider informationally neutral sentences, that is, sentences uttered out of the blue. We will deal with the interaction between information structure and sentential stress in chapter 5. We start by looking at primary stress only, but will discuss the implications of the proposed system for the computation of secondary stress in section 4.10. Secondary stress will also play a role in our discussion of the interaction between sentential stress and information structure in chapter 5.

4.2 Phases and multiple spell-out: brief overview

The mechanism proposed here for the assignment of sentential stress crucially relies on the notions of phases and multiple spell-out. While these notions were introduced in chapter 1, section 1.2.1, a quick review of the core concepts is in order here.

According to the theory of phases and multiple spell-out, syntactic structure is sent off in chunks to PF and LF for phonological and semantic interpretation, respectively. We confine our discussion to the phonological side for our purposes here. Derivation proceeds bottom-up in a phase-by-phase manner. When the derivation reaches a phase, the (syntactic) complement of the phase head is shipped off for phonological interpretation. We called this syntactic chunk the SPELLEE. This process is shown schematically in the diagram in (1).

(1)

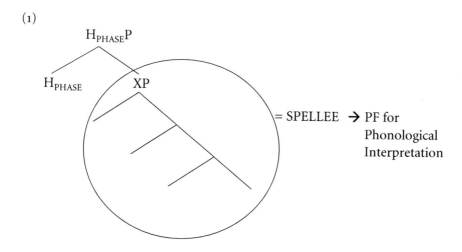

As to the question of what constitutes a phase, we adopted Chomsky's (2001, 2002) proposal that CPs and (transitive) vPs constitute phases. According to this view, unaccusative and passive verb phrases do not induce phasal boundaries.[1] This is a crucial assumption for the system developed below.

4.3 Phase-based computation of sentential stress

To overcome the problems discussed in chapters 2 and 3 and to account for some stress facts in Persian and other languages which cannot be captured by the other analyses in the literature, I propose the following mechanism for the assignment of sentential stress.

(2)   Sentential stress rule
      Sentential stress is assigned at the phase to the highest phonologi-
      cally non-null element (i.e. the phonological border) of the spelled out
      constituent or the SPELLEE.
      [$_{HP}$ XP [H YP]]: if HP is a phase, YP = SPELLEE.

In order better to understand the notion of highest element, consider the schematic tree diagram in (3), where constituents are shown abstractly using capital letters. In this tree diagram, the circled constituent, B, is the highest element.[2] We will illustrate the application of this rule to some actual examples. Meanwhile, it is worth considering a more formal definition of the notion of "highest" at this point. First, we should note that only elements on the non-branching side of the tree (i.e. heads, specifiers, or adjuncts) enter into our computation. Therefore, in our diagram in (3), competition arises only for B, D, E, H, J, K, L, N and not A, C, G, I, or M. An element X is considered to be higher than an element Y if X asymmetrically c-commands or dominates Y. Therefore, in this system, the highest element corresponds to the element that asymmetrically c-commands all the elements it does not dominate. In a right-branching structure assumed in this monograph (à la Kayne 1994), this would be the first left branch of the SPELLEE, B. If this node is phonologically null, the computation of the highest element applies one level lower: the first branch of its sister, F, which would then count as the highest element, and so on.[3] The following discussion and actual examples should help in clarifying this notion.

---

[1] I am abstracting away from the distinction between strong and weak phases (see ch. 1, n. 6).
[2] Note that our system makes no prediction about which element within B, namely C or D, receives more prominence (see 1.4).
[3] I have intentionally avoided references to directional notions such as "leftmost" or "rightmost" prevalent in the phonological literature. While at first glance it may look as if B is the leftmost element in the domain, it is not clear why D should not be taken as the leftmost element. Under our definition, B dominates and is therefore higher than D.

(3)

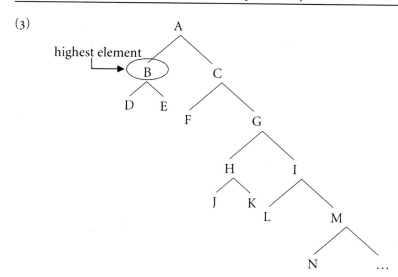

For the sake of illustration, consider a simple transitive sentence in SVO and SOV languages, exemplified by English and Persian in (4). Recall the generalization that main stress falls on the object in both of these language types. We also saw in chapter 2 that the subject receives more prominence than the verb. We return to the issue of the secondary stress on the subject in section 4.10. and will see how the proposed system correctly accounts for it.

(4)   a.   John bought <u>a book</u>.

      b.   Ali   <u>ye ketaab</u>   xarid.
           Ali   a book   bought
           'Ali bought a book.'

Following Kayne's (1994) antisymmetric theory of syntax, I am assuming that both SOV and SVO start off as SVO and the difference in word order is the result of movement (see ch. 1). Following Travis (1991, 1992; also Borer 1994; Koizumi 1995; Megerdoomian 2002; Jelinek and Carnie 2003, among others), I am assuming a split verbal structure with an inner aspectual head between the lexical head V and the functional head v (which introduces the external argument, Kratzer's 1994 voice head).[4] The verbal structure is thus divided into a lower (inner) verbal structure, projecting the internal arguments and inner aspectual elements, and a higher (outer) verbal structure, projecting the external argument. These verbal domains (roughly) correspond to the structural decomposition of events, with an inner event representing the change of

---

[4] We need a more articulated structure to allow for other internal arguments and adverbials, but this much is sufficient for our purposes at this point.

state in the predicate and an outer event denoting causation and agency (see Borer 1994; Megerdoomian 2002, among others). The phasal head v, which projects the external argument, thus determines the boundary between the inner event and the outer event (for the correlation between phase structure and event structure, see Butler 2003). The SPELLEE (i.e. the complement of the v head), therefore, contains all the internal arguments and the inner aspectual heads. I further take the object to move out of VP to the specifier position of the AspP for case assignment.[5] The structure and the relevant movement are shown schematically in (5). At the vP phase, the spelled-out constituent or the SPELLEE is the inner verbal domain or AspP. The object, the highest element in the SPELLEE, receives stress according to the sentential stress rule in (2). It is worth noting here that, throughout this monograph, in the context of stress assignment, the two terms stress domain and SPELLEE will be used interchangeably. It is important to remember that "stress domain" is not a primitive of the system, but derived from the phase-based system in a manner elaborated above.

(5)   vP   SPELLEE (Inner verbal domain) = Stress Domain

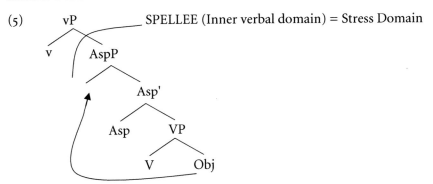

Before we proceed with the application of the stress rule to a wider range of examples, let us briefly consider the word-order difference between an SVO and an SOV language. Given that the object is proposed to move to the specifier of the AspP in both SVO and SOV languages, a question arises as to how we get the word-order difference in the two language types. If as standardly assumed the verb undergoes head-to-head movement to the v head, SOV order in a language like Persian is unexpected. It is worth noting that this question arises for any theory that adopts Kayne's (1994) antisymmetric syntax. In a system which takes both SVO and SOV to start off as SVO, the

---

[5] On movement of the object see also Johnson (1991) and Jelinek and Carnie (2003), among others; on the correlation between direct object/accusative case and aspect see Tenny (1994); Ritter and Rosen (2001); Pesetsky and Torrego (2001); Svenonius (2001, 2002), among others.

word-order difference has to be seen as the result of the movement of the V to a position higher than the object in SVO (but not in SOV) languages. One way of capturing this difference is to take the verb to move overtly to the v head only in SVO languages. Under this formulation, the verb does not move overtly to the v head in SOV languages and as a result appears after the object which is in the specifier of AspP in (4). It is worth noting, however, that this difference in word order does not interact with the stress system proposed here. Regardless of whether the verb is higher or lower than the object, stress falls on the object as the highest element in the SPELLEE.

In what follows I apply the sentential stress rule in (2) to a wide range of structures, including those discussed in the previous chapters as well as some new ones to show how the proposed system can account for the facts in a straightforward manner. As a starting point, we consider the Persian facts which were shown to be problematic for all the syntactic accounts discussed in chapter 3.

4.4 Sentential stress rule: the case of Persian

We considered the core cases of sentential stress assignment in Persian in chapter 3, where main stress was shown to fall on the leftmost element within a specific stress domain. According to the proposal in (2) above, the spelled out constituent or the SPELLEE is the stress domain, with the highest element in this domain receiving stress. At the phase v, the SPELLEE was identified as the inner verbal domain or AspP. The core pattern of sentential stress in Persian is illustrated in (6).

(6) a. Ali [$_{AspP}$ <u>xord</u>].
        Ali   ate

    b. Ali [$_{AspP}$ <u>mi</u>-xord]
        Ali   DUR-ate
        'Ali would eat/was eating.'

    c. Ali [$_{AspP}$ <u>qazaa</u> xord].
        Ali   food   ate
        'Ali ate food.'

    d. Ali [$_{AspP}$ <u>xub</u> qazaa xord].
        Ali   well food   ate
        'Ali ate well.'

Example (6a) shows a simple sentence with a verb with the stress on the verb. This is expected under (2), with the verb being the only and thus trivially the highest element in the stress domain. Example (6b) shows that if a durative marker (or an adverbial prefix, not shown in these examples; see Kahnemuyipour 2003) is prefixed to the verb, stress falls on the prefix. Kahnemuyipour (2003) argues that in order to maintain the simple generalization that stress is on the final syllable in Persian words, the best way to treat these verbal prefixes is to take them to constitute separate morphosyntactic words (see Kahnemuyipour 2003 for details). The verbal prefix thus occupies a separate functional head such as Asp.[6] As a result, the verbal prefix, being the highest element in the SPELLEE, receives stress. Sentence (6c) is an example of an SOV sentence with a non-specific object. Stress falls on the object, as discussed above and shown schematically in (5). Finally, the crucial example in (6d) shows the addition of a manner adverbial, argued to mark the left edge of the verbal domain (see e.g. Holmberg 1986 and Webelhuth 1992, among others). We can see that when a manner adverb appears to the left of the object, it receives stress. Some more examples with other manner and measure adverbs are provided in (7).

(7)   a.   Ali   <u>ziyaad</u>   dars   mi-xun-e.
           Ali   a lot   lesson   DUR-read-3SG
           'Ali studies a lot.'

      b.   Ali   <u>kam</u>   qazaa   xord.
           Ali   little   food   ate
           'Ali ate little food (lit. Ali ate food a little).'

      c.   Ali   <u>aarum</u>   ketaab   mi-xun-e
           Ali   slowly   book   DUR-read-3SG
           'Ali reads slowly.'

      d.   Ali   <u>bad</u>   futbaal   baazi   mi-kon-e.
           Ali   bad   football   play   DUR-do-3SG
           'Ali plays football badly.'

The syntax of adverbials will be discussed in more detail in section 4.6. We will see that, in comparison to other adverbials (e.g. speaker-oriented adverbs), manner adverbs and measure adverbs are argued to be low in the syntactic structure. The stress pattern in (6d) and (7) is expected under a system which predicts stress on the highest element within the stress domain, under the assumption that the manner or measure adverbial is inside and marks the left boundary of the stress domain in Persian. Recall from chapter 3 that

---

[6] Whether the prefix is in the Asp head or some independent functional head has no bearing on our discussion.

the same type of example created serious problems for both Cinque's system, which predicted stress on the constituent to the immediate left of the verb, and Zubizarreta's system, which predicted stress on a non-final element only if it were selectionally ordered with respect to the material following it. The adverbial is not selectionally ordered with respect to $[DP_{obj} V]$, and thus sentence-final stress is predicted by Zubizarreta's system, contrary to fact. Examples such as (6d) and (7), with stress on the leftmost element within a specific domain, crucially point to a structural account of sentential stress which, unlike Cinque's NSR and Zubizarreta's C-NSR, refers to the highest element in the stress domain derived from the phase-based spell-out system. We will see how this new formulation of the sentential stress rule is necessary to account for some other stress facts in different languages.

The stress behaviour of manner adverbials in different languages introduces some interesting complications to which we will return in section 4.6. We will see that while manner and measure adverbials are low in the structure in comparison to other types of adverbs, there is parametric variation with respect to whether they are inside or outside the stress domain. It will be proposed that this is due to a variation in the merge position of manner adverbials in different languages. While in Persian and Eastern Armenian, these elements are merged below vP, thus inside the stress domain, in English and German they are merged above vP, outside the stress domain. I put off a more detailed discussion of the behaviour of manner adverbials to section 4.6.

It is worth noting here that the stress behaviour of the German separable prefixes discussed by Cinque can now receive an account similar to the one proposed above for the Persian verbal prefixes. The basic German fact from Cinque is repeated in (8), indicating stress on the separable prefix.

(8)   ...Wann   werden   wir $[_{AspP}$ <u>an</u> + kommen]?   (Cinque's n. 20, (ia))
          when   will   we   arrive?

According to the stress system in (2), the separable prefix receives stress by virtue of being the highest element in the stress domain. Cinque accounted for (8) by suggesting that the separable prefixes are heads of intransitive PPs selected by the verb. We saw in chapter 3, however, that when an object is added to the left of the separable prefix, stress falls on the object. The relevant facts are repeated in (9). Recall that according to Cinque, the most deeply embedded element in the clause receives stress. This is translated into the element to the immediate left of the verb in an SOV-type sentence. Given his analysis of the separable prefix as the complement of the verb, the stress would be wrongly predicted on the separable prefix in (9).

(9)   a.   Karl   wird   [$_{AspP}$ <u>Kleider</u>   um-arbeiten].
         *Karl   wird   Kleider   <u>um</u>-arbeiten.
         Karl   will   dresses   alter
         'Karl will alter dresses.'

      b.   Karl   hat   [$_{AspP}$ <u>ein Buch</u>   ein-gekauft].
         *Karl   hat   ein Buch   <u>ein</u>-gekauft.
         Karl   has   a   book
         'Karl shopped for a book.'

      c.   Ein   Mädchen   hat   [$_{AspP}$ <u>einen Ballon</u>   auf-gepumpt].
         *Ein   Mädchen   hat   einen Ballon   <u>auf</u>-gepumpt.
         a   girl   has   a   balloon   inflated
         'A girl inflated a balloon.'

Our new formulation, on the other hand, takes stress to fall on the highest/leftmost element in the stress domain or the SPELLEE, correctly identifying the object as the element receiving primary stress in the examples in (9).

We have seen in this section how the proposed sentential-stress rule—coupled with some reasonable syntactic assumptions—can account for the core stress facts in Persian (as well as several cases in German), where stress appears to be leftmost within a particular domain. These facts created problems for the other syntactic accounts discussed in chapter 3. Specific and non-specific objects exhibit an interesting difference in their stress behaviour, which receives a straightforward account under the above proposal. This is the topic of the next section.

4.5 Specific vs. non-specific objects

There is a striking contrast between the stress pattern of a non-specific object (10a) (repeated from (6c)) and a specific one (10b) which receives a straightforward account under the proposed analysis. It has been proposed in the syntactic literature that specific objects are in a higher syntactic position than their non-specific counterparts (see Mahajan 1990 for Hindi; Koopman and Sportiche 1991, and de Hoop 1996, for Dutch; Enç 1991 and Diesing 1992 for Turkish, among others). This claim was specifically made for Persian by Browning and Karimi (1994) (for arguments in favour of this position, see also Ghomeshi 1996, Karimi 1996, Megerdoomian 2002; for a different view see Karimi 2003). Following this widely accepted view, I take the specific object to move to a higher syntactic position outside the stress domain, such as the (second) specifier of vP. This analysis is supported by the position of the object relative to manner adverbs. In (10c), with a non-specific object, the adverb precedes the object. In (10d), on the other hand, the specific object precedes the adverb. This is not surprising if the specific object is outside of vP, and thus outside the stress domain. The difference in the stress behaviour of specific and non-specific objects is thus expected in the proposed system, as it is tied to a syntactic difference between the two. The highest element in the SPELLEE is the non-specific object in (10a), the verb in (10b) and the manner adverb in (10c) and (10d).[7]

(10) a. Ali [AspP qazaa xord].
          Ali   food   ate
          'Ali ate food.'

      b. Ali qazaa-ro [AspP xord]
          Ali food-ACC   ate
          'Ali ate the food.'

      c. Ali [AspP xub qazaa xord]
          Ali   well food   ate
          'Ali ate food well.'

      d. Ali qazaa-sh-o [AspP xub xord]
          Ali food-his-ACC   well ate
          'Ali ate his food well.'

The contrast illustrated in (10) for Persian has been noted for other languages such as German and Dutch, and a positional analysis has been proposed. In Persian, the specific object obligatorily moves to a higher position and receives a special marking *-ra* (colloquially *-ro* or *-o* depending on the phonological environment).[8] In German and Dutch, on the other hand, the movement is not obligatory and may depend on factors other than specificity (see, for example, de Hoop 1996; Reinhart 1996). The crucial point is that in these languages, just as in Persian, when the object moves to a higher position, it does not receive stress. The data in (11) and (12) from German and Dutch illustrate this pattern.

(11) German (adapted from Cinque 1993: 254–5):
      a. Der Arzt wird [einen Patienten untersuchen].
          the doctor will   a   patient   examine
          'The doctor will examine a patient.'

---

[7] The initial *r* in the accusative marker is dropped in colloquial Persian when preceded by a consonant, leading to (10d).

[8] *-ra* is an accusative marker that appears only on specific objects (for different analyses of Persian *-ra*, see Karimi 1990, 1996; Dabir-Moghaddam 1992; Ghomeshi 1996). The fact that non-specific objects are either morphologically unmarked or marked differently from their specific counterparts is not peculiar to Persian: see Ritter and Rosen (2001) and references cited there.

    b. Der Arzt   wird den Patienten [<u>untersuchen</u>].
        the   doctor will   the   patient   examine
        'The doctor will examine the patient.'

(12)   Dutch (adapted from Reinhart 1996):
    a. dat ik gisteren   [<u>het boek</u> las]
       that I   yesterday the book read
    b. dat ik het boek gisteren   [<u>las</u>]
       that I   the book yesterday read
       'that I read the book yesterday'

In the German pair in (11), the objects differ in definiteness. While in (11a) the object is indefinite, the one on (11b) is definite. As in Persian, the indefinite object is stressed and the definite object is not. In the Dutch pair in (12), on the other hand, both objects are definite but their position relative to the adverb shows that the object in (12b) has undergone movement to a higher position (see also Kiparsky 1966; Cinque 1993; Reinhart 1996) with similar implications for sentential stress.

    The account of the difference between specific and non-specific objects in Persian and other languages underlines an important property of the system proposed in this monograph for the assignment of sentential stress. According to this approach, sentential stress is not sensitive to the underlying (or merge) position of a constituent, and thus elements such as specific objects, which move out of the stress domain for independent syntactic reasons, may escape sentential stress. We will consider another case of this phenomenon for wh-questions in chapter 5. In this respect, the theory developed here agrees with Cinque (1993) and Zubizarreta (1998) and stands in sharp contrast to a proposal from Bresnan (1971, 1972) (adopted by Legate 2003), which takes nuclear stress to be sensitive to the underlying structure of a sentence.

    The above proposal for the assignment of sentential stress raises an immediate question with respect to sentential stress in a language such as English. Putting unaccusative and passive sentences aside, sentential stress is sentence-final in English, the prime motivation for Chomsky and Halle's (1968) original formulation of the Nuclear Stress Rule (see ch. 2). While the above system correctly predicts stress on the object in a simple SVO sentence, it is not clear how it can handle all the other cases of sentence-final stress. To address this issue, I start with a discussion of adverbials. By providing a comparative study of their stress behaviour in Persian and English, I show how the correct conceptualisation of the above system does in fact make the right predictions for both languages.

4.6 Adverbials: a comparative look at Persian and English

We ended the previous section with a question about how the application of the phase-based sentential stress rule in (2) could correctly predict sentence-final stress in English sentences. In this section we explore this question by comparing the behaviour of adverbials in Persian and English and accounting for their stress patterns. We will see that with the correct analysis of the syntax of adverbials and an additional assumption about the implementation of our sentential stress rule, their stress behaviour will fall into place in the proposed theory. The particular conception of the syntax of adverbials is based on Cinque's (1999, 2002, 2004) seminal work on the topic. I start with a brief review of the relevant principles of Cinque's theory of adverbials. It is important to note at the outset that Cinque's (1999, 2002, 2004) work on adverbs is based on an underlying assumption which is incompatible with his work on nuclear stress. While his work on stress relies crucially on the head parameter, in his work on adverbs, Cinque (following Kayne 1994) dispenses with the head parameter and lays out his theory in an antisymmetric framework (see 3.2 for a discussion of Cinque's 1993 crucial reliance on the head parameter). Moreover, Cinque's particular proposal about the syntax of adverbs, as we will see below, is radically different from what he assumed to account for their stress. Recall that in his work on stress, he took the adverbs to be the lowest constituent in a Larsonian VP-shell, thus receiving stress as the most deeply embedded item (see 3.2). This is precisely the type of structure he argues against on syntactic grounds in his later work on adverbs (in particular Cinque 2002, 2004). In what follows, I am departing from the syntactic assumptions in Cinque's work on nuclear stress and will use his work on the syntax of adverbs as a framework to account for the stress behaviour of adverbials within the system I am proposing in this monograph.

4.6.1 *The syntax of adverbials: Cinque (1999, 2002, 2004)*

In this section, we briefly review the basic tenets of Cinque's (1999, 2002, 2004) theory of adverbs. In his work on the syntax and order of adverbs, Cinque (1999) argues for locating adverbs in the specifiers of distinct functional projections within a well-articulated theory of clause structure. The functional heads corresponding to these adverbs, Cinque argues, encode different types of functional notions such as mood, modality, tense, aspect, voice, etc. He uses the rigid ordering of these functional projections to account for the ordering of the inflectional morphemes and the adverbials across languages. Cinque's (1999) detailed breakdown for a universal order of the functional projections and their corresponding adverbs is compatible with a less refined hierarchy of adverbs, generally accepted in the literature (see Jackendoff 1972 and subsequent work). In this less refined hierarchy, each class represents several adverbs in Cinque's system. This hierarchy, given in (13), is sufficient for our purposes.[9]

(13)   Hierarchy of adverbs
       speaker-oriented   adverbs   >   subject-oriented   adverbs   >
       manner/measure adverbs.

According to (13), the speaker-oriented adverbs appear to the left of subject-oriented adverbs, which in turn appear to the left of manner adverbs. In structural terms, the adverbs on the left are merged higher than those on the right. In particular, as we will see below, crucial to our discussion is a distinction between manner adverbs—the lowest in the hierarchy in (13)—and other type of adverbs.

There is a class of adverbials of place, time, and manner, known as circumstantial adverbials, which are typically PPs and appear after the complement of the verb in English. The structure and order of these adverbial PPs are the topic of Cinque (2002, 2004) (see also Barbiers 1995, and Nilsen 2000). A detailed discussion of Cinque's work will take us too far afield from our main topic—sentential stress—but the points relevant to our discussion are summarized below. For illustration purposes, we will consider a simple sentence involving only two such prepositional phrases, a locative PP (PP_{LOC}) and a temporal PP (PP_{TEMP}), as exemplified in (14).

(14)   I gave a talk [$_{PP_{LOC}}$ at MIT] [$_{PP_{TEMP}}$ on Thursday].

Cinque (2002, 2004) considers two possible structures for these adverbials. These possibilities are given in (15). The right-adjunction structure in (15a), originally from Chomsky (1981), and the VP-shell structure in (15b), from Larson (1988, 1990), make different predictions with respect to c-command and binding relations. We will return to this issue below.

---

[9] In general, the proposals made in this monograph do not rely on the detailed cartography proposed by Cinque (1999), but rather a broader perspective which distinguishes several general domains, with each housing one broad type of adverbial (see e.g. Grohmann 2003).

(15)   a. Right-adjunction structure

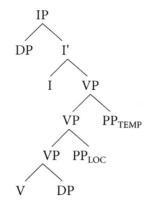

b. VP-shell structure

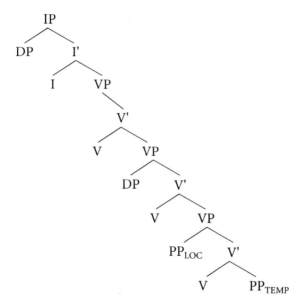

Cinque (2002, 2004) points out that two different sets of evidence have been put forth, each providing support for one of the structures in (15) (also referred to as Pesetsky's paradox). On the one hand, the lack of Principle C effects (e.g. Lakoff 1968; Reinhart 1983), constituency diagnostics (e.g. Pesetsky 1995; Nilsen 2000) and relative scope (e.g. Manzini 1995; Pesetsky 1995; Brody 1997) favour the structure in (15a), that is, a structure in which the PP on the right is higher than and c-commands the PP on the left, which in turn is higher than the direct object. A pair showing the lack of Principle C effects between the direct object and an R-expression contained in the adverbial PP is given in (16) (adapted from Cinque 2002). The example in (16) should lead to a principle C violation if *him* c-commands *John* as predicted ¹ *y* the structure in (15b). The right-adjunction structure in (15a), on the other hand, makes the correct prediction with respect to Principle C.

(16)   They killed him$_k$ on the very first day John$_k$ was being released from prison.

On the other hand, anaphor binding (e.g. Pesetsky 1995), pronominal binding (e.g. Stroik 1990; Pesetsky 1995) and licensing of negative polarity items (e.g. Stroik 1990; Pesetsky 1995) seem to favour the structure in (15b), a structure in which the PP on the left is higher than and c-commands the PP on the right. A pair showing the facts with respect to the binding of anaphors is given in (17) (adapted from Pesetsky 1995). The facts in (17) indicate that *these people* should c-command *each other* in compliance with the structure in (15a), not (15b).

(17)   a.   John spoke to Mary about *these people* in *each other's* houses on Tuesday.

          b.   *John spoke to Mary about *each other* in *these people's* houses on Tuesday.

A question arises as to how we can capture both sets of facts at the same time. To resolve the above paradox and to account for some ordering restrictions, Cinque proposes that these adverbials are preverbal at Merge and that their postverbal surface position is the result of the movement of the lower VP (the verb and its argument) around them (see also Nilsen 2000). This way the Merge position provides us with the required configuration to capture the effects corresponding to (15a), whereas the final surface configuration handles the effects corresponding to (15b). The Merge position is shown schematically in (18). Note also that the order of the PPs in (18) is the mirror-image of their post-verbal order in English. The English order is obtained via movement of the VP to a specifier position between the PP$_{LOC}$ and PP$_{TEMP}$, followed by the movement of the whole [VP PP$_{LOC}$] complex to a specifier higher than PP$_{TEMP}$. This manner of deriving the order of adjuncts (also known as roll-up) is now fairly standard within a type of syntactic framework initiated by Cinque's work on adjuncts within the noun phrase and the verb phrase (see Cinque 1999, 2000; Rackowski and Travis 2000; Pearce 2002; Shlonsky 2004; Kahnemuyipour and Massam 2006, among

others).[10] The crucial point here is that adverbials are base-generated preverbally, with their surface position the result of the movement of VP around
them, as shown in (18).

(18) $DP_{subject}$ ... T ... PP_{TEMP} ... PP_{LOC} ... VP

I adopt the analysis in (18) and will show in the next section how the stress
facts in Persian and English with respect to adverbials can be accounted
for.

4.6.2 *Stress facts: Persian vs. English*

We are now ready to consider the stress behaviour of different types of adverbials in Persian and English in light of the syntactic analysis presented above.
A close analysis reveals several patterns of stress in Persian and English. The
first pattern is found in structurally high adverbs, which are stressed neither
in Persian nor in English. The second observed pattern concerns adverbs that
are not stressed in Persian, but are stressed and sentence-final in English. The
most intriguing case, however, is the stress behaviour of manner/measure
adverbs, the lowest adverbs in the hierarchy in (13). While these adverbs
are consistently stressed in Persian, they exhibit dual behaviour in English:
they are stressed when in sentence-final position, but not in sentence-medial
position. Each of these stress patterns will be the subject of one of the following subsections, with the goal of showing how their stress behaviour can be
accounted for in the proposed system.

4.6.2.1 *Not stressed in Persian, not stressed in English*   In looking at the stress
behaviour of adverbials in Persian and English, we come across a group which
is stressed neither in Persian nor in English. This pattern occurs with the high
adverbs, in other words, speaker- and subject-oriented adverbs in (13). An
example of a speaker-oriented adverb *probably* is provided in (19), with the
stress domain marked by square brackets.

(19) a. I'll probably take [the subway].
      b. man   ehtemaalan   [esteyk   mi-xor-am]
          I   probably   steak   DUR-eat-1SG
          'I'll probably have steak.'

---

[10] The various accounts of deriving the surface order of elements from a universal base order differ
in details that are not of interest to us here.

The stress pattern in (19) is expected; the high adverbs are outside the stress domain and thus unstressed.[11]

4.6.2.2 Not stressed in Persian, stressed and sentence-final in English   The stress behaviour of circumstantial adverbials (see 4.6.1) reveals an interesting difference between Persian and English. While these adverbials are stressed and sentence-final in English, they surface in their Merge position (see (18)) and are not stressed in Persian. This contrast is shown in the examples in (20).

(20) a. I walked the dog in the <u>park</u>.

     b. maa tu   paark <u>futbaal</u> baazi kard-im
          we   in   park   soccer   play   did-1PL
          'We played soccer in the park.'

From a structural perspective, we have noted that these adverbials are merged higher than manner adverbs in compliance with the adverbial hierarchy. We also noted in section 4.4 that the manner adverbs mark the edge of the stress domain or the SPELLEE in Persian (see also section 4.6.2.3). Therefore, the circumstantial adverbials, having been merged higher than the manner adverbs, are expected to be outside the stress domain. The fact that they do not receive stress in Persian (20b) is therefore expected. Their stress pattern in English, on the other hand, is a surprise. To account for the stress pattern of circumstantial adverbials in English I propose the following.

We have seen so far that sentential stress is assigned to the highest element in the stress domain: the SPELLEE. The circumstantial adverbials are assumed to be merged outside the stress domain in both Persian and English. Meanwhile, if we adopt Cinque's analysis of circumstantial adverbials, in other words, if their final position in English is the result of the movement of lower material to a position higher than the adverbials, at the time of stress assignment the stress domain will be phonologically empty. It is in these cases that I propose stress is realized on the closest phonologically non-null element, for example on the locative in (20a). This mechanism is illustrated schematically in (21). In (21), the two copies of the VP are marked in angled brackets with the higher pronounced copy highlighted.[12]

---

[11] In both English and Persian, these speaker-oriented adverbs can occur in other positions, namely, sentence-initially or sentence-finally. These informationally marked options do not affect stress and have thus been left out of the discussion (see section 5.5 for a discussion of the interaction between movement and stress).

[12] The proposed mechanism may appear to be counter-cyclic, raising the question of how the lower SPELLEE (which is phonologically null in this case) can access the higher SPELLEE for the realization of stress. It should be noted, however, that this repair mechanism takes place at a point when cyclicity is not an issue. The process can be best understood in the framework of the copy theory of movement, where the two copies are identical up to the point of lexical insertion at PF. When the lower SPELLEE is

(21)

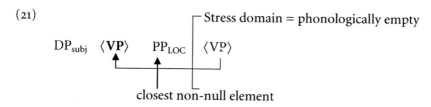

Stress domain = phonologically empty

DP~subj~ ⟨**VP**⟩   PP~LOC~   ⟨VP⟩

closest non-null element

The mechanism schematized in (21) accounts for stress on constituents that are merged high (i.e. outside the stress domain) according to the hierarchy in (13) but appear sentence-finally in English. In their Persian counterparts, on the other hand, these constituents surface in their high merge position and are thus not stressed, as expected.[13] English manner adverbs, which allow for two possible surface positions (see section 4.6.2.3 and references cited there), provide additional support for the above proposal. These adverbs are stressed in sentence-final but not in sentence-medial position, underlining the relation between stress and surface position as predicted by the above mechanism. The dual behaviour of English manner adverbs with respect to stress highlights the fact that adverb type does not directly dictate stress, and provides a strong case for the relation between (derived) syntactic structure and sentential stress. Manner adverbs will be discussed in more detail in section 4.6.2.3.

It is worth noting here that the stress behaviour of some temporal adverbials (such as *today*, *yesterday* and *tomorrow*) in English appears to pose a problem for the above proposal. In Persian, their behaviour is as expected. Like locative and other temporal adverbials, they appear high in the clause, are outside the stress domain and thus unstressed. This is shown in (22).[14]

sent off to PF, the sentential stress rule applies and assigns stress to the highest element in the SPELLEE. Crucially, lexical insertion has to occur at a point when both copies and thus both phases are accessible. If at this point, the whole lower SPELLEE is phonologically null, sentential stress is realized on the closest phonologically non-null element.

[13] The proposal that the circumstantial PPs are merged higher than the VP coupled with the fact that the VP does not move around them in Persian implies that we should not get binding or negative polarity licensing from the VP-internal object into the PPs (that is, the evidence used in favour of the VP-shell structure and one motivation for Cinque's proposal for the syntax of English circumstantial adverbials). Given that in Persian the VP-internal object is non-specific and that the licensing of negative polarity items is possible only by negation on the verb, the tests cannot be applied.

[14] The order of the Persian temporal adverbials with respect to the locative adverbials provides further support for Cinque's hierarchy. The relative order in Persian is: [DP~subj~ PP~TEMP~ PP~LOC~ DP~obj–nonspec~ V]; e.g.

(i) *man diruz   tu   baaq-e   vahsh meymun   didam*
     I   yesterday in   garden-Ez wild   monkey   saw-1sg.
     'I saw monkeys in the zoo yesterday.'

The order in English is the mirror-image of the Persian order, which is expected under the roll-up analysis proposed by Cinque.

(22) a. Ali diruz   <u>ketaab</u> xund
          Ali yesterday book   read
          'Ali read books yesterday.'

      b. man fardaa   <u>maashin</u> mi-xar-am
          I   tomorrow car   DUR-buy-1SG
          'I am buying a car tomorrow.'

In English, on the other hand, these temporal adverbials appear sentence-finally but are typically unstressed in focus-neutral contexts, contrary to what is predicted by the above system, where the movement of the VP around the adverbial results in the stress on the adverbial as the closest phonologically non-null element. Some examples are provided in (23).[15]

(23) a. John ran into <u>Mary</u> yesterday.

      b. Mary is moving to <u>the US</u> tomorrow.

Before attempting to provide an explanation, let us see how the other accounts of sentential stress fare with the facts in (23). A phonological account such as Chomsky and Halle's (1968) NSR would wrongly predict stress on the rightmost constituent, the adverbial. Zubizarreta's (1998) modular NSR would wrongly predict stress on the adverbial as well. Recall that she translates precedence into hierarchical structure. Thus the adverbial, which is at the end of the sentence, is taken to be the lowest in the structure. Meanwhile, her S-NSR cannot apply to the structure, as the metrical sisters [V] and [DP$_{obj}$ Adv] are not selectionally ordered. The C-NSR then predicts stress on the lowest element in the syntactic structure, that is, the adverbial. Evaluating Cinque's (1993) account is somewhat more difficult as it depends crucially on the structure he would attribute to these examples. If we extend his right-branching structures for English (including those involving manner adverbs) to these cases, his system would wrongly predict stress on the adverbials as the most deeply embedded constituent. If, on the other hand, we allow these adverbials to right-adjoin above the verb phrase, then the stress and the word order can be captured at the same time. In fact, if we allowed for such a structure, the systems proposed by Zubizarreta and the one we proposed above would also be able to capture the facts. For Zubizarreta, the adverbial would no longer be structurally the lowest constituent, thus not predicted to receive stress under the C-NSR. For us, the adverbial would be outside the stress domain and thus expected not to receive stress. In other words, the

---

[15] The Persian order is marginally acceptable in English, much more common in journalistic discourse. An example is *George Bush yesterday denied reports*.... The adverbials are unstressed in these cases. I am putting aside such examples in the ensuing discussion.

stress, which is the same in Persian and English, could be attributed to the high attachment of the adverbials in both languages, while the order difference would be handled by allowing the adverbials to left-adjoin in Persian and right-adjoin in English.

There are two problems with allowing such a structure, however. First, it would go against Kayne's antisymmetric system and against much of the motivation for Cinque's (1999, 2002, 2004) proposal with respect to the syntax of adverbials adopted in this monograph. More importantly, it would be hard to capture the stress behaviour of these adverbials and maintain the account for the regular stress pattern found with other temporal adverbials in English. As exemplified in (24), other sentence-final temporal adverbials in English receive stress in focus-neutral contexts.

(24)   John is defending his thesis in <u>July</u>.

To maintain a Cinque-style analysis, one would have to suggest that while the time adverbials such as 'yesterday' are right adjoined in a position higher than the verb phrase, the temporal adverbial in (24) is the complement of a verb in a Larsonian shell (see ch. 3) and thus the most deeply embedded element in the clause. We, on the other hand, would have to propose different directions of adjunction and different derivations for *yesterday*-type adverbials and the one in (24). These would be ad hoc stipulations. In fact, the existence of the regular pattern shown in (24) strongly suggests that there is something special about *yesterday*-type adverbials that leads to their stress behaviour. I concur with Zubizarreta (1998), who ties the stress behaviour of these adverbials to their deictic nature, that is, the fact that they pick out their referents in relation to the context of utterance. In other words, these adverbials avoid sentential stress in the same way that anaphoric pronouns do (cf. *John saw Mary.* vs. *John <u>saw</u> her*). This logic also predicts that locative adverbials such as *here* and *there* should fail to receive sentential stress in a focus-neutral context as well. This prediction is borne out, as shown in the examples in (25).

(25)   a.   John ate <u>an apple</u> here.

       b.   John gave <u>a talk</u> there.

4.6.2.3 *Stressed in Persian, stressed/unstressed in English*   Manner adverbs as well as some measure adverbs (e.g. *a lot*) exhibit the most intriguing stress pattern. While in Persian these adverbs are consistently stressed in a focus-neutral context, in English they exhibit dual behaviour: they are stressed in sentence-final position but not in sentence-medial position. In this subsection, we will consider this type of adverb and provide an account of its stress behaviour in Persian and English.

Consider Persian first. Some sentences involving manner/measure adverbs are provided in (26).

(26) a. Ali <u>aarum</u> qazaa mi-xor-e.
          Ali slowly food DUR-eat-3SG
          'Ali eats slowly.'

      b. Ali <u>xub</u> baazi kard.
          Ali well play did
          'Ali played well.'

      c. Ali <u>xeyli</u> sib dust daare.
          Ali a lot apple friend has
          'Ali likes apples a lot.'

Manner adverbs were taken to be the lowest in the hierarchy of adverbs in (13). In section 4.4 it was suggested that in Persian these adverbs mark the left edge of the stress domain (i.e. the SPELLEE) and are thus stressed based on our sentential stress rule which assigns stress to the highest element in this domain. I will assume for the sake of illustration that manner adverbs are located in the specifier of a functional projection above AspP, hereafter called ManP. The SPELLEE is the complement of the v head, or the ManP, with its highest element being the manner adverb. There is nothing surprising about the stress behaviour of manner adverbs in Persian. The proposed structure is shown schematically in (27).[16]

(27) ...[$_{vP}$ v | [$_{ManP}$ Adv$_{Man}$ [$_{AspP}$ DP$_{obj}$ Asp [$_{VP}$ V t$_{obj}$]
                  | SPELLEE = Stress domain

We now turn to English. In English, as noted above, the manner adverbs exhibit dual behaviour with respect to stress. When these adverbs appear in a sentence-final position, they receive stress. This is shown in the examples in (28).

(28) a. John answered the questions <u>cleverly</u>.

      b. John ate the cake <u>slowly</u>.

      c. John played the game <u>well</u>.

      d. John likes apples <u>a lot</u>.

[16] In compliance with Cinque (1999), I have assumed that adverbs are in the specifiers of their respective functional projections. Nothing in our proposals crucially hinges on this assumption, however. The system can be maintained with minor adjustments under a theory in which adverbs are taken to involve adjunction structures. For example, if the manner adverb is taken to be adjoined to AspP, it would still be the highest element in the SPELLEE, the complement of v.

Given the facts in (28), one may be tempted to suggest that these adverbs are assigned stress in English in the same position as their Persian counterpart and the order difference, as proposed by Cinque (2002, 2004), is the result of the movement of the lower elements around these adverbs in English. This proposal for the stress pattern of these adverbs runs into trouble, however, in the face of the other surface possibility for these adverbs in English. As noted above, (some of) these adverbs may appear in the sentence-medial position, and crucially, in this position, they do not receive sentential stress, as shown in the examples in (29).[17] It is important to note that the adverbs in (29) allow for a subject-oriented reading as well. At this point, however, we are only interested in the manner reading, which is possible both sentence-medially and sentence-finally (see Jackendoff 1972 and subsequent authors). We will return to the different interpretations of adverbs later in this section.[18]

(29)   a.   John cleverly answered <u>the questions</u>.

     b.   John slowly ate <u>the cake</u>.

The facts in (29) indicate that the stress on the manner adverbs when they appear sentence-finally cannot be attributed to their Merge position as the highest element of the SPELLEE or the stress domain because if manner adverbs were the highest element in the SPELLEE in English, as is the case in Persian, we would expect the manner adverbs to receive stress in (29). In the previous subsection, however, we introduced a different mechanism for the assignment of stress to the sentence-final circumstantial adverbs. These adverbs are merged outside the stress domain. It was suggested that they receive stress in the sentence-final position due to the movement of the lower elements around the adverbs, making them the closest phonologically non-null element to the otherwise emptied stress domain. If we extend this mechanism to the manner adverbs, their dual behaviour can be accounted for. The manner adverbs are thus proposed to be merged outside the stress domain (or SPELLEE) in English. As such, they do not receive stress in that position,

---

[17] The possibility of the manner reading of the adverb in the sentence-medial position is discussed in Jackendoff (1972) and confirmed by most native speakers of English I have consulted. The discussion in this monograph is based on the possibility of the manner reading in both positions. Some speakers, however, allow the manner reading only in the sentence-final position. Given the discussion, it could be the case that for these English speakers the manner adverb is placed lower within the stress domain or the SPELLEE, as is the case in Persian. This has repercussions for the discussion of VP-fronting below. I will not pursue this issue any further.

[18] Note that some manner adverbs (e.g. *well*) and measure adverbs (e.g. *a lot*) appear only in the sentence-final position. This suggests that we may need a breakdown of these adverbs into more finely defined groups in English (see Cinque 1999). I put this issue aside and focus on the difference between English and Persian.

explaining the stress facts with the manner adverbs in sentence-medial position in (29). When the lower elements move around them, on the other hand, these adverbs appear in sentence-final position and receive stress according to the mechanism detailed above (see (28)). This dual behaviour of English manner adverbs with respect to stress and their correlation with position in the sentences provides support for the mechanism proposed in (21). It also undermines any attempt to connect the stress behaviour of manner adverbs directly to their adverb type without close consideration of the (derived) syntactic structure of the whole clause. The type of adverb determines its position which will in turn impact its stress behaviour. Meanwhile, their ultimate syntactic behaviour in a particular clause can only be determined when all other details of the (derived) syntactic structure are taken into consideration.

The proposed account crucially relies on a difference between what is spelled out in Persian and English. It was suggested that in Persian, the SPELLEE contains the manner adverb, while in English it does not. This raises a question about how this difference can be implemented in our system. I will explore several possibilities and opt for the most promising. One way to treat this difference is to adhere to the rigid universal ordering of adverbs and take manner adverbs to merge at exactly the same position in Persian and English. Under this view, the difference in their stress would have to be a result of a difference between what is spelled out in the two languages, with Persian spelling out the complement of the phase-head v, but English skipping the adverbial projection ManP and spelling out the rest.[19] This option is schematically shown in (30), with V-movement not indicated.

(30)   Manner adverbs: explaining cross-linguistic difference; first attempt

$$\ldots[_{vP}\ V \;\Big|\; [_{ManP}\ Adv_{Man}]\; \Big|\; \overbrace{[_{AspP}\ DP_{obj}\ Asp\ [_{VP}\ V\ t_{obj}]}^{\text{English SPELLEE}}$$

with the whole bracketed region labelled *Persian SPELLEE*.

By adopting the proposal in (30), we would have to give up a unified approach to the spelled-out constituent as the complement of the v head. In (30), only the Persian SPELLEE meets this requirement. In other words, there appears to be no way of determining what is spelled out, independent of the stress facts. Moreover, if we take the word-order difference between English SVO and Persian SOV to be the result of the movement of the verb to v only in English, (30) faces a word order problem, as it would wrongly

---

[19] For a somewhat similar proposal set in a very different context to allow variation across languages as to what is spelled out at a phase head, see Megerdoomian (2002).

predict the V–Adv$_{Man}$–Obj order in English. The example in (31) shows the ungrammaticality of this order.

(31)   *John answered cleverly the questions.

For the above reasons, I do not adopt the analysis in (30). Alternatively, I propose a difference between Persian and English in the position that the manner adverb merges. I suggest that while in Persian the manner adverb is merged below vP, in English it is merged above it. These structures are given in (32).

(32)   Manner adverbs: Persian vs. English
   a.   Persian: ... [$_{vP}$ t$_{subj}$ v [$_{ManP}$ Adv$_{Man}$ [$_{AspP}$ DP$_{obj}$ Asp [$_{VP}$ V t$_{obj}$]
   b.   English: ... [$_{ManP}$ Adv$_{Man}$ [$_{vP}$ t$_{subj}$ v [$_{AspP}$ DP$_{obj}$ Asp [$_{VP}$ V t$_{obj}$]

Given the structures in (32), let us see how we can account for the stress facts. Under this view, we can maintain the unified account of what constitutes the SPELLEE. In both Persian and English, the SPELLEE is the complement of the phase head v. The difference in stress follows in a straightforward manner. In Persian, the highest element in the SPELLEE is the manner adverb, which receives stress. In English, on the other hand, the adverb is outside the stress domain, and thus does not receive stress in the sentence-medial position. The manner in which they receive stress sentence-finally was explained above. This analysis does not face the problem with respect to English word order either, as the adverb is placed above the v head, home to the verb.

Supporting evidence for the fact that manner adverbs are in different positions in Persian and English comes from the behaviour of VP-fronting in these languages. While in English VP-fronting can leave the manner adverb behind as shown in (33), in Persian, a language which otherwise tolerates a wide range of word order possibilities due to scrambling, VP-fronting obligatorily pied-pipes the manner adverb with it, as shown in (34).

(33)   English VP-fronting: manner adverb can be stranded
   a.   Answer the questions, John did cleverly but ...
   b.   Eat the cake, John did slowly but ...

(34)   Persian VP-fronting: manner adverb cannot be stranded
   a.   Ali   aarum   qazaa   mi-xor-e.
        Ali   slowly   food   DUR-eat-3SG
        aarum   qazaa   mi-xor-e   Ali.
        *qazaa   mi-xor-e   Ali   aarum
        'Ali eats slowly.'

    b. Ali <u>xub</u> baazi kard.
        Ali well play did
        xub   baazi kard Ali.
        *baazi kard Ali   xub
        'Ali played well.'

The facts in (33) and (34) receive a straightforward account under the proposed structures in (32). Assuming that VP-fronting targets the same maximal projection in both languages, for instance vP, it is not surprising that in Persian, unlike English, the manner adverb cannot be left stranded.[20, 21]

It is worth noting that the proposal that manner adverbs are merged at different positions in English and Persian deviates from a rigid view of the universal Merge positions for adverbs. It is, however, in compliance with a relativized view which allows for some differences across languages, as long as the relative order of the adverbs is maintained (see, for example, Ernst 2001).[22]

The above proposal with respect to the assignment of stress to adverbs paves the ground for a straightforward account of a striking correlation between the stress behaviour and interpretation of some adverbs in Persian. Let us consider the case of English first. It has been noted in the literature that the same lexical item can be used as an adverb in different positions in English with different interpretations (Jackendoff 1972; Cinque 1999). This is shown in (35) and (36).

(35)   a. John cleverly answered their questions. → subject-oriented or manner

        b. John answered their questions cleverly. → manner

(36)   a. He quickly ran away.

        b. He ran away quickly.   (Travis 1988)

While (35a) can roughly mean 'It was clever of John to answer their questions', (35b) can only mean 'John answered their questions in a clever manner'. Similarly, (36a) roughly means 'He immediately ran away', whereas (36b) means

---

[20] In English, the manner adverb does not have to be stranded; it can be pied-piped with the verb phrase (e.g. *Answer the questions cleverly, though John did* . . .). This simply shows that chunks larger than the verb phrase can be fronted as well. This additional possibility does not affect the above argument, and has thus been left out. The crucial point is that in Persian (as opposed to English), the smallest movable constituent includes the manner adverb.

[21] A question may arise with respect to the learnability of the two types of language, namely the Persian-type with the manner adverb merged lower than v and the English-type with the manner adverb merged outside vP. Under the proposed system, primary stress can be viewed as a robust cue for setting the parameter appropriately.

[22] The fact that the manner adverb is merged above vP in English may be tied to the movement of the verb to the v head. Under this view, the generalization would be that the manner adverb merges above the head that is home to the main verb. This would make a close connection between SVO and SOV order and the Merge position of the manner adverb, an issue I leave for future research.

'He ran away fast'. This difference in interpretation receives a straightforward account in a theory which takes adverbs to follow a hierarchy such as the one in (13). Under this view, the interpretation of adverbs is tied with their structural position (see Cinque 1999; Ernst 2001, among others). The same lexical item, for example *cleverly*, can be merged in a higher position and receive a subject-oriented reading, or it can be merged lower and receive a manner reading. In English, the surface sentence-medial position in (35a) can be attributed to either reading (each with a different Merge position), but, crucially, assuming that the VP only moves above the manner adverb and not higher, the sentence-final position in (35b) can only have the manner reading.

We now turn to Persian. It was suggested that in Persian the manner adverb marks the edge of the SPELLEE, and thus receives stress as the highest element in the stress domain. Given that the manner adverb surfaces in the position it merges in Persian, it is expected that the same kind of difference in interpretation observed in English should be marked by a difference in stress in Persian. In other words, one expects to find some lexical items that are merged as adverbs in different positions leading to different interpretations, while in the surface this difference is only marked by stress. This prediction is borne out, as shown in (37) and (38).

(37) a. Ali <u>sexaavatmandaane</u> komak kard.
          Ali generously   help   did
          'Ali helped generously.'

      b. Ali sexaavatmandaane <u>komak</u> kard.
          Ali generously   help   did
          'It was generous of Ali to help.'

(38) a. Ali tond <u>qors</u> xord.
          Ali fast pill   ate
          'Ali immediately took a pill.'

      b. Ali <u>tond</u> qazaa xord.
          Ali fast   food   ate
          'Ali ate quickly.'

In this section we contrasted the behaviour of adverbials in Persian and English. It was shown that their stress behaviour can be accounted for given reasonable assumptions about their syntax and how the proposed system of stress assignment works. In looking at the behaviour of circumstantial adverbials in section 4.6.2.2, it was noted that adjunct prepositional phrases are merged outside the stress domain and as a result do not receive stress in Persian. A comparison of adjunct and argument PPs reveals an interesting contrast which is the topic of the following section.

4.7 Argument vs. adjunct PPs

I have proposed that stress is assigned to the highest element in the spelled-out constituent, the SPELLEE. The head v (Kratzer's 1994 voice), which projects the external argument, on the other hand, was identified as the phase-defining head (following Chomsky 2001, 2002). The SPELLEE (i.e. the complement of the v head) contains all the internal arguments and the inner aspectual heads. It is therefore expected that the highest internal argument in the stress domain receive stress according to the proposed system. In this section we explore some consequences of this claim by looking at data from Persian, German and English.

One consequence of the above proposal is that it predicts a contrast between the behaviour of adjunct and argument PPs with respect to stress. The expectation is that the argument PP, which is part of the stress domain, should receive stress, while the adjunct PP should not. This prediction is borne out, as shown in the Persian pair in (39).[23]

(39) a. Argument PP

Ali [ru tez-esh   kaar mi-kon-e].
Ali on thesis-his work DUR-do-3SG
'Ali works on his thesis.'

b. Adjunct PP

Ali tu daftar-esh [kaar mi-kon-e].
Ali in office-his work DUR-do-3SG
'Ali works in his office.'

Ditransitive verbs provide us with more evidence of this contrast between adjunct and argument PPs. In (40), we see two more examples of adjunct PPs which are outside the stress domain and thus do not receive stress. The examples in (41), on the other hand, illustrate cases of ditransitive verbs, with the argument PP receiving stress.

(40) Adjunct PPs

a. Ali tu paark futbaal baazi kard.
Ali in park   soccer   play   did
'Ali played soccer in the park.'

[23] It is important to note that here, as elsewhere in this chapter, focus-neutral stress is intended (Context question: *What happened?*). Otherwise, for instance, stress on the adjunct in (39b) would lead to a grammatical sentence, given the appropriate context (e.g. with the adjunct contrasted or in response to a question such as *Where does Ali work?*). For a discussion of sentential stress in non-neutral contexts, see chapter 5.

b. Ali   ru   zamin   <u>ye ketaab</u>   peydaa   kard.
Ali   on ground   a book   find   did
'Ali found a book on the ground.'

(41)   Argment PPs
a. Ali   shir-o   tu   <u>yaxchaal</u>   gozaasht.
Ali   milk-ACC   in   fridge   put
'Ali put the milk in the fridge.'
b. Ali   tup-o   be   <u>Hassan</u>   daad.
Ali   ball-ACC   to   Hassan   gave
'Ali gave the ball to Hassan.'

It is worth noting that in the examples in (41), the direct object, even though an argument of the verb, does not receive stress. The crucial point is that the objects in (41) are specific. We saw in section 4.5 that Persian specific objects move out of the stress domain to a higher position, thus avoiding stress. In fact, if we look at ditransitive sentences with non-specific objects, where the object is expected to remain in the stress domain, the non-specific object receives stress. This is shown in the examples in (42).

(42)   a. Ali   <u>ketaab</u>   tu   qafase   mi-zaar-e.
Ali   book   in   shelf   DUR-put-3SG
'Ali puts books on shelves.'
b. Ali   <u>ye keyk</u>   tu   yaxchaal   gozaasht.
Ali   a   cake   in   fridge   put
'Ali put a cake in the fridge.'

In the previous section it was noted that manner adverbs mark the left edge of the stress domain in Persian and receive stress as the highest element in this domain. The examples in (43) illustrate that the same generalization holds for ditransitive sentences involving a manner adverb. Examples (43a) and (43b) show ditransitive sentences with no manner adverb. In (43a) (similar to (42)), the direct object is non-specific, thus inside the SPELLEE and stressed, while in (43b) (similar to (41)), it is specific, therefore outside the SPELLEE and not stressed. Sentences (43c) and (43d) show that once a manner adverb is added to these sentences, it marks the edge of the stress domain and receives sentential stress in a manner expected under the proposed system.

(43)   a. Ali   [<u>ye tup</u>   be   Hassan   daad].
Ali   a   ball   to   Hassan   gave
'Ali gave a ball to Hassan.'

b. Ali tup-o   [be <u>Hassan</u> daad].
    Ali ball-ACC to Hassan gave
    'Ali gave the ball to Hassan.'

c. Ali [<u>xub</u> tup be Hassan daad].
    Ali well ball to Hassan gave
    'Ali assisted Hassan in the (football) game well.' (Lit. 'Ali gave ball
    to Hassan well.')

d. Ali tup-o   [<u>xub</u> be Hassan daad].
    Ali ball-ACC well to Hassan gave
    'Ali gave (passed) the ball to Hassan well.'

The same type of contrast in the stress behaviour of PP adjuncts and
arguments has been noted for German verb-final sentences, as shown in the
minimal pair in (44) (adapted from Wagner 2003), supporting the proposed
analysis.[24] In (44a), the PP complement is part of the stress domain, thus
receiving stress, whereas the PP adjunct in (44b) is outside the stress domain
and as a result the stress falls on the verb.

(44) a. German: PP argument
          Peter/er ist [in   den <u>Garten</u> getanzt].
          Peter/he is into the garden   danced

          'Peter/he danced into the garden.'

      b. German: PP adjunct
          Peter/er hat im   Garten [<u>getanzt</u>].
          Peter/he has in.the garden danced

          'Peter/he danced in the garden.'

The sentence in (44a) is very much reminiscent of the example from Krifka
(1984) we discussed in chapter 3, repeated in (45). The difference between (44a)
and (45) is that in the latter the verb has two internal arguments and stress falls
on the highest element in the stress domain, thus the object DP in this case.

(45) Maria hat [das <u>auto</u> in   die garage gefahren].
      Mary has the car   into the garage driven
      'Mary has driven the car into the garage.'

In chapter 3, we used this type of ditransitive sentence, exemplified in (42)–
(43) for Persian and (45) for German, to argue against Zubizarreta's system,
which would predict stress on the selectionally lowest argument, in these cases

---

[24] I have changed the notational conventions and marked primary stress only in conformity with
the conventions used in this monograph.

the prepositional phrases (see ch. 3 for more examples).[25] This type of example provides support for the proposal put forth in this monograph, predicting stress on the highest constituent in the stress domain which includes all the internal arguments.

We have seen so far that German V-final sentences behave like Persian with respect to stress. Before we turn to English, which appears to pose a problem for the proposed system, let us consider the status of manner adverbs in German. In Persian, we noted that manner adverbs mark the left edge of the stress domain and receive stress as the highest element in this domain. The examples in (46) show that, unlike Persian, manner and measure adverbs do not receive stress in German V-final sentences. Sentences (46a) and (46b) involve cases with moved objects, while in (46c) and (46d) the objects are inside the stress domain. The crucial point here is that the manner adverbs do not receive stress.

(46) a. Karl hat Spaghetti schnell <u>gekocht</u>.
          Karl has spaghetti   quickly   cooked
          'Karl cooked spaghetti quickly.'

      b. Hans hat die Spaghetti völlig   <u>aufgegessen</u>.[26]
          Hans has the spaghetti completely up-eaten
          'Hans ate the spaghetti completely.'

      c. Karl hat viel <u>Fußball</u> gespielt.
          Karl has a lot soccer   played
          'Karl played soccer a lot.'

      d. ... dass er sehr gerne <u>Äpfel</u> mag.
              that he very much   apples likes
          '... that he likes apples a lot.'

To account for this difference in the behaviour of manner adverbs in German and Persian, I posit that in German, manner/measure adverbs are merged outside the vP and as a result are outside the stress domain. In other words, German patterns like English with respect to the behaviour of manner/measure adverbs. In both languages these adverbs are merged outside the vP domain and as a result do not receive stress. In Persian, on the other hand, they merge lower than the v head and are thus included in the spelled out constituent. We will see in section 4.9. that (Eastern) Armenian patterns like Persian with respect to the behaviour of manner adverbs.

---

[25] Zubizarreta (1998) would have no problem accounting for (44).
[26] On the status of the German separable prefixes, see section 4.4.

The proposal that manner adverbs in German, like their counterparts in English, are merged outside the vP, makes a prediction about their behaviour with respect to VP-fronting. Recall from section 4.6.2.3 that in English, unlike Persian, manner adverbs can be left stranded in the context of VP-fronting. This difference between English and Persian was attributed to the difference in the merge position of manner adverbs in the two languages. If the merge position of manner adverbs in German is the same as English, it is expected that German manner adverbs can be left stranded in the context of VP-fronting as well. This prediction is borne out, as shown in the examples in (47).

(47)   German VP-fronting: manner adverb can be stranded
    a. Karl ißt   Äpfel   schnell.
        Karl eats apples quickly

        Äpfel   essen   tut   Karl schnell
        apples eat (INF) does Karl quickly

    b. Karl hat viel   Fußball gespielt.
        Karl has a lot football played

        Fußball gespielt hat Karl viel
        football played   has Karl a lot

Finally, let us turn to the status of argument PPs in English. In English, argument PPs are sentence-final and stressed; in other words, no contrast is found between argument PPs and adjunct PPs with respect to their stress behaviour. This is shown in the examples in (48) and (49). Sentence (48) illustrates an example of a sentence with an adjunct PP with sentence-final stress and (49) shows two ditransitive sentences with stress on the sentence-final argument.

(48)   Adjunct PP
    John saw Mary in the <u>park</u>.

(49)   Argument PPs
    a. John put the milk in the <u>fridge</u>.
    b. John gave the ball to <u>Bill</u>.

The stress pattern in (48) is not unexpected. In section 4.6.2.2 it was argued, following Cinque (2002, 2004), that circumstantial adverbs such as the locative PP in (48) are merged above vP and their sentence-final position is the result of lower elements moving around them. It was proposed that when the movement of lower element leaves the stress domain empty, stress falls on the closest phonologically non-null element, in this case the locative PP. A question arises as to how we can account for the stress behaviour of the argument PPs in (49).

In particular, it is reasonable to ask whether the argument PPs in (49) lend themselves to the same type of analysis as the adjunct PP in (48). To address this question we need to have a closer look at the structure of ditransitive sentences.

It is widely accepted in the generative literature that, in a ditransitive sentence, the direct object is higher than (and in a c-commanding relation with) the indirect object, as suggested by facts from anaphor/quantifier binding, weak crossover, superiority, and negative polarity items (see Barss and Lasnik 1986; Larson 1988, and subsequent authors). For the ditransitive sentence in (49b), I assume the structure given in (50), adapted from Koizumi (1995) (see also Harley 1995).[27] For the sake of convenience, I am leaving out the subject from this and other structures below.

(50)

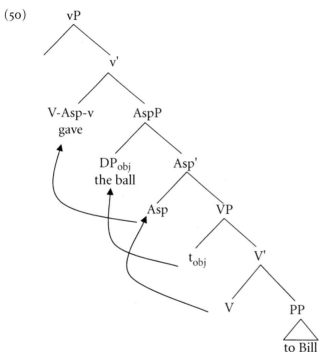

The structure in (50) provides us with the correct surface word order: V DP_{obj} PP. Once we add a manner adverb to the picture, however, the word order possibilities suggest that this cannot be the whole story. The sentences in (51) show that the manner adverb can appear in three different positions.[28]

---

[27] Koizumi (1995) calls the projection between VP and vP, which is responsible for the assignment of accusative case, AgrOP. I have dubbed Koizumi's AgrOP to AspP in compliance with the notations used in this monograph.

[28] Koizumi (1995) discusses these word-order possibilities and provides an account for them under very different assumptions about the syntax of adverbs.

(51) a. John slowly gave the ball to Bill.

  b. John gave the ball to Bill slowly.

  c. John gave the ball slowly to Bill.

Let us put aside the possibility in (51c) for a moment and see how we can account for (51a) and (51b). Our assumptions about the syntax of adverbs do not allow us to adjoin adverbs freely in different positions. Following Cinque (1999, 2002, 2004) (and in the spirit of Pollock 1989, 1997), adverbs are taken to occupy fixed positions, with a one-to-one relation between their position and interpretation. Thus, for instance, English manner adverbs were suggested to occupy the specifier of a projection dominating vP (see section 4.6). Different word-order possibilities are the result of the movement of other elements around the adverbials rather than the movement of the adverbs themselves.[29] Given these assumptions, the word order in (51a) can be taken as the base order, with the manner adverb added to the structure in (50), as in (52).

(52) Base order: Adv$_{Man}$ [$_{vP}$ V DP$_{obj}$ PP]

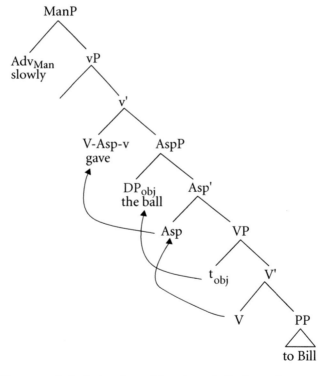

---

[29] Movement of adverbs is only possible under topicalization or focus movement (see Cinque 1999).

The structure in (52) can be taken to represent the surface word order in (51a). The example in (51b), on the other hand, can be accounted for by allowing the whole vP to move around the manner adverbs. This is shown schematically in (53).

(53) Accounting for (51b): not adopted in this monograph

      Derived order: Adv_{Man} [$_{vP}$ V DP_{obj} PP]

While the analysis illustrated in (52) and (53) can account for the surface order in (51a) and (51b) respectively, it runs into trouble in the face of the surface order in (51c). In fact, the order in (51c) cannot be derived directly from the base order in (52) at all. The problem is that the verb and the object do not form a constituent independent of the indirect object in this structure. In order for us to allow them to move independently from the indirect object, we need them to form a constituent without the indirect object. To achieve this goal, I propose that, starting with the base order in (50), the argument PP first moves to a position higher than vP, leading to the order given in (54). The structure in (54) is then used as the base in deriving the other orders in a manner elaborated below.

(54)   PP [$_{vP}$ V DP_{obj} t_{PP}]

Before accounting for the different word order possibilities in (51), it is worth noting that the proposal in (54) paves the way for an account of certain syntactic facts noted by Pesetsky (1995). Pesetsky points to some "backward binding" facts (originally from Burzio 1986) and quantifier scope facts (originally from Aoun and Li 1989) which indicate that the indirect object is in a c-command relation to the direct object at some point in the derivation. This can be achieved by the structure in (54).

We now turn to the three word-order possibilities in (51). The base order to be used to derive these three possibilities is given in (55), which is essentially the order in (54) with the manner adverb added.

(55)   Base order: Adv_{Man} [$_{IOP}$ PP [$_{vP}$ V DP_{obj} t_{PP}]]

Here is how the three possible word orders can be derived. The movement of the vP to the specifier position of a projection FP between the manner adverb and the PP results in the order in (51a). This is shown in (56a). If FP further moves around the manner adverb, we get the order in (51b), which is the mirror image of the base order in (55). This is shown in (56b). Finally, the word order in (51c) is the result of the movement of the vP to a position higher than the manner adverb. This is shown in (56c).

(56)   Deriving the word order possibilities in (50) from the base order in (54)

a.   Adv$_{Man}$ [$_{FP}$———[$_{IOP}$PP [$_{vP}$ V DP$_{obj}$ t$_{PP}$]]] → (51a):
          |_____↑_____|
                                                    Adv$_{Man}$ V DP$_{obj}$ PP

b.   Adv$_{Man}$ [$_{FP}$———[$_{IOP}$PP [$_{vP}$ V DP$_{obj}$ t$_{PP}$]]] → (51b):
     |_____| ↑_____|
                                                    V DP$_{obj}$ PP Adv$_{Man}$

c.   Adv$_{Man}$ [$_{IOP}$PP [$_{vP}$ V DP$_{obj}$ t$_{PP}$]] → (51c): V DP$_{obj}$ Adv$_{Man}$ PP
     |_____|

We started our discussion with a question as to how we can account for the stress behaviour of English ditransitive sentences, exemplified in (57), repeated from (49b).

(57)   John gave the ball to <u>Bill</u>.

We have argued that the construction in (57) involves movement of the goal PP to a position higher than vP followed by the movement of the vP around it. Given the proposed derivation, the stress pattern is not unexpected. We are once again dealing with a case where the stress domain has been emptied. As a result, the stress is assigned to the closest phonologically non-null element, leading to the observed sentence-final stress in English (see section 4.6.2.2).

In this section, we looked at constructions involving more than one internal argument. In Persian and verb-final German sentences, it was shown that stress falls on the highest internal argument as predicted by the stress system developed in this monograph. When a manner adverb is brought into the picture, Persian behaves differently from German. In Persian, the manner adverb is merged lower than v and thus receives stress, while in German, like English, it merges outside the vP and, as a result, does not receive sentential stress. In both languages, we noted a contrast between adjunct and argument PPs, with the former merging outside the stress domain and thus avoiding sentential stress. Turning to English, we noted that the contrast between adjunct and argument PPs is lost. In English, adjunct and argument PPs appear sentence-finally and are stressed. This was shown to be the result of certain movement operations, leaving the stress domain empty, with sentential stress falling on the closest phonologically non-null element.

In reviewing previous phonological and syntactic accounts of sentential stress in chapters 2 and 3, a recurring problem was their failure to account for the stress pattern of passives and unaccusatives. We saw in chapter 2 that the phonological accounts were incapable of capturing the facts unless they resorted to construction-specific phonological rules, an undesirable result. Cinque's (1993) syntactic account suffered from the same type of problem, which was one of the reasons for Legate's (2003) and Zubizarreta's (1998) alternative proposals. We noted that in solving the passive/unaccusative problem, the latter accounts created new problems. What we have not seen so far is how the system proposed in this monograph handles these cases. This is the topic of the following section.

4.8 Passives and unaccusatives

In chapter 3 we considered a range of examples from English and German which showed stress on the subject when the verb was passive or unaccusative. This stood in sharp contrast to sentences involving transitive and unergative verbs. Some examples from English are repeated in (58) (for more English and some German examples, see chs. 2 and 3).

(58)   Passives and unaccusative: $\underline{DP}_{subj}$ V
        Context: What happened?
   a.   <u>My bike</u> was stolen.
   b.   <u>A boy</u> disappeared.
   c.   <u>The mail</u> arrived.

Before providing an account for the stress facts illustrated in (58), let us explore the issue in Persian by looking at the behaviour of unaccusative sentences with respect to stress.[30] First, we need to find some verbs that qualify as unaccusative in Persian. It has been argued that certain diagnostics such as *-er* nominalization or adjectival participle formation can be used to distinguish unaccusative from unergative verbs (see, for example, Grimshaw 1987; Levin and Rappaport Hovav 1986, 1988, 1995). While *-er* nominalization targets external arguments and can only apply to unergative predicates (e.g. *runner, dancer* vs. **arriver, *appearer*), adjectival participle formation is only compatible with unaccusative predicates (e.g. *wilted lettuce, a fallen leaf* vs. **coughed patient, *swum contestant*). Karimi-Doostan (1997) uses these diagnostics to identify unergative and unaccusative verbs in Persian (see also Megerdoomian 2001). The equivalent to the *-er* nominalization is formed in Persian by adding

[30] I am putting aside passives due to their controversial status in Persian syntactic literature, with some scholars arguing for the existence of syntactic passives and others classifying them with "inchoative" constructions (see e.g. Moyne 1974; Dabir-Moghaddam 1982; Vahedi-Langrudi 1999).

the suffix-*ande* to the present stem of the verb and the adjectival participle
is formed by adding the suffix -*e* to the past stem. The application of these
diagnostics is shown in (59) and (60).

(59)   -*er* nominalization: Persian

Unaccusative	*Unergative*
*aay-ande *'comer'	dav-ande 'runner'
*res-ande *'arriver'	raqs-ande 'dancer'
*riz-ande *'spiller'	*xand-ande *'laugher'
*baar-ande *'precipitator'	
*chek-ande *'dripper'	

(60)   Adjectival participle: Persian

Unaccusative	*Unergative*
ʔaamad-e *'come'	*david-e *'run'
resid-e ? 'arrived'	*raqside *'danced'
rixt-e 'spilt'	*xandid-e *'laughed'
ʔbaarid-e *'precipitated'	
chekid-e *'dripped'	

The examples in (59) show that the agentive -*ande* suffix can be added only
to unergative verbs; (60) shows that the adjectival participle can only be
formed with the unaccusative verbs.[31] It is worth noting that not all forms
meet all the criteria. For instance, the verb *xandidan* 'laugh' patterns with
unaccusatives with respect to -*er* nominalization, but with respect to adjectival
participle formation and another diagnostic we will consider next, it patterns
with unergatives and is identified as such accordingly.

In addition to the above diagnostics, Karimi-Doostan (1997) and
Megerdoomian (2001) use another test to distinguish unaccusative from
unergative verbs in Persian. There is a type of manner adverb, with an agentive
sense, in Persian which is formed by adding the suffix -*aan* to the present stem
of the verb. An example is given in (61).

(61)   Ali   xand-aan   vaared   shod
        Ali   laugh-aan   enter   became
        'Ali entered laughing.'

Given the agentive nature of these adverbs, their formation is compatible only
with unergative verbs. This is shown in (62).

---

[31] The grammaticality judgements have been provided based on the relevant meaning of the forms.
For example, the form *aayande* has been marked ungrammatical based on the relevant agentive sense
*'comer'. Its common meaning, 'future', is irrelevant here.

(62) Manner adverbs with -*aan*: Persian

Unaccusative	*Unergative*
*aay-aan 'coming'	dav-aan 'running'
*res-aan 'arriving'	raqs-aan 'dancing'
*riz-aan 'spilling'	xand-aan 'laughing'
*baar-aan 'precipitating'	
*chek-aan 'dripping'	

We are now ready to examine the stress behaviour of unaccusative sentences in Persian. Some sentences involving the verbs classified as unaccusative by the above tests are given in (63). The stress pattern is similar to English, with sentential stress falling on the subject. The examples in (64) show that in sentences with unergative verbs sentential stress falls on the verb. It is important to note that, here as elsewhere in this chapter, we are dealing with a focus-neutral context (Context: *chi shod?* **what became** 'What happened?' OR *che xabar?* **what news** 'What's new?').

(63) Unaccusative

    a. <u>Ali</u> umad.
       Ali came
       'Ali came.'

    b. <u>Ye baste</u> resid.
       one package arrived
       'A package arrived.'

    c. <u>Qahve</u> rixt.
       coffee spilled
       'Coffee spilled.'

    d. <u>Barf</u> mi-baar-e.
       snow DUR-precipitate-3SG
       'It's snowing (formal).'

    e. <u>Aab</u> mi-chek-e.
       water DUR-drip-3SG
       'Water's dripping.'

(64) Unergative

    a. Ali <u>david</u>.
       Ali ran

    b. Ali <u>raqsid</u>.
       Ali danced

    c. Ali <u>xandid</u>.
       Ali laughed

We have so far established that Persian unaccusatives pattern like their counterparts in English and German. In all these languages, sentential stress falls on the subject in an unaccusative sentence. We now turn to the question of how the system developed in this monograph fares with these facts. The unaccusative/passive stress pattern receives a straightforward account under our proposed system for assignment of sentential stress, which assigns sentential stress to the highest element in the SPELLEE. Recall that in our system, following Chomsky (2000, 2001), only CPs and transitive vPs constitute phases. Under this view, passive/unaccusative verb phrases are crucially not taken to induce phasal boundaries. As a result, in our calculation of sentential stress, the first phasal head is C, with its complement or SPELLEE being TP. The highest element in the TP domain is the subject, and it thus receives stress according to our system of stress assignment. The system proposed in this monograph, therefore, has the advantage of being able to account for the passive/unaccusative facts in English, German and Persian without facing the problems the other syntactic accounts introduced (see ch. 3).

In our discussion of the stress behaviour of passive/unaccusative sentences, we have so far only considered clauses consisting of a subject and a predicate. Zubizarreta (1998), however, makes an interesting observation about the position of nuclear stress in passive/unaccusative sentences with additional material. While the stress is on the subject in the simple clauses, once more constituents such as manner adverbs are added to the sentence, primary stress is no longer on the subject. Some examples from English and Persian are given in (65) and (66) (see Zubizarreta 1998 for more English as well as German examples). These examples differ from (58) and (63) solely by an additional manner adverb. In other words, if we eliminate the manner adverbs, stress falls on the subject, as expected.[32]

(65)   a.   A boy mysteriously <u>disappeared</u>.

     b.   The mail quickly <u>arrived</u>.

---

[32] In fact, it may be the case that a more complex tense/aspect will have the same effect. This is shown in the English example in (i) and the Persian example in (ii). The status of these examples is not very clear. In what follows, I am putting these cases aside and will focus on the type of sentence first noted by Zubizarreta (1998).

(i)   ?<u>My bike</u> would have been stolen.

(ii)   Ali   <u>xaahad</u>   umad.   vs.   ??<u>Ali</u>   xaahad   umad.
    Ali   want-3SG   come
    'Ali will come.'

(66) a. Ali <u>dir</u> umad.
       Ali late came
       'Ali came late.'

    b. Aab <u>tond</u> mi-chek-e.
       water fast DUR-drip-3SG
       'Water's dripping fast.'

We reviewed Zubizarreta's (1998) account of the facts exemplified in (65) in chapter 3. She proposes that once an adjunct is added to the sentence, the S-NSR fails to apply to the metrical sisters [DP$_{subj}$] and [adjunct V], as they are not selectionally ordered. As a result the C-NSR applies and assigns stress to the structurally lowest or the final constituent in the clause. We saw in chapter 3 that Zubizarreta's system faced a range of other empirical and conceptual problems. It is worth noting here that, even with respect to the problem at hand, her system would fail to capture the Persian facts in (65), as the stress is not sentence-final in Persian.

The question arises as to how we can account for these cases under the system proposed in this monograph. A closer look at the examples in (65) and (66) reveals that these sentences essentially behave as if they are transitive or unergative. In other words, they behave as if they involve two phasal boundaries. If we take these sentences to involve two phases, just like transitive and unergative sentences, the stress facts follow straightforwardly. Given that in English the manner adverb was proposed to be just outside the lower SPELLEE, the stress on the verb is expected.[33] In Persian, on the other hand, it was shown that the manner adverb marks the left edge of the SPELLEE, receiving stress as the highest element in this domain, according to the system developed in this monograph. We are thus led to the following hypothesis: it is only in its barest form that a passive/unaccusative verb phrase does not constitute a phase. These bare forms were exemplified in (58) and (63) for English and Persian, respectively. Once modifiers are added, imposing additional structure, the verb phrase becomes phasal, leading to the stress pattern exemplified in (65) and (66).[34]

---

[33] The other possible word order and stress pattern in English, shown in (i), is the result of the lower elements moving around the adverb, thus leading to sentence-final stress in a manner discussed in section 4.6.2.2.

(i) a. A boy disappeared <u>mysteriously</u>.
    b. The mail arrived <u>quickly</u>.

[34] The idea that adverbial modifiers should be tied with phasal domains has already been proposed. To account for some syntactic adjacency facts in Greek, Alexiadou and Anagnostopoulou (2001) argue for a general principle prohibiting adverbial modifier insertion in 'incomplete semantic domains'. They suggest that certain heads, such as the verb and the aspectual and voice heads should combine first

The essence of the this proposal is that the addition of modifiers turns an unaccusative structure to an unergative one. There is some evidence from word formation that points to such a correlation between modification and unergativity. As mentioned above, there is a widely held assumption that English -*er* nominalization can apply only to unergative predicates. The contrasts in (67) are of special interest here. The ungrammatical cases in (67) are expected, as they all involve -*er* nominalization applied to an unaccusative verb. The grammatical examples, on the other hand, all involve the same unaccusative verb, with an additional modifier. These examples suggest that the addition of the modifier changes the structure. In the terms used here, the presence of the modifier has helped them qualify as unergative predicates at least for the application of -*er* nominalization, thus providing support for the correlation between modifier insertion and (loss of) unaccusativity/unergativity.[35, 36]

(67)   a.   *comer   vs.   newcomer, latecomer
       b.   *arriver   vs.   late arriver
       c.   *riser   vs.   early riser
       d.   *developer   vs.   late developer
       e.   *bloomer   vs.   late bloomer
       f.   *grower   vs.   low grower ($=$ a shrub)

Another related aspect of the above proposal is the connection it makes between structural complexity and unaccusativity/unergativity, where structural complexity results in an unaccusative verb behaving like an unergative one (with respect to stress). Data from Dutch provide some support for this correlation in a different context. In Dutch (like Italian), unergativity or unaccusativity of the verb determines the choice of auxiliary, with *hebben* 'have' used for unergatives and *zijn* 'be' for unaccusatives. The data in (68) and (69) (originally from Everaert 1992, cited in Borer 1994) show that while an unaccusative predicate, used as a simplex verb, takes *zijn* as auxiliary, the same

to form a complete semantic domain before the adverbial can be merged. Alexiadou and Anagnostopoulou correlate these domains with Chomsky's phases.

[35] Some examples are adapted from Levin and Rappaport Hovav (1988), who point to their problematic nature but provide no account for them. Some verbs such as *develop* and *grow* have a transitive usage as well. Only the unaccusative usage is intended here.

[36] Juan Uriagereka (p.c.) has pointed out another set of facts which seem to support this correlation. While expletive constructions are often used as a diagnostic for unaccusative predicates, it appears that these sentences become ungrammatical with the addition of manner adverbs, as shown in (i).

(i)   a.   There arrived (?*late) an army (?*late).
      b.   There developed (?*late) a blooming community (?*late).

predicate, when used in a light-verb construction, takes *hebben* as auxiliary. Everaert (1992) notes that for any aspectual calculus, the sentences in (68) and (69) are synonymous. These examples provide further support for the idea that increasing the structural complexity of an unaccusative predicate may turn it into an unergative one.

(68) a. Het   vliegtuig   is   geland.
          the   plane   is   landed

      b. Het   vliegtuig   heeft   een   landing   gemaakt.
          the   plane   has   a   landing   made
          'The plane landed.'

(69) a. De   voorstelling   is   aangevangen.
          the show   is   begun

      b. De   voorstelling   heeft   een   aanvang   genomen.
          the show   has   a   beginning   took
          'The show began.'

We can now revisit Legate (2003) in the light of our proposal that an unaccusative verb phrase does not constitute a phase in its barest form but rather becomes phasal when additional structure is involved. Recall that Legate attributes the stress on the subject in passives and unaccusatives to their Merge position as the internal argument of the verb. A crucial assumption for Legate is that unaccusative and passive verbs, just like their transitive counterparts, constitute phases (see ch. 3 for more details). She provides several syntactic arguments to prove her case. Using evidence from reconstruction effects, quantifier raising in antecedent-contained deletion and parasitic gaps, Legate (2003) argues that subjects of unaccusative/passive (just like transitive) verb phrases leave intermediate traces at the edge of the verb phrase and concludes that unaccusative/passive verb phrases, just like transitive ones, constitute phases. It is worth noting, however, that due to the nature of the tests used as diagnostics for the phase edge, all the sentences she considers involve additional syntactic structure. In other words, none of the sentences involve a bare unaccusative/passive sentence. I suggest that the conclusion she draws is too strong and that based on the evidence, only a weaker claim is warranted: unaccusative/passive sentences involving additional syntactic structure constitute phases. In other words, her theory leaves open the question of whether unaccusative/passive verb phrases constitute phases in their barest form. As discussed above, there is enough reason to believe that a distinction needs to be made between the phasal structure of bare unaccusatie/passive verbs and those involved in a more complex structure.

We have so far only considered the stress facts in passives/unaccusatives in English, German and Persian.[37] Let us now turn to Romance languages, in particular, Italian, Spanish, and French. The expected pattern for unaccusatives, if Romance languages behaved like English and Persian, would be [$\underline{DP}_{subj}$ V_{unacc}]. A closer look, however, reveals some interesting deviations from the expected pattern, not only with respect to stress, but in some cases also word order. In fact, there are differences between Spanish and Italian, on the one hand, and French, on the other.

In Italian and Spanish, the contrast between unaccusative and unergative sentences uttered out of the blue is realized in a difference in word order. It has been widely accepted in the literature that in Italian and Spanish the neutral order for an unaccusative sentence, as opposed to an unergative one, is VS (see Contréras 1976; Suñer 1982; Burzio 1986; Bonet 1990; Cinque 1993; Pinto 1994; Levin and Rappaport Hovav 1995).[38] As for the stress pattern, in the case of the unergative sentences where the neutral order is SV, stress is on the verb. This is similar to English and Persian and receives a straightforward account under our stress system.[39] In the unaccusative cases, the neutral order is VS and stress falls on the subject, as shown in (70).[40]

(70)   Unaccusative: Italian and Spanish [V $\underline{DP}_{subj}$]

    a. E'   morto   <u>Johnson</u>.[41]   (Italian: Cinque 1993: 260)
        is   dead   Johnson
        'Johnson died.'

    b. Llegó   <u>el   correo</u>.   (Spanish)
        arrived   the   mail
        'The mail arrived.'

In French, on the other hand, there is no difference between an unaccusative sentence and an unergative one, neither in sentential stress, nor in word

---

[37] While German examples were not discussed in this chapter, recall from chapter 3 that the facts are identical to Persian and English.

[38] Different terms are sometimes used to refer to these two classes of verbs, in particular in works that predate Perlmutter's (1978) Unaccusative Hypothesis.

[39] If we assume syntactic V-to-T movement in Romance languages, then with the subject in Spec–TP and the verb in T, the verb receives stress as the closest phonologically non-null element to the otherwise empty stress domain.

[40] In chapter 3, we discussed Spanish examples from Zubizarreta (1998) who provided the SV order for the unaccusative with the stress on the verb. I follow the literature in taking the VS order to be the neutral order. This has also been verified with a native speaker of Spanish. Meanwhile, if we considered the Zubizarreta facts, they would be identical to the French example in (71) and thus would have to be treated likewise.

[41] For a discussion of the context in which this sentence is uttered, see chapter 5 and references cited there.

order. As the unergative word order and stress pattern is identical to English
and Persian and can thus receive a similar account, we will only consider an
unaccusative example. This is shown in (71).

(71)   Unaccusative: French [DP$_{subj}$ $\underline{V}$]

     Le   courier   est   <u>arrivé</u>.
     the   mail   is   arrived

     'The mail has arrived.'

To sum up the Romance unaccusative facts, in Spanish and Italian, neutral
word order is VS, while in French it is SV. With respect to stress they all
have stress on the final constituent. Given the difference in word order, in
Spanish and Italian, the final element is the subject, while in French it is the
verb.

A question arises as to how we should handle the above Romance facts
within the system proposed in this monograph. Given that in Romance languages stress is always sentence-final, even in unaccusative sentences, one way
to deal with the difference between these languages and the other languages
we have considered so far is to suggest that the systems governing sentential stress in the two types of languages are different. Zubizarreta's (1998)
attempt to address this difference falls under this type of approach. Under
her modular system of sentential stress, she suggests that Romance languages,
unlike English and German, lack the S-NSR, the module that is sensitive to
selectional restrictions, and as a result, stress falls on the final constituent in
the sentence, according to the C-NSR, the module sensitive to hierarchical
constituent structure (see ch. 3 for details). In fact, any other rule, even a
phonological one, which puts stress on the final element in the sentence, can
correctly account for these facts.

Alternatively, if the same system of stress assignment is to account for the
stress facts in Romance, then the unaccusative facts have to follow from a
syntactic difference between Romance languages and the other languages we
have looked at so far. Below, I explore the plausibility of this alternative given
the stress system proposed here.

I start with the Italian and Spanish stress pattern in (70). At first glance,
these stress facts may not seem to pose a problem for our system. Recall that
unmodified unaccusative verbs do not induce phasal boundaries. Therefore,
the only phasal head is C, with its complement TP being the SPELLEE. Now,
if we further assume that, just like English and Persian, the subject is in
the specifier of TP, it is expected to receive stress as the highest element in
the SPELLEE. The VS order then has to be attributed to some independent

movement of the verb (phrase) to a position in the CP domain.[42] In other words, under this account, the stress facts follow the stress system developed in this monograph and the order difference is irrelevant. In fact, this account may have some appeal for Italian if Zubizarreta (1998) is correct in suggesting that in Italian (but not Spanish) nominative case is checked overtly in Spec–TP and the postverbal subject is the result of the lower elements moving to a higher position.

Under the more standard assumption about the position of the subject in (70), according to which the subject remains in its VP-internal merge position, we cannot maintain the idea that the subject receives stress as the highest element in the SPELLEE TP. Under this view and based on the assumption that, like English and Persian, unaccusative verbs in Italian and Spanish do not induce a phasal boundary, one would expect the stress to fall on the verb, as the highest element in the TP SPELLEE, contrary to fact. Therefore, if the subject is assumed to be in the VP-internal position, the only way to reconcile the facts with our stress system is to suggest that in Italian and Spanish, unlike English and Persian, unaccusative verbs do induce phasal boundaries. If we further follow the standard assumption that in Romance languages the verb moves to v and/or to T, the stress on the subject, as the highest element in the complement of v, would be easily accounted for. In fact, the same assumption will pave the way for capturing the French fact in (71) as well. Note that the subject in French is assumed to be in Spec–TP. Thus, if the unaccusative verb is phasal, the stress on the verb is expected.[43] Whether there is further support for the idea that unaccusative verbs induce phases in Romance languages is a question I leave for future research.[44] The answer to this question has important implications for the possible extension of the proposed system of sentential stress to Romance languages.[45]

---

[42] Whether this movement occurs in the syntax or in PF movement has no bearing for our theory of stress.

[43] Even if we assume that the verb has moved to v or T, the stress domain will be devoid of any phonologically non-null elements and stress in these cases, is expected to fall on the closest non-null element, in this case the verb.

[44] In the spirit of what was suggested for English and Persian unaccusative sentences involving adjuncts, a potential avenue to explore may be that the unaccusative sentences in Romance languages involve a more complex structure. Alternatively, given that in all these Romance languages, the verb is proposed to move to T, it would be tempting to tie the phasal nature of the unaccusative verb phrase in Romance languages to this movement. One way to achieve this would be to suggest that the movement from V to T forces the projection of little v, perhaps due to a constraint on movement from a lexical head V to a functional head of a different domain T.

[45] The fact that the main stress of the sentence is consistently on the final word of the clause in Romance languages appears to undermine any syntactic account of sentential stress for these languages, including the one proposed in this monograph. It is worth noting that the system proposed here, as discussed in more detail in section 4.10, also correctly accounts for secondary stress on the subject,

So far, we have looked at the application of the proposed system of stress assignment to several languages, focusing mainly on Persian, English, and German and to some extent Spanish, Italian, and French. Of these languages, Persian and German verb-final sentences have provided us with the source of SOV languages. We have also noted that the stress behaviour of manner adverbials is different in these languages. While in Persian manner adverbials receive sentential stress, in German V-final sentences they do not. In fact, Persian has been our sole example of a language in which manner adverbials receive sentential stress in a non-final position, which we attributed to their merge position being inside the SPELLEE or the stress domain. Given the importance of the stress facts in Persian and in particular the behaviour of manner adverbials in this language, both in our rejection of previous syntactic accounts of sentential stress and in the development of the proposed alternative, our position would be strengthened if we could find another language which replicates these patterns. Eastern Armenian, an SOV language which is the topic of the next section, appears to be one such language.[46]

4.9 Sentential stress rule: the case of Eastern Armenian[47]

In this section we will briefly look at the behaviour of sentential stress in Eastern Armenian. We will see that the stress facts in Eastern Armenian are strikingly similar to Persian, thus providing further support for the theory developed in this monograph. To avoid repetition, I will only review the facts in Eastern Armenian, noting that they can be captured in our system in a manner elaborated above for Persian.

In a simple SOV sentence in Armenian, stress falls on the object. This is shown in (72) (from Megerdoomian 2002: 126).

which nicely extends to Romance languages. As for the sentence-final primary stress, in the text above, I have explored the possibility of it being the result of the application of the proposed sentential stress rule. It is also conceivable that the sentence-final main stress is the result of some surface phonological/phonetic rule whose application obviates the effect of the sentential stress rule in these languages. A more thorough consideration of these possibilities is left for future research.

[46] Turkish may yet be another language with a similar stress pattern, amenable to the system proposed in this monograph (Asli Untak Tarhan, p.c.).

[47] Armenian is an Indo-European language which constitutes a separate and independent branch of its own. It is spoken by the vast majority of the population in Armenia as well as sizeable communities in Iran, Lebanon, Syria, Turkey, and across the world. There are two main dialects of Armenian, Eastern (spoken mainly in Armenia and Iran) and Western (spoken among the Armenian diaspora everywhere else). The data presented here are from the Eastern Armenian dialect spoken in Iran. I am grateful to Karine Megerdoomian for providing the data and the stress judgments. Where indicated, the data are from Megerdoomian (2002).

(72)   a.   Ara-n   <u>girk</u>   gn-ets.
            Ara-NOM   book   buy-AOR.3SG
            'Ara bought a book/books.'

       b.   k'at'u-ner-ə   norits   <u>muk'</u>   bʀn-ets-in.
            cat-PL-NOM   again   mouse   catch-AOR-3PL
            'The cats caught a mouse/mice again.'

       c.   k'at'u-n   norits   <u>mi muk'</u>   bʀn-ets.
            cat-NOM   again   one mouse   catch-AOR.3SG
            'The cat caught a mouse again.'

The examples in (72) all involve non-specific objects. In Eastern Armenian, like Persian, specific objects behave differently from their non-specific counterparts with respect to stress. While non-specific objects exemplified in (72) receive stress, specific objects shown in (73) do not (from Megerdoomian 2002: 126). As a result, stress falls on the verb.

(73)   a.   Ara-n   girk-ə   <u>ayr-ets.</u>
            Ara-NOM   book-ACC   burn-AOR.3SG
            'Ara burnt the book.'

       b.   k'at'u-ner-ə   mk'-an   <u>bʀn-ets-in.</u>
            cat-PL-NOM   mouse-ACC   catch-AOR-3PL
            'The cats caught the mouse.'

       c.   menk   yerek'   yerk'u hat'   gini-n   <u>verčatsr-ets-ink.</u>
            we.NOM   yesterday   two   CLASSIF   wine-ACC   finish-AOR-3PL
            'We finished two bottles of wine yesterday.'

The distinct behaviour of specific and non-specific objects with respect to stress is clearly shown in Eastern Armenian by the auxiliary 'be', which is used in all verb tenses in the indicative mood, with the exception of the aorist. What makes this auxiliary very interesting for our purposes is the fact that it is a prosodic enclitic which appears after the element bearing the main stress in the clause (see Tamrazian 1994; Megerdoomian 2002).[48] The auxiliary, therefore, is an excellent indicator of sentential stress on the preceding element. The specific–non-specific distinction is illustrated clearly in the examples in (74) and (75) (from Megerdoomian 2002: 128). The auxiliary is highlighted in these examples for clarity. In the examples in (74), which involve a specific object, the auxiliary follows the stress-bearing verb. In the examples in (75), which

---

[48] The question of how the intriguing behaviour of this auxiliary can be accounted for is left open for future research.

involve a non-specific object, on the other hand, the auxiliary follows the stress-bearing object.

(74) a. Ara-n   girk-ə   <u>ayr-el</u>   e.
          Ara-NOM book-ACC burn-PERF be-PRES-3SG
          'Ara has burnt the book.'

      b. Ara-n   payt'-ov   mi   mart-u   <u>tzetz-elu</u> e.
          Ara-NOM stick-INSTR one man-ACC hit-FUT   be-PRES.3SG
          'Ara will beat up a man with a stick.'

(75) a. Ara-n   <u>girk</u>   e   gn-um.
          Ara-NOM book   be-PRES-3SG buy-IMPERF
          'Ara is buying a book/books.'

      b. yerexa-n   poqots-um   <u>gndak'</u> er   xaq-um.
          child-NOM street-LOC ball   be-PAST.3SG play-IMPERF
          'The child was playing ball in the street.'

Megerdoomian (2002) provides several arguments showing that specific and non-specific objects occupy distinct positions in Eastern Armenian. While the specific object, she argues, is in a vP-external position, the non-specific one is in a vP-internal position. The stress pattern in Eastern Armenian, therefore, receives an account similar to Persian: the specific object is outside and the non-specific object inside the lower SPELLEE, the domain of sentential stress.

It was noted in the previous sections that Persian stands in contrast to English and German with respect to the stress behaviour of manner adverbials. In Persian, unlike English and German, manner adverbials are inside the stress domain and receive sentential stress. To evaluate the status of manner adverbials in Eastern Armenian, consider the sentences in (76).

(76) a. Ara-n   <u>arag</u> e   girk   gn-um.
          Ara-NOM fast   be-PRES.3SG book buy-IMPERF
          'Ara is buying a book/books quickly.'

      b. yerexa-n   <u>lav</u>   er   gndak' xaq-um.
          child-NOM good be-PAST.3SG ball   play-IMPERF
          'The child was playing ball well.'

The examples in (76) reveal that Eastern Armenian behaves like Persian with respect to the stress pattern of manner adverbs. While in the absence of a manner adverb, sentential stress falls on the non-specific object (see (75)), when manner adverbs are added, they receive sentential stress. This is clearly marked by the position of the 'be' auxiliary. While in (75) the auxiliary follows the non-specific object, in (76) it follows the manner adverb. These facts lead us to the conclusion that in Eastern Armenian, just like Persian, manner adverbs are merged lower than the phase head v.

The proposal with respect to the position of the manner adverb in Eastern Armenian leads to a prediction about VP-fronting in this language. It was noted in section 4.6.2.3 that, in Persian, VP-fronting cannot leave the manner adverb stranded. This fact was tied to the vP-internal position of the manner adverb. If, as proposed above, the manner adverb is in a vP-internal position in Eastern Armenian as well, it is expected that VP-fronting cannot leave the manner adverb stranded in this language. This prediction is borne out, as shown in (77).[49]

(77)   Eastern Armenian VP-fronting: Manner adverb cannot be stranded

    a. Ara-n   arag e   girk gn-um.
        Ara-NOM fast be-PRES.3SG book buy-IMPERF

          arag e   girk gn-um Ara-n
       * girk gn-um Ara-n arag   e

          'Ara is buying a book/books quickly.'

    b. yerexa-n lav   er   gndak' xaq-um.
        child-NOM good be-PAST.3SG ball   play-IMPERF

          lav   er   gndak' xaq-um yerexa-n
       * gndak' xaq-um yerexa-n lav   er

          'The child was playing ball well.'

In the discussion of manner adverbs, we noted that the same lexical item can be used as an adverb in different positions with different interpretations. It was shown that this difference is marked by a difference in stress in Persian.

---

[49] My consultant points out that sentence-final manner adverb with the VP fronted to the beginning of the clause, as shown in (i) below, is much improved in the context that the manner adverb is topicalized or uttered as an afterthought. The position of the auxiliary in (i) (cf. (77)), shows that the manner adverb is unstressed, confirming its topicalized status. These cases can be analysed as the manner adverb first moving out of vP to a topic position, followed by the fronting of the vP. The crucial case for our purposes is the one exemplified in (77).

(i) a. ?Girk e   gn-um   Ara-n   arag.
         book be-PRES.3SG buy-IMPERF Ara-NOM fast

    b. ??Gndak' er   xaq-um   yerexa-n   lav.
         ball   be-PAST.3SG play-IMPERF child-NOM good

Given that Eastern Armenian manner adverbs behave like Persian, one expects to find some lexical items in Eastern Armenian that are merged as adverbs in different positions, leading to different interpretations, while in the surface this difference is only marked by stress. This prediction is borne out. The examples in (78) show one such lexical item *vst'ah* 'confident' which could take the manner adverb interpretation 'with confidence' (78a) or the sentential interpretation 'surely', 'certainly' (78b) depending on its merge position. This difference is marked by a difference in stress, also highlighted by the position of the 'be' auxiliary.

(78) a. Ara-n   <u>vst'ah</u>   e vot'anavor art'asanel.
          Ara-NOM confident is poem   recited
          'Ara recited a poem/poems with confidence.'

      b. Ara-n   vst'ah   <u>vot'anavor</u> e art'asanel.
          Ara-NOM confident poem   is recited
          'Ara certainly recited a poem/poems.'

Finally, while a thorough study of unaccusative verbs and their stress behaviour in Eastern Armenian is beyond the scope of this monograph, preliminary data show that, like English, German, and Persian, in an unaccusative sentence uttered in a focus-neutral context, stress falls on the subject. In (79) we can see examples of unaccusative verbs, with main stress on the subject, marked by the 'be' auxiliary following the subject.

(79) Unaccusative: Eastern Armenian
      a. <u>mart</u> e galis.
          man is coming
          'A man/someone is coming.'

      b. aysteq <u>ptuq</u> e choranum.
          here   fruit is drying
          'In here, fruits are dried.'

We have been able to show so far that with the sentential stress rule in (2) and some reasonable assumptions about phrase structure we can account for a wide range of cross-linguistic stress facts in simple clauses. One robust property of the system developed in this monograph is that it assigns stress in a phase-based manner. The iterative nature of phase-based multiple spell-out, meanwhile, predicts that stress assignment should also be iterative. This prediction will be explored in the following section. We will see that the iterativity of the proposed system has the added benefit of being able to account for secondary stress. Secondary stress will also be discussed in the context of the interaction between information structure and sentential stress in chapter 5.

4.10 Multiple spell-out and iterative stress assignment

It was proposed in (2) that sentential stress is assigned in a phase-based manner. Phase-based multiple spell-out is an iterative operation. When the derivation reaches a phase, the complement, here called the SPELLEE, is sent off to PF, and as suggested here it undergoes the stress rule which assigns stress to the highest element in the SPELLEE. According to Chomsky (2000, 2001), CPs and (transitive) vPs constitute phases. So far, we have only considered one phase, namely, the light verb phrase vP. Even in a simple clause, however, there is another phasal boundary that we have to deal with, namely, CP. One would expect the same stress-assignment procedure to apply to CP, and in the case of more complex sentences, to higher phases, that is, vPs and CPs of higher clauses. This iterative nature of stress assignment is the topic of this section.

Consider a simple clause, a CP. When the derivation reaches C, its syntactic complement, namely TP, is spelled out. The SPELLEE or the stress domain in this case is therefore TP. This is shown in (80).

(80)

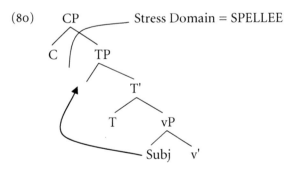

If according to the proposed system sentential stress is assigned to the highest element in the SPELLEE, one would expect the subject, which occupies the highest surface position in TP, to receive stress. In other words, while stress is assigned to the object at the vP phase, at the CP phase, stress is assigned to the subject. This is illustrated clearly in the tree structure in (81), where the vP and CP phases have been combined into one tree.

(81)

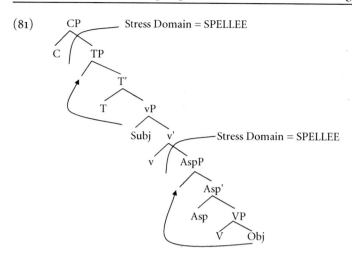

According to the structure in (81), in a simple transitive sentence, we expect stress on both the object and the subject. This prediction is in fact borne out. In a simple transitive sentence, while the object receives primary stress, the subject is more prominent than the verb and receives secondary stress. In more general terms, in a simple clause, the internal argument (or, to be more precise, the highest element in the lower SPELLEE, which could be the object, the argument PP, the manner adverb in Persian-type languages, etc.) receives primary stress and the external argument (or the subject) receives secondary stress. This is shown for English and Persian in the examples in (82) and (83), where I am using numbers to show primary and secondary stress (82b is adapted from Halle and Vergnaud 1987).

(82)   a.   <u>John</u> saw <u>Mary</u>.
             2   1

       b.   <u>Jesus</u> preached to the people of <u>Judea</u>.
             2   1

(83)   a.   <u>Ali</u> <u>ye ketaab</u> xarid.
             2   1
             Ali   a book   bought
             'Ali bought a book.'

       b.   <u>Ali</u> <u>xub</u> qazaa xord.
             2   1
             Ali well food   ate
             'Ali ate well.'

If we build more structure on top of a single clause, that is, if we deal with more complex sentences with complement clauses, the generalization is clear. There is one stressed element for each phase (or for each SPELLEE to be more precise). Take a sentence with a complement clause, exemplified for English and Persian in (84). Here, we are dealing with four phases, two for the lower clause and two for the higher one. Two elements in each clause receive stress according to the proposed system.

(84)   a.   [_{CP} John [_{vP} told Maryam [_{CP} that Jane [_{vP} saw Bill]]]].
                       2   2   2   1

       b.   Ali   be   Maryam   goft   ke   Mina   qazaa   mi-xaad.
             2   2   2   1
            Ali   to   Maryam   said   that   Mina   food   DUR-want.3SG
            'Ali said to Maryam that Mina wants food.'

We have been able to show using some basic examples that the iterativity built into the system correctly accounts for the elements that receive some level of stress in simple or complex clauses. This is a good outcome, an advantage over proposals such as Zubizarreta's (1998) which cannot account for elements receiving secondary stress. Nothing in our system, however, predicts that one of the stressed elements has more prominence that the others, for example the fact that in (84a), *Bill* receives primary stress and the rest secondary stress. Descriptively, it is clear which element receives primary stress in all the languages we have looked at. Of all the elements that are marked for stress by the sentential stress rule, it is always the last one in the clause that receives primary stress. Below I will consider several different ways this generalization can be incorporated into our system.

Consider the simple SVO sentence in (85) repeated from (82a).

(85)   John saw Mary.
         2   1

Our stress system correctly predicts stress on the object and the subject. One way to capture the fact that stress on the object is stronger than the subject is to put the burden on the phonological component. Under this view, the sentential-stress system is solely responsible for determining which constituents receive stress and makes no predictions as to which of these constituents receives primary stress. Primary stress, on the other hand, is handled by the phonological component, assigning higher prominence to the rightmost stressed constituent in the sentence. The generalization about the final stressed element in the clause receiving primary stress, according to this solution, is translated into a (global) phonological rule, namely, rightmost. Meanwhile, this rule should be teased apart from the types of rule proposed in the phonological approaches to sentential stress discussed in chapter 2. There is a crucial difference between allowing for a *parametric* phonological rule to determine sentential stress and a phonological/phonetic principle which invariably puts more prominence on the rightmost of otherwise syntactically determined stressed elements. The parametric nature of the rules in the phonological accounts needs to be highlighted. The phonological accounts use a phonological rule which in one language could be rightmost and in another leftmost (at different prosodic levels) to determine which elements receive prominence and which of those the highest prominence of a phrase/clause. We discussed two major problems with these approaches in chapter 2, namely, "overgeneralization" and the inability to account for "leftmost" prominence in unaccusative sentences in an otherwise "rightmost" prominence language such as English. In a syntactic account of the kind proposed in this monograph, the stressed elements in a sentence are determined in a purely syntactic manner. Meanwhile, in the phonetic realization, I put forth the possibility that what accounts for which element receives primary stress may be a phonological/phonetic principle which is the same for every language and has the effect of a (perceived) higher prominence on the last or rightmost element in line. Such a proposal is totally compatible with the proposed system.

Alternatively, one may attempt to find a syntactic translation for the notion of "last stressed element in the clause" in the kind of multiple spell-out system proposed in this monograph. Let us start with the hypothesis that it is the "lowest" phase that receives primary stress, with all the rest receiving secondary stress. Meanwhile, "lowest" appears to be a global notion, to be determined only once the whole structure is built. At the vP phase, how does the system know that this is the lowest phase of the whole clause? In order to maintain local computation, the simplest conceivable choice would be to interpret "lowest" as "first" in a bottom-up multiple spell-out system.[50] That is to say, it is the first SPELLEE that is marked for primary stress with all the rest being marked for secondary stress. Applying this condition to the simple clause in (85) with the derivation in (81) yields the right result without encountering any problems. The derivation proceeds bottom-up: the verb merges with the object, Asp merges, Obj moves to the Spec–AspP, the phasal head v merges and the complement of v is shipped off to PF, with the highest element, the object, being marked for primary stress following our sentential

---

[50] I am adopting a bottom-up multiple spell-out system following standard assumptions. The core idea, however, may be readily transferable to a top-down multiple spell-out system (see e.g. Cowper and Hall 2001; Richards 2002), if we take "lowest" to mean "last". I will not pursue this option here.

stress rule. From this point to the end of the derivation, in other words, when the Lexical Array LA is exhausted, the constituent receiving sentential stress following the sentential-stress rule will be marked for secondary stress. The procedure yields the right result for the more complex clauses in (84), which involved four phasal domains. The first SPELLEE in the bottom-up derivation is marked for primary stress and the rest for secondary stress.

The situation gets more complicated when we consider sentences involving complex subjects or objects. Consider a clause involving a complex subject, exemplified in (86).

(86)   That <u>the Leafs</u> beat <u>the Flyers</u> initiated <u>an uproar.</u>

              2   2   1

In (86), we are dealing with a subject which itself contains a clause. Let us first consider how we can account for stress on the underlined elements in (86) regardless of the degree of stress. Our system predicts stress on the object of the main clause, *an uproar*, and on the subject which itself constitutes a clause. Thus assuming that the clausal subject undergoes the stress system independently, the stress on its object *the Flyers* and the subject *the Leafs* is expected. The question is how we can account for *primary* stress on the object of the main clause and *secondary* stress on all the other stressed elements. If we assume a strictly bottom-up derivation in which the construction of the clause would literally start from the bottom and the subject would only be built when we reached its Merge position Spec-vP, we can maintain our generalization that it is the first SPELLEE that receives primary stress, with all the other elements receiving secondary stress. If, on the other hand, we follow more standard assumptions (Chomsky 1995) in assuming that there is no inherent ordering between the construction of the main clause or the clausal subject, we cannot resort to the notion of "first" to ensure that it is the "lowest" SPELLEE that is marked for primary stress. Under this view we would need to introduce a readjustment mechanism that would ensure that the object of an embedded clause is distinguished from the object of the main clause. One way to achieve this goal is to suggest that whenever a clause merges into an already existing structure, any element within the clause loses its "first" status and thus avoids primary stress. Therefore, in the case of the clausal subject in (86), the object of the clausal subject, *the Flyers*, loses its first status by lowering the degree of stress by one level. This will lead to the object of the main clause receiving primary stress and the other stresses being realized as secondary. It is worth noting that the phonological solution proposed above will handle these cases without a problem by taking the rightmost/last stressed element as the one receiving primary stress.

We have seen in this section that the system proposed in this monograph has the added advantage of accounting for stresses on elements other than the one receiving primary stress.[51] In fact, as far as the proposed system is concerned, all these stresses are treated on a par, in other words, they are all marked for stress by the sentential stress rule. With respect to the question of which of these elements receives primary stress, two different options were explored. According to the first option, the system for the assignment of sentential stress does not discriminate the element receiving primary stress. What the system does is simply to mark the elements that receive stress, secondary or primary. Of the elements marked for stress, under this view, the rightmost/last one receives the highest prominence following an invariable cross-linguistic phonological/phonetic principle. According to the second option, the choice of which element receives primary stress is built into the phase-based multiple spell-out system. Under this view, the notion "last stressed element" is translated into "first" in a strictly bottom-up system of syntactic derivation. Several complications were discussed. Both of these options are compatible with the system proposed in this monograph and the choice of which one is on the right track requires further development of syntactic derivation in a multiple spell-out framework as well as independent motivations, to be explored in future research.

4.11 Conclusion

In this chapter, a new syntactic account of sentential stress, one based on the notion of phases and multiple spell-out, was introduced. It was proposed that sentential stress is assigned to the highest element in the spelled out constituent, referred to as the SPELLEE. The SPELLEE is the complement of a phasal head, which, following Chomsky, was taken to be transitive v and C. It was shown that this new formulation of the sentential stress rule provides a systematic way for accounting for a wide range of cross-linguistic facts while avoiding the problems raised for the analyses discussed in the previous chapters. In particular, from an empirical point of view, the SOV facts exemplified in this chapter by Persian, German V-final sentences, and Eastern Armenian—where stress is neither on the element immediately preceding the verb (as predicted by Cinque 1993) nor on the lowest selectionally ordered element (as predicted by Zubizarreta 1998)—receives a straightforward

---

[51] Even in Romance languages, in which primary stress appears to be invariably sentence-final in focus-neutral contexts, there is secondary stress on the subject, providing empirical support for the application of the proposed sentential-stress rule in these languages.

account in the proposed system, in which stress is assigned to the highest element within the stress domain, defined on syntactic terms in a phase-based system.

A question arose with respect to sentence-final stress in an SVO language such as English. It was shown that with certain assumptions about the syntax of SVO languages and how the system of stress assignment operates, we can account for the apparent rightmost stress. It was suggested that the apparent rightmost stress is the result of the movement of lower elements to higher positions, thus emptying the stress domain. In these cases, stress was proposed to fall on the closest phonologically non-null element.

With respect to the stress behaviour of manner adverbs, it was noted that in some languages such as Persian and Eastern Armenian they are stressed, while in others such as German and English they are not. This difference was tied to a difference in the position where manner adverbs are merged in these languages. While in the former type of languages, manner adverbs merge inside vP—in other words, inside the stress domain—in the latter type of languages they merge outside it. Independent evidence from VP-preposing was presented in support of this proposal. These explanations underline the purely structural characteristic of the proposed system.

Moreover, to account for the stress behaviour of specific objects in Persian and Eastern Armenian, it was proposed, following standard syntactic assumptions, that specific (unlike non-specific) objects occupy a vP-external position (in surface structure) and thus avoid sentential stress. This points to another important characteristic of the proposed system. Like Cinque (1993) and Zubizarreta (1998), but unlike Bresnan (1971, 1972) and Legate (2003), the system proposed here is insensitive to underlying syntactic structure and relies solely on surface structure.

The stress behaviour of passives/unaccusatives in English, German, and Persian provides more support for the proposal that sentential stress is assigned to the highest element in the stress domain, defined here within a phase-based system. The fact that sentential stress falls on the subject in unaccusative/passive sentences is expected under the proposed system, given that unaccusative/passive verb phrases do not induce phasal boundaries, leaving C as the only phasal head in the clause and the subject as the highest element in the spelled-out TP. It was noted, however, that the stress on the subject in an unaccusative sentence is lost once a manner adverbial is added to the structure. It was suggested that the addition of the manner adverbial imposes a phasal boundary, resulting in the unaccusative sentence behaving like an unergative one with respect to stress. Some independent syntactic evidence was presented in support of this position.

Finally, given the nature of multiple spell-out, the proposed stress system predicts that stress should be assigned iteratively. It was shown that the iterativity of the system of stress assignment paves the way for an account of secondary stress facts, an added advantage to some previous accounts of sentential stress.

So far, we have considered only sentences that are focus-neutral, that is, sentences in which no constituent is informationally more prominent than any other. It is a well-known fact that sentential stress/accent interacts with information structure. This interaction is the topic of the following chapter.

5

Sentential stress and information structure

5.1 Introduction

In the previous chapters, we considered only sentences with neutral focus, where no phrase in the clause is informationally more prominent than any other or, more technically, where the context question is 'What happened?' (known as the out-of-the-blue context). It is a well-known fact that information structure interacts with sentential stress in sentences with non-neutral focus, and there are various proposals to account for such interactions (see e.g. Jackendoff 1972; Selkirk 1984, 1995; Rooth 1992; Cinque 1993; Lambrecht 1994; Reinhart 1995; Truckenbrodt 1995; Büring 1997; Zubizarreta 1998; Schwarzschild 1999; Kadmon 2001). In this chapter, we consider sentences uttered in non-neutral contexts. While the default Sentential Stress Rule introduced in chapter 4 accounts for stress in focus-neutral sentences, an additional rule, the Focus Stress Rule, is proposed to handle the interaction between sentential structure and information structure. The Focus Stress Rule, which is also proposed to apply in a phase-based manner, ensures that a focussed constituent receives the highest clausal prominence in languages which mark focus prosodically. It is shown that sentential stress is determined in an interplay between the default Sentential Stress Rule and the Focus Stress Rule. I also provide a novel account for the intriguing behaviour of wh-questions with respect to the distribution of sentential stress.

One of the properties of the system developed in this chapter is that it takes the relationship between syntax and phonology to be unidirectional, in compliance with the Y-model of grammar adopted in one way or another in the generative tradition. According to this model, the syntactic component feeds into the phonological and semantic components. It is thus unexpected, under this view, to have prosodic considerations motivating syntactic operations, as suggested, for instance, by Zubizarreta's (1998) p-movement. In this chapter, I provide several arguments against her proposal and present a new way of accounting for the word-order facts, which attributes the movements solely to syntactic motivations. Focus is thus treated as a syntactic property interpreted in the semantic and phonological components, realized by prosodic prominence in some languages. Therefore, the Focus Stress Rule takes the focus structure as input and incorporates its effect in the calculation of sentential stress for the whole clause. The direction is crucially from focus to sentential stress/accent. This stands in contrast to other approaches, such as the Focus Projection Algorithm (see Selkirk 1984, 1995; Rochemont 1986, 1998), which take sentential stress/accent as the input to an elaborate algorithm which derives the focus structure of a sentence. In this chapter, I provide several conceptual and empirical arguments against this type of approach and show how the proposed system fares better with the data. It is worth noting that the main goal of this chapter is to account for the prosodic consequences of focus rather than its syntactic/semantic implications. These different approaches are discussed and compared with the proposed system insofar as facts regarding sentential stress/accent are concerned. Detailed discussions of issues such as the scope or representation of focus are beyond the scope of this monograph. Before we proceed, it is worth noting that the particular formulation of the default Sentential Stress Rule developed in the previous chapter is orthogonal to the discussions in this chapter. The arguments and the proposals in this chapter can thus be regarded as independent from the particular proposal with respect to the manner of stress assignment in chapter 4.

5.2 Focus and sentential stress

It is a well-known fact that the information structure of a sentence can affect sentential stress, which concerns the element that receives the highest prominence in a sentence.[1] Thus, for instance, all variants of the sentence *John kissed Mary* given in (1) would be considered felicitous depending on the context of the utterance. Recall that underlining marks sentential stress.

(1) a. John kissed <u>Mary</u>.
     b. John <u>kissed</u> Mary.
     c. <u>John</u> kissed Mary.

In the previous chapters, we dealt only with the variant in (1a), which we understood to be the one with neutral focus, uttered in an out-of-the-blue context. No attempt was made to formalize the notions of neutral focus and out-of-the-blue context. While a thorough review of the literature regarding

[1] This is not necessarily true of all languages. In some languages focus structure does not influence sentential stress and is marked otherwise. We will return to this issue later.

the notion of "focus" is beyond the scope of this monograph,[2] I will attempt to provide a basic framework in which a discussion of the main issue at hand—namely, the interaction between information structure and sentential stress—is made possible.

Following Chomsky (1971, 1976) and Jackendoff (1972), I will assume that focus is defined as the nonpresupposed part of the sentence, where the presupposed part of the sentence consists of the speaker's and hearer's shared assumptions at the point at which the sentence is uttered in a discourse.[3] Also following Chomsky and Jackendoff, I use the wh-question/answer test to determine the focus structure of a sentence, in other words, how a sentence is divided in terms of focus and presupposition.[4] The wh-question is known as the context question. It is worth noting here that while the wh-question/answer test provides us with a convenient tool to determine the focus structure of a sentence, one we will employ in the remainder of this chapter, it should not be regarded as a flawless replacement for such an intricate notion as context. Often one needs to look beyond the context question and consider the actual context of the utterance to determine the focus structure of a sentence. We will consider some complexities regarding the identification of focus in section 5.3.

Some possible context questions for the string *John kissed Mary* (with sentential stress left unmarked) are given in (2), with (2a) the out-of-the-blue context.[5]

(2)   a. What happened?
       b. What did John do?
       c. Who did John kiss?
       d. Who kissed Mary?
       e. What did John do to Mary?

The presupposition in a context question can be paraphrased by replacing the wh-phrase with an indefinite, as shown by the sentences in (3), which correspond with the questions in (2).

---

[2] There is no consensus on terminology here. Sometimes, scholars use different terms to refer to what I call focus, such as new information, rheme, and topic, and sometimes they use these terms to mean slightly different things. These controversies are irrelevant for our purposes here; a working definition of this notion will be provided below. (For a review of these and other discourse-related terms, see Vallduví and Engdahl 1996.)

[3] For arguments against defining focus in terms of presupposition (based on the behaviour of factive predicates), see Schmerling (1976) and Rochemont (1986). For a response to such arguments, see Zubizarreta (1998: 159, n. 3).

[4] The wh-question/answer test dates back at least to Paul (1970).

[5] We are leaving out one possible context (What happened to Mary?) which will lead to disjoint focused constituents. This context will be dealt with at the end of the section.

(3)   a. Something happened.
      b. John did something.
      c. John kissed someone.
      d. Someone kissed Mary.
      e. John did something to Mary.

Based on the context questions in (2) and the presuppositions in (3), we can now build the focus structure of a sentence. We defined focus as the nonpresupposed part of the sentence. Thus, the focused part of the sentence is the part that is not shared with the context question. The focus structures for the string *John kissed Mary* corresponding to the context questions in (2) are shown in (4), where, following Jackendoff, Selkirk (1984), and Zubizarreta (1998), among others, [F] marks the focused constituent.[6] I refer to the cases in (4a) and (4b), where the focus of the sentence is the verb phrase or the whole clause, as *broad focus* and the other cases in (4c–e), which involve focus on smaller constituents, as *narrow focus*. The terms broad and narrow are used descriptively, and do not constitute primitives in our system.[7] It is worth noting here that (4a–c) correspond to the stress pattern in (1a), (4d) to (1c), and (4e) to (1b), to be accounted for below. For convenience, these stress patterns are repeated in (4), with secondary stress ignored at thispoint.[8]

(4)   a. [F John kissed Mary] → John kissed <u>Mary</u>⎤
                                               ⎬ Broad focus
      b. John [F kissed Mary] → John kissed <u>Mary</u>⎦

      c. John kissed [F Mary] → John kissed <u>Mary</u>⎤
      d. [F John] kissed Mary → <u>John</u> kissed Mary⎬ Narrow focus
      e. John [F kissed] Mary → John <u>kissed</u> Mary⎦

---

[6] Unless specified otherwise, I am assuming a two-way distinction where marked [F] will be interpreted as focused and not marked [F] as presupposed. Some scholars, e.g. Zubizarreta 1998, make a three-way distinction: [+F], [−F], and unmarked for [F].

[7] The terms "broad" and "narrow" are often used in a relative sense. Thus, for instance, focus on the DP object can be seen as narrow, compared to focus on the whole verb phrase, but as broad, compared to focus on an adjective within the DP object. In this monograph, the term broad is used solely to refer to cases of verb phrase or clausal focus, and focus on all other smaller constituents is referred to as narrow.

[8] In all the sentences in (4a–c) it is the object noun phrase that receives the highest prominence in the sentence, leading to the given stress pattern. Meanwhile, no claim is made at this point as to whether there are differences in the phonetic realization of the accent on the object in these sentences. In fact, differences between broad-focus accent (examples 4a, b) and narrow-focus accent (example 4c) have been reported, in particular for languages other than English. We are abstracting away from such differences for now, but will return to this issue in the ensuing discussions.

Questions arise as to how the focus structure should be represented at the conceptual-intentional interface. Chomsky (1976), for instance, suggests that the focus–presupposition partitioning of a sentence can be represented at LF by applying the rule of Quantifier Raising (QR) to the focused constituent. Other scholars have offered other alternatives (see e.g. Culicover and Rochemont 1983; Rooth 1985, 1992, 1995; Kratzer 1991; Tancredi 1992; Erteschik-Shir 1998, among others). Zubizarreta (1998) argues for a more abstract level called Assertion Structure which is derived from LF via some interpretive mechanisms. A discussion of these different views would take us too far afield our main goal, an account of the interaction between information structure and sentential stress. In what follows, I put aside the interpretive side of the issue and focus on the phonetic realization of focus relevant for our purposes here.

Let us have a closer look at the facts in (4) before attempting to account for them formally. The first thing to note is that the default Sentential Stress Rule alone cannot account for these stress facts. Recall from chapter 4 that the Sentential Stress Rule predicts primary stress on the object. This prediction is only compatible with the examples in (4a–c). Example (4d) with the subject focussed and example (4e) with the verb focussed are the problematic cases. On the other hand, focus alone does not seem to be able to capture the facts either. Thus, for instance, if we hypothesize that focussed constituents receive the main prominence of the sentence, we can capture the examples in (4c–e), in which the focussed constituent consists of a single word, but need an additional rule to determine which word within the focussed constituent receives primary stress when it consists of more than a single word. Thus, in (4a), for example, where the whole clause is focussed, an additional rule is needed to determine which word within the focussed clause receives prominence.[9] Meanwhile, there is one generalization that is true of all the examples in (4): the primary stress of the sentence is always within the domain of the focussed constituent. This generalization is more formally captured in the Focus Prosody Correspondence Principle in (5) (adapted from Zubizarreta 1998: 38, originally proposed by Chomsky 1971 and Jackendoff 1972).

[9] This point can also be illustrated with examples in which a focussed noun phrase consists of more than a single word. An example with a focussed subject is given in (i), with both focus and stress marked simultaneously. In (i), we need an additional rule concerning stress within the DP to determine which word within the focussed subject receives primary stress. We are not concerned with default stress within DP in this monograph (see 1.4 for a discussion of this methodological choice).

(i)   Context: Who brought the cake?
     [F The man in the red <u>shirt</u>] brought the cake.

(5)   Focus Prosody Correspondence Principle (FPCP)

   The F-marked constituent of a sentence must contain the most prominent word in that sentence.

We can now reconsider the facts in (4) in light of this preliminary discussion
and the principle in (5). There are two ways of approaching these facts. One
way is to take the sentential stress or accent as given and ask the question
how we can capture the focus-structure possibilities in (4). This is the line
taken by the proponents of focus projection algorithms, discussed in detail
in section 5.6, where several arguments against this type of approach will be
provided. The second approach is to take the focus structure as given and ask
the question how we can capture the stress facts in (4). This is the line taken
in this monograph. Recall that while the FPCP is a correct generalization, it
is not sufficient to determine the element with the highest prominence in a
sentence. To account for the relation between focus structure and sentential
stress, I propose the Focus Stress Rule in (6), which I take to apply, like the
sentential stress rule, in a phase-based manner (see below).

(6)   Focus Stress Rule

   At the phase HP, mark a focussed subconstituent C to receive focus stress.

The rule in (6) leads to the marking of the focussed constituent to receive
focus stress in languages with prosodic realization of focus. Thus, in addition
to the default Sentential Stress Rule discussed in the previous chapters, we
have the Focus Stress Rule in (6) which affects which constituent in a sentence
receives stress. I suggest that each rule applies independently from the other
and marks a constituent to receive the corresponding stress. Application of
one rule does not preclude or precede application of the other. Nor does
application of one rule, let us say the Focus Stress Rule, define the domain
of the application the other rule, the default Sentential Stress Rule. The two
rules apply totally independently, with interaction arising only in the final
phonetic realization of the stress markings. The final stress pattern of the
sentence is determined when these stress markings are interpreted at PF, with
the constituent marked for focus stress receiving the highest prominence of
the sentence. We will look at the interaction between these two rules in more
detail below.[10]

---

[10]   There is something inherently different between the default Sentential Stress Rule and the Focus
Stress Rule. While focus stress is the phonetic realization of a syntactic property "focus", which also has
semantic implications, default sentential stress is simply a formal property with no corresponding
feature in the syntactic or semantic domains. This raises the interesting question of why default
sentential stress (or nuclear stress) exists at all. This monograph has provided an account for how

We can now examine the effect of the two rules by applying them to the examples in (4). In the following discussion, I will continue to use underlining to indicate stress. Meanwhile, to make a distinction between the two rules, I will use FS to specify elements marked for stress by the Focus Stress Rule and SS to specify elements marked for stress by the default Sentential Stress Rule. As for the latter, I will use numbers as subscripts to distinguish primary and secondary stress. A point of clarification is in order here. In chapter 4, section 4.10, we discussed at some length how the distinction between primary and secondary stress may be captured in our system. Recall that the default Sentential Stress Rule itself does not distinguish between primary and secondary stresses. For illustration purposes, in the ensuing discussion, I will mark primary and secondary stress as if they are given by the Sentential Stress Rule itself. This does not signify a change in our position with respect to the issue of primary and secondary stress and is done solely for the sake of comprehensibility and ease of illustration. Let us start with a more straightforward case, the sentence with the focussed subject in (4d), repeated in (7).

(7)   [_FJohn] kissed Mary.

As discussed above, the two rules apply independently in a phase-based manner and in no particular order. At the vP phase, there is no focussed constituent within the phasal domain; thus the rule in (6) does not apply. The Sentential Stress Rule, on the other hand, applies and puts primary stress on the object, marked as SS_1 in (8). At the CP phase, the subject is marked for Focus Stress (thus FS in (8)) as well as for secondary sentential stress, marked as SS_2 in (8).

(8)   <u>John</u>   kissed <u>Mary</u>   →   <u>John</u>   kissed <u>Mary</u>
       FS, SS_2 SS_1 1   2

Crucially, at the point of phonological interpretation at PF, an element that is marked for focus stress receives more prominence than one that is marked for sentential stress. This has two implications. First, an element marked for FS receives higher prominence than one marked for SS. Moreover, if a single element is marked for both FS and SS, only the phonetic interpretation of the FS marking will be realized. The system thus correctly predicts primary stress on the focussed subject *John* and secondary stress on the object *Mary*.[11] The

default sentential stress is computed, but has nothing to contribute with respect to its existence per se. One possible consequence of this inherent difference between the two types of stress is that focus stress is phonetically more prominent than default sentential stress, rather than the other way around. If default sentential stress were more prominent, focus information would be lost as a result of the interaction between the two rules.

[11] We are solely interested here in what elements receive the highest and second highest prominence in the sentence, but this may be an oversimplification. The phonetic interpretation of Focus Stress

secondary stress on the object provides further support for the claim that the Sentential Stress Rule is also at work here and that the stress facts cannot be determined solely on the basis of focus structure. We will return to the issue of secondary stress in such examples in section 5.4.

Let us now turn to the sentence with the verb focussed in (4e), repeated in (9).

(9)   John [$_F$ kissed] Mary

The Focus Stress Rule applies and marks the verb for focus stress. The Sentential Stress Rule, on the other hand, marks the object for primary stress and the subject for secondary stress. The result is shown in (10). At PF, the FS marking is interpreted as the highest prominence of the sentence, whereas the Sentential Stress Rule correctly predicts higher stress on the object compared to the subject.

(10)   John   kissed   Mary   → John   kissed   Mary
       SS$_2$ FS   SS$_1$ 1   2

All the remaining examples in (4) have primary stress on the object and secondary stress on the subject. We will see, however, that according to our proposal with respect to sentential stress and its relation with focus, the stress patterns come about in slightly different ways. In particular, the primary stress on the narrowly focussed object in (4c) has a source different from that of the examples with broad focus in (4a) and (4b). Consider first the example in (4c), repeated in (11).

(11)   John kissed [$_F$ Mary]

The application of the Focus Stress Rule and the Sentential Stress Rule generates the result shown in (12), with the object marked for both FS and SS$_1$ and the subject marked for SS$_2$. This will result in primary stress on the object and secondary stress on the subject at PF.

(12)   John   kissed   Mary
       SS$_2$ FS, SS$_1$

The primary stress on the object is of special interest here. Given the system developed above, FS takes precedence over SS and thus the primary stress on the object is due to it being marked for focus stress. We will see below that in broad focus cases illustrated by the examples in (4a) and (4b), primary stress on the object is the result of the Sentential Stress Rule. Thus, one may expect to see the difference between the FS marking in one case and the SS marking

may be different from that of Sentential Stress in qualitative ways. Thus, for instance, primary stress determined by FS may be different from SS in phonetic details. We will return to this issue briefly in the discussion of example (4c).

in the other manifest itself in the phonetic realization. There is evidence in
the literature suggesting that this is in fact the case. While the evidence for
English is inconclusive, with most linguists indicating no difference between
the two (e.g. Chomsky 1971; Jackendoff 1972; Ladd 1996; but see Selkirk 2002),
different accents for broad and narrow focus have been reported in a number
of other languages: Bengali (Hayes and Lahiri 1991); Central Basque (Irurtzun
2003); European Portuguese (Frota 1995); Finnish (Välimaa-Blum 1993); Greek
(Baltazani 2002); (some dialects of) Italian (Grice et al. 2004; Brunetti 2003,
and references cited there). The system developed here readily allows for such
differences, with FS and SS sending different instructions to PF for phonological interpretation.[12] We will return to this issue in the discussion of focus
projection algorithms in section 5.6.

Now consider the sentences with broad focus in (4a) and (4b). In these
broad-focus sentences, sentential stress is determined by the Sentential Stress
Rule alone. In (4a), repeated in (13), the domain of focus is the whole clause.

(13)   [$_F$ John kissed Mary]

The Focus Stress Rule in (6) fails to mark any constituent for focus stress in
this sentence. At both phasal levels, vP and CP, there is no single subconsituent
that is focussed but rather the whole domain. As a result, no constituent is
marked for focus stress and the application of the Sentential Stress Rule results
in primary stress on the object and secondary stress on the subject, as shown
in (14). This is the out-of-the-blue context discussed in the previous chapters.

(14)   <u>John</u>   kissed   <u>Mary</u>   →   <u>John</u>   kissed   <u>Mary</u>
         SS$_2$ SS$_1$ 2   1

The sentence in (4b), repeated in (15), has the whole verb phrase as its
focussed domain.

(15)   John [$_F$ kissed Mary]

At the vP phase, the whole domain is focussed; thus no subconstituent gets
marked for focus stress according to the Focus Stress Rule in (6). At the CP
phase, there is no focussed constituent, given that in our cyclic multiple spell-
out system, the focussed verb phrase belongs to the lower cycle and is not
accessible at this point. As a result, no constituent is marked for focus stress
and the sentential stress rule correctly predicts primary stress on the object

---

[12] It is worth noting that the existence of languages like English (if English truly does not make any
distinction in the realization of broad and narrow focus) does not provide evidence against the proposed system. The proposed system simply allows for languages to realize this difference phonetically.
It does not, however, rule out the possibility of a language not marking this difference.

and secondary stress on the subject. This result is identical to the one for the example with sentence focus shown in (14).

Before we end our discussion of the English examples in (4), it is worth highlighting once again that the default Sentential Stress Rule is blind to the focus structure of the clause and applies to all of these examples in an identical way. Meanwhile, differences arise in the phonetic interpretation of the cases discussed above as a result of the application of the Focus Stress Rule. Thus, for instance, the object is marked for stress by the default sentential stress rule in the broad focus cases in (4a–b) as well as the subject focus sentence in (4d). Meanwhile, the SS marking is realized as primary stress in the former case, where focus stress marking is absent, and as secondary stress in the latter context, where there is focus on the subject.[13]

We have illustrated how the Focus Stress Rule in (6) and a particular understanding of the way it interacts with the default sentential stress rule can account for the interaction between focus structure and sentential stress in English. We will see how the proposal can be readily extended to data from Persian, another language with prosodic marking of focus. The Persian sentences corresponding the English examples in (4) are given in (16), with focus structure and stress marked on the sentences simultaneously.

(16) a. [F<u>Ali</u> Maryam-o <u>busid</u>].
         2   1

      b. <u>Ali</u> [F<u>Maryam-o</u> <u>busid</u>].
         2   1

      c. Ali [F<u>Maryam-o</u>] <u>busid</u>.
                      1   2

      d. [F<u>Ali</u>] Maryam-o <u>busid</u>.
              1   2

      e. <u>Ali</u> Maryam-o [F <u>busid</u>].
         2   1
         Ali Maryam-ACC kissed

To avoid repetition, I will not go into the details of how the Focus Stress Rule and the Sentential Stress Rule apply to the Persian sentences in (16).

---

[13] Given the global nature of the phonetic realization of different stress markings, the system allows for qualitative differences in the realization of sentential stress on the object in the two different contexts. It is conceivable that SS on the object in the context of no focus marking can be qualitatively different from SS on the object in the context of focus stress on the subject. I leave a closer examination of this issue for future research.

It is sufficient to recall from chapter 4 that in Persian SOV sentences with specific objects, the sentential stress rule predicts primary stress on the verb and secondary stress on the subject. The Focus Stress Rule marks the focussed constituent for focus stress in a manner elaborated above for English. The result of the application of these rules to the sentences in (16) is shown in (17). The phonological interpretation of the stress markings in (17) leads to the stress facts shown in (17), with FS marking interpreted as primary stress, and SS_1 or SS_2 as secondary stress. In the absence of FS marking, SS_1 is interpreted as primary stress and SS_2 as secondary stress.

(17) a. <u>Ali</u> Maryam-o <u>busid</u> → <u>Ali</u> Maryam-o <u>busid</u>.
        SS_2 SS_1 2   1

    b. <u>Ali</u> Maryam-o <u>busid</u> → <u>Ali</u> Maryam-o <u>busid</u>.
        SS_2 SS_1 2   1

    c. <u>Ali</u> <u>Mrayam-o</u> <u>busid</u> → Ali <u>Maryam-o</u> <u>busid</u>.
        SS_2 FS SS_1 1   2

    d. <u>Ali</u> Maryam-o <u>busid</u> → <u>Ali</u> Maryam-o <u>busid</u>.
     FS, SS_2 SS_1 1   2

    e. <u>Ali</u> Maryam-o <u>busid</u> → <u>Ali</u> Maryam-o <u>busid</u>.
        SS_2 FS, SS_1 2   1
        Ali   Maryam-ACC kissed

All the examples we have considered so far involved cases where the domain of focus consists of a single syntactic constituent. For example, in the examples in (4a) and (4b), where the domain of focus was larger than a single word, these domains corresponded to single syntactic constituents, namely, the whole clause and the verb phrase. A question arises as to what happens with disjoint focussed constituents, in other words, where the focussed/non-presupposed part of the sentence does not form a single syntactic constituent. The relevant context and the corresponding stress facts are illustrated in the English example in (18) and even more clearly with the two constituents separated in the surface form in the Persian example in (19).

(18) Context: What happened to Mary?
    [$_F$ <u>John</u>] [$_F$<u>kissed</u>] Mary.
         2   1

(19) [$_F$<u>Ali</u>] Maryam-o   [$_F$<u>busid</u>].
      2   1
    Ali   Maryam-ACC kissed

Consider the example in (18). The Focus Stress Rule marks the verb and the subject for focus stress. The stress on the verb and the subject is thus expected. A question arises as to how we can account for the levels of stress in (18), that is, the fact that the verb receives *primary* stress, while the subject receives *secondary* stress. It was proposed in (6) that the Focus Stress Rule, like the Sentential Stress Rule, applies in a phase-based manner. To account for the levels of stress in the application of the Sentential Stress Rule, it was suggested in chapter 4, section 4.10 that it is the stress in the lower SPELLEE that is realized as primary stress, with all the other stresses realized as secondary. Different ways of implementing this notion were discussed in section 4.10. I suggest that the same mechanism is responsible for the realization of focus stress. In other words, the FS marking of the lower phase is realized as primary stress and the other one is realized as secondary stress. The same can be extended to the Persian example in (19). The results are shown in (20) and (21).

(20)   John kissed Mary → John kissed Mary.
       FS$_2$ FS$_1$ 2   1

(21)   Ali Maryam-o busid → Ali Maryam-o busid.
       FS$_2$ FS$_1$ 2   1

The facts in (18) and (19) are thus accounted for without adding an extra mechanism to our system. It is worth noting that since there are two focussed constituents in each of these sentences and that, in the phonetic interpretation, marking by the Focus Stress Rule overrides that of the Sentential Stress Rule, the latter plays no role in determining primary and secondary stress in these sentences.

To sum up, we have seen that the stress pattern of a sentence is determined in an interplay between the Sentential Stress Rule discussed in chapter 4 and the Focus Stress Rule introduced in this section. In the case of broad focus, that is, when the domain of focus is as large as the vP or CP, the Sentential Stress Rule applies and determines which constituents within this domain receive primary and secondary stress. In cases where the focussed constituent is smaller than vP or CP, the Focus Stress Rule may impose stress on an element other than the one predicted by the sentential stress rule. In such cases, the effect of the sentential stress rule will be realized as secondary stress. We have also seen that in disjoint focussed contexts, the Focus Stress Rule correctly predicts stress on both focussed constituents, with different levels of stress following the phase-based system in the way discussed for the default Sentential Stress Rule. In the above discussion, following a long tradition, we relied on the wh-question/answer test for determining the focus structure of a sentence. While the wh-question/answer test can be employed as a convenient tool for this purpose, one we will continue to use in the remainder of this chapter, the notion of context often involves intricacies which can be over-looked by a blind application of this test. Let us take a pause here and briefly consider some of these complexities in the following section.

5.3 Focus structure and context

To determine the focus structure of a sentence, we have so far followed tradition and used the wh-question/answer test. While this test is certainly a convenient tool and adequate in most non-complex cases, often one needs to look beyond the context question and consider the actual context of the utterance to determine the focus structure of a sentence.[14] In this section we will examine some of these more intricate cases. The point is not to cover all the possible cases where the blind application of the wh-question/answer test may fail, but simply to illustrate that this test is just a shorthand way of representing the context and by no means a substitute for it. My intention is not to discredit the wh-question/answer test, which has been proven very useful over the years and certainly in the present monograph. The goal is to highlight some problems and remind the reader that by using a convenient test we cannot claim to have captured the intricacies of a complex notion like "context".

Let us start with the case of the out-of-the-blue context. While we take the question *What happened?* to represent such a context, it is worth noting that a sentence uttered in response to this question may or may not be informationally neutral, depending on the shared assumptions of the speaker and the hearer. Take the example of the passive sentence *My bike was stolen* (Legate 2003), which was used in the previous chapters as a canonical passive example with stress on the subject in an out-of-the-blue context "What happened?" Note, however, that one could easily conceive of a context in which the bike is so much part of the world of discourse of both the hearer and the speaker (e.g. of a couple, one has recently bought the bike) that the speaker may utter the sentence in response to *What happened?* with stress on the predicate. This pattern is predicted based on the Focus Stress Rule if we identify the predicate as the focussed constituent in this particular context. In other words, this particular case should not be seen as an out-of-the-blue context. A true

---

[14] The intricacies regarding the notion "context" have consequences for grammaticality judgements involving different information structures. Speakers often unintentionally attach a particular context to a given utterance. Thus, they could consider an utterance with a particular prosody as an appropriate response to the out-of-the-blue context question "What happened?", where the respective context is not truly out of the blue.

out-of-the-blue context is one in which no constituent is informationally more or less prominent than any other. To illustrate the point more clearly, consider a well-known contrast, due to Schmerling (1976) (also discussed in Cinque 1993 and Zubizarreta 1998, among others).

(22)   a. <u>Johnson</u> died.
        b. Truman <u>died.</u>

The contexts for the utterances in (22) were quite different. In Schmerling's words, "Johnson's death came out of the blue; it was not news that we were waiting for... When Truman died, on the other hand, his condition had been the subject of daily news reports for some time." (Schmerling 1976: 90) Given the circumstances, the only true out-of-the-blue context is the one in which (22a) is uttered, and this is precisely the one whose stress pattern is predicted by the system developed in chapter 4, where sentential stress falls on the subject of an unaccusative verb like *die*. The sentence in (22b), however, is uttered under the assumption that Truman's deteriorating health condition is part of the shared knowledge of the speaker and the hearer. This example, therefore, does not constitute an out-of-the-blue sentence with neutral, but rather one with the predicate focussed and thus stressed. The fact that both sentences in (22a) and (22b) could be uttered in response to the question *What happened?* should not be taken as the determining factor. Context questions are really used to represent contexts and not to identify them. A question such as *What happened to Truman?* more accurately represents the context we are dealing with in (22b).

In response to these and other similar problems, some scholars have attempted to use other tools to define the focus structure of a sentence. Rochemont (1986), for example, defines focus in terms of "new" versus "old" (or "given") information. According to this approach, the material in a sentence S that corresponds to the new information in a given discourse context constitutes the focus in S. New information is that which is not old information. Old information, on the other hand, is defined in terms of the notion c-construable (Rochemont 1986: 47). A string P is c-construable in a discourse D if P has a "semantic antecedent" in D, with the definition of "semantic antecedent" given in (23).

(23)   A string P has a semantic antecedent in a discourse D, D = $\{D_1, \ldots, D_n\}$, if and only if there is a prior and readily available string P′ in D, such that the uttering of P′ either formally or informally entails mention of P.

Rochemont discusses some interesting cases of informal entailment. Thus, for example, the mention of *VW* in (24) is enough to make *car* c-construable.

(24)   Harry wants a VW, but his wife would prefer an <u>American</u> car. (Rochemont 1986)

As Zubizarreta (1998) correctly points out, part-whole relations should also be subsumed under the notion "informally entails mention of", where mention of the "whole" informally entails mention of the corresponding part. Thus, in (25), *legs* functions as old information by virtue of being part of *cat*.

(25)   Poor cat! It has only <u>three</u> legs. (Zubizarreta 1998)

Zubizarreta also notes that the notion "c-construable" does not need to be defined solely in linguistic terms. A perceptually salient or familiar referent may function as old information even if it has not been previously mentioned. For example, if two people see a cat, one of them may say, *How strange! It has only <u>three</u> legs* (Zubizarreta 1998: 161). I argued above that contextual familiarity or salience may arise even if the referent is not present at the time of utterance. For example, in the case of the passive "bike" sentence, the "bike" may be salient or familiar by virtue of the particular context in which it is uttered.

We have seen some of the complexities involved in determining the focus structure of a sentence and considered some attempts to capture these intricacies more formally. I will continue to use the wh-question/answer test in the remainder of the book, while keeping in mind that it is merely a means of representing and not replacing an intricate notion such as context. I leave a more definitive answer to the question of how context can be accurately defined in a formal manner for future research.

In section 5.2 we looked at how the stress pattern of a sentence is determined in the interplay of the Sentential Stress Rule and the Focus Stress Rule. In the following section we will look at how Zubizarreta's (1998) stress system deals with such interactions. We start by considering how she handles the interaction between information structure and sentential stress in English-type languages. We then turn to her proposal with respect to syntactic movements being triggered by prosodic considerations in some Romance languages. The model we have proposed so far to handle the interaction between information structure and sentential stress is framed within a Y-model of grammar, in which the interaction between syntax and phonology only goes in one direction, from syntax to phonology. Accordingly, focus is seen as a syntactic property with semantic and phonological implications. Under this view of the grammar, adopted in one way or another in the generative tradition, one does not expect to find cases in which a syntactic operation, movement, is triggered by prosodic considerations, as suggested by Zubizarreta's prosodically-motivated movement, or p-movement (see also Reinhart

1995; Szendrői 2003; Samek-Lodovici 2005). I provide arguments against p-movement and will propose a new way of handling the facts without facing these problems.

5.4 Against prosodically motivated movement

The main question we intend to address in this section is whether prosodic considerations can trigger movement of some constituents in certain languages. Reinhart (1995), for instance, proposes that scrambling of the definite object in Dutch is prosodically motivated, that is, it occurs to escape a position which would receive stress according to the nuclear stress rule (see also Neeleman and Reinhart 1998). The most explicit theory of prosodically motivated syntactic movement, however, is proposed by Zubizarreta (1998) (see Samek-Lodovici 2005 for an optimality theoretic version of her proposal). She uses this notion (what she refers to as p-movement) to account for certain facts in Spanish and Italian, namely, that a focussed constituent in these languages is always sentence-final. In order to understand her proposal, we need briefly to review the way in which her system handles the interaction between information structure and sentential stress/accent. This discussion also provides us with a basis to compare our account of this interaction with Zubizarreta's.

Recall from chapter 3 that in order to account for the stress facts in focus neutral sentences in some Germanic and Romance languages, Zubizarreta proposed a modularised Nuclear-Stress Rule, repeated in (26).

(26) Zubizarreta's Modularised NSR   (Zubizarreta 1998: 19)
      S-NSR: Given two sister categories C_i and C_j, if C_i and C_j are selectionally ordered, the one lower in the selectional ordering is more prominent.
      C-NSR: Given two sister categories C_i and C_j, the one lower in the asymmetric c-command ordering is more prominent.

The intention here is not to review how the NSR in (26) can account for the stress facts in neutral focus sentences. For that and related problems, the reader is referred to chapter 3. The crucial point here is that the rules in (26) cannot account for the stress facts in sentences with non-neutral focus such as those discussed in section 5.2, and illustrated again by the English and French examples in (27) (adapted from Zubizarreta 1998).

(27) Context: Who ate an apple?
      a. [F John] ate an apple.

b. [$_F$ Jean] a   mangé une pomme.
   Jean   has eaten an   apple

In both examples in (27), the NSR in (26) would wrongly predict stress on
the object *apple*. We have seen already that in such sentences with non-neutral
focus, we need an additional rule to represent the effect of focus on sentential
stress. Zubizarreta proposes the Focus Prominence Rule in (28) to capture this
relationship, where [+F] is marked as [F] in our system and [−F] is unmarked.

(28) Focus Prominence Rule (FPR)   (Zubizarreta 1998: 21)
      Given two sister categories C_i (marked [+F]) and C_j (marked [−F]), C_i
      is more prominent than C_j.

Here is how Zubizarreta's system accounts for the facts in (27). The NSR in
(26) and the FPR in (28) impose contradicting requirements on the subject
and the predicate as metrical sisters. While the FPR requires that the focussed
subject receive greater prominence, the NSR requires greater prominence on
the predicate. According to Zubizarreta, different languages offer different
solutions to such contradictions. In English and French, exemplified in (27),
this is done by treating defocalized constituents (i.e. constituents marked
[−F] in Zubizarreta's system and not F-marked in our system) as metrically
invisible. Thus, in the examples in (27), everything but the subject becomes
metrically invisible. The C-NSR applies and puts stress on the only metrically
visible element, the subject.

Zubizarreta's treatment of primary stress in the examples in (27) looks
somewhat similar to our account of the same facts. Recall that according
to the system developed in this monograph, primary stress is predicted to
fall on the focussed constituent, here the subject, following the Focus Stress
Rule in (6). It should be noted, however, that our system also accounted for
the secondary stress on the object. It was argued that while the Focus Stress
Rule assigns primary stress on the subject, the default sentential stress rule
is responsible for the secondary stress on the object. In Zubizarreta's system,
on the other hand, the conflicting requirements of FPR and NSR lead to the
domain of the application of the NSR being confined to the subject, which
receives primary stress accordingly. Zubizarreta, therefore, needs a different
explanation for the secondary stress on the object. She attributes the secondary
stress to what she refers to as "echo stress". According to Zubizarreta, the
secondary stress on the object is the echo of the primary stress on the object in
the corresponding context question *Who ate an apple?* Putting aside its ad hoc
nature, Zubizarreta's proposal to capture secondary stress is also questionable
on empirical grounds. Consider a sentence with the object in focus. A possible

context question is given in (29), with primary stress marked by underlining. The corresponding response and its focus structure are provided in (30).

(29)   Context: Who did John <u>kiss</u>?

(30)   John kissed [F Mary].

Zubizarreta's system correctly predicts primary stress on the object *Mary*. However, if secondary stress is the result of primary stress in the context question being echoed in the response, as Zubizarreta suggests, the prediction is that the verb *kiss* should receive secondary stress. This prediction is not borne out. In the sentence in (30), it is the subject *John* that receives secondary stress, correctly predicted by our system, which attributes this secondary stress to the application of the Sentential Stress Rule, in a manner elaborated in section 5.2. The system developed here, therefore, fares better than Zubizarreta's in accounting for the interactions between information structure and sentential stress in English-type languages, at least as far as secondary stress is concerned. In sentences involving focussed constituents, secondary stress is the result of the application of the default Sentential Stress Rule, which correctly predicts stress on the object in (27) and on the subject in (30).[15]

I now turn to Zubizarreta's prosodically motivated movement, which, she suggests, arises as a result of the way contradictions between the FPR and the NSR are resolved in Spanish and Italian. In English and French, focus was realized as sentential stress/accent on the focussed constituent. The parallel facts in Italian and Spanish are given in (31).

(31)   Context: Who ate an apple?
    a. *<u>Gianni</u> ha   mangiato una mela.   (Italian)
        Gianni has eaten   an   apple
    b. *<u>Juan</u> comió una manzana.   (Spanish)
        Juan ate   an   apple

Zubizarreta uses the ungrammaticality of the examples in (31) to show that in Italian and Spanish, unlike English and French, focus on a non-sentence-final element such as the subject cannot simply be indicated by sentential stress/accent. In other words, in these languages, the contradiction between the FPR and the NSR cannot be resolved by deeming the non-focussed

---

[15] Zubizarreta's system may also run into trouble in accounting for the primary and secondary stress facts in sentences with disjoint focussed constituents. Since it is not clear how these cases should be treated in her system, I leave them out of our discussion.

material metrically invisible.[16] The grammatical equivalents of the sentences in (31) are given in (32).

(32)   Context: Who ate an apple?

    a.   ?Ha mangiato una mela <u>Gianni</u>.   (Italian)

    b.   Comió una manzana <u>Juan</u>.   (Spanish)

To account for the facts in (32), Zubizarreta resorts to the notion of prosodically motivated movement or p-movement. According to her proposal, Italian and Spanish resolve a contradiction between the FPR and the NSR by moving the defocalized constituent to a higher position, thus leaving the focussed phrase in a position to receive sentential stress via the NSR. To be more precise, first the focussed phrase moves out to the specifier of FocP and then the remnant TP undergoes p-movement and is adjoined to FocP, as shown in (33) for the Italian example.[17]

(33) $[_{FocP}[_{TP}\ t_i\ [ha\ mangiato\ una\ mela]]_j\ [_{FocP}\ Gianni_i\ [_{TP}\ t_j]]]$

There is an immediate empirical problem with Zubizarreta's account, namely that prominence on a non-final element in the clause is possible in both Italian and Spanish. A distinction is often made in the literature between information focus (also called presentational focus), which merely conveys non-presupposed information, and contrastive focus (also called identificational focus), which provides new information *by denying part of the hearer's presupposition* (see, for example, Halliday 1967; Rochemont 1986; Kiss 1998). The impossibility of non-final sentential stress, illustrated in (31) and (32) above, is only true of informationally-focussed constituents. Contrastively focussed elements, on the other hand, allow for non-final sentential stress, as illustrated by Zubizarreta's examples in (34) (see also Brunetti 2003 and references therein; Domínguez 2004; among others).

(34)   Contrastive focus

    a.   <u>Gianni</u>   ha   mangiato una mela (non Piero).   (Italian)
         Gianni has eaten   an   apple (not   Piero)

    b.   <u>Juan</u> comió una manzana (no Pedro).   (Spanish)
         Juan   ate   an   apple   (not Pedro)

---

[16]   The examples in (31) are compatible with a contrastive focus interpretation, an issue we will return to later in this section.

[17]   To account for the non-perfect status of the Italian example in (32a), Zubizarreta suggests that in Italian, as opposed to Spanish, VOS order is sensitive to the relative heaviness of VO with respect to S. She further suggests that this is due to the different sources of VOS in these languages. She proposes that in Spanish VOS is derived from VSO via leftward movement of O across S, whereas in Italian (which lacks VSO) VOS is derived from SVO via leftward movement of VO across S. I am abstracting away from these details.

To account for the facts in (34), Zubizarreta suggests that contrastive focus is determined by a different rule from non-contrastive focus. She collapses contrastive stress with emphatic stress and calls the rule responsible for the assignment of this type of stress the Emphatic/Contrastive Stress Rule (E/CSR). The crucial point is that, according to Zubizarreta, only contradictions between the FPR and the NSR result in p-movement. In other words, Spanish and Italian tolerate stress induced by the E/CSR even if it does not fall on the final word in the sentence as predicted by the NSR. There is a sharp contrast in this sense between the FPR and the E/CSR with only the former triggering p-movement. This raises an important question as to whether making such a strong distinction between contrastive and non-contrastive focus with respect to stress is justified. If we set aside the difference in word order for a moment, with respect to sentential stress, the facts in (32) and (34) look identical. In both cases, we are dealing with a focussed constituent receiving the main prominence of the clause. This obvious stress similarity already undermines any differential treatment of the two types of focus in this respect. We will consider the issue more closely below.

Brunetti (2003) provides several arguments to show that information and contrastive focus should be considered a uniform phenomenon from a prosodic point of view.[18] Brunetti first considers some of the differences that have been attributed to contrastive and information focus. The first difference concerns the issue of focus projection. We deal with the notion of focus projection in more detail in the discussion of Selkirk's (1995) Focus Projection Algorithm in section 5.6. For illustration purposes, consider a well-known example from Chomsky (1971). As noted by Chomsky, the focus of (35) with accent on the final head noun *shirt* can be taken as any of the bracketed phrases, supported by the fact that the sentence can be followed by any of those in (36) depending on the context.

(35)   He was [warned [to look out for [an ex-convict with [a red [shirt]]]]].

(36)   a. No, he was warned to look out for an ex-convict with a red [tie].
       b. No, he was warned to look out for an ex-convict with [a carnation].
       c. No, he was warned to look out for [an automobile salesman].
       d. No, he was warned [to expect a visit from the FBI].
       e. No, he was [simply told to be more cautious].

It has been suggested that focus projection of the kind illustrated in (35) is only possible with information/non-contrastive focus and that focus with

---

[18] In fact, Brunetti's goal is to show that contrastive and information focus are a uniform phenomenon from a syntactic and semantic point of view as well. I am setting aside this aspect of her proposal (see n. 23).

emphatic/contrastive prominence cannot project (see e.g. Kiss 1998; Donati and Nespor 2003). A corollary of the claim that contrastive focus does not project is that it cannot be larger than a word. To illustrate these claims, Donati and Nespor (2003) provide the examples in (37), where contrastive focus is indicated by capital letters.

(37)   a. I always thought John was [ANTI]_F-communist.

    b. I always thought John was [WELSH]_F.

    c. I always thought John was *[A YOUNG JOURNALIST]_F.

The crucial example is (37c), which is supposed to show that contrastive focus on the head noun *journalist* cannot be projected to the whole DP *a young journalist*, in contrast to the information focus example we saw in (35).

    The claim that contrastive focus cannot project or be larger than a word is readily challenged by Brunetti's Italian example in (38), where (38a) provides the context in which (38b) is uttered.[19]

(38)   a. Maria ha   incontrato il   Prof. Rossi.
        Maria has met   the Prof. Rossi
        'Maria met Prof. Rossi.'

    b. No, ha   incontrato [_DP IL   MAESTRO [_PP DELLA
        no   has met   the teacher   of the
        FIGLIA   [_PP DI PIETRO]]].
        daughter   of Pietro
        'No, she met Peter's daughter's teacher.'

Given the context in (38a), the focus in (38b) is clearly contrastive and it involves the whole DP. Focus is realized on the focussed DP prosodically as primary stress on *Pietro*. From a focus projection perspective, one can see the focus stress on *Pietro* being projected to the whole DP. In fact, as pointed out by Brunetti, the stress facts for the sentence in (38b) would not have changed if it were uttered in the context of a wh-question, thus conveying information focus. This is shown in (39), with the informationally focussed part in bold.

(39)   a. Chi ha   incontrato tua   sorella?
        Who has met   your sister
        'Who did your sister meet?'

<hr>

[19] The contrastively focussed constituent can appear preverbally as well. The optionality of the position of contrastively focussed elements is an issue I will not deal with in this monograph.

b. Ha incontrato [DP **il   maestro** [PP **della   figlia**   [PP **di**
   has met   the teacher   of-the daughter   of
   Pietro]]].
   Pietro
   'She met Peter's daughter's teacher.'

The same point made by Brunetti for Italian can be easily extended to
English. Thus, for instance, the phrase [a young journalist] used in (37c) to
show that contrastive focus cannot be larger than a word, can easily be used
contrastively in response to the sentence in (40a). The contrastive response is
given in (40b).

(40)   a. John met an old police officer.
       b. No, he met [A YOUNG JOURNALIST]

Moreover, as shown in (41), regardless of whether the sentence is uttered
contrastively or to provide new information, the stress facts are the same.

(41)   a. Who did John meet?
       b. John met [**a young journalist**].

Brunetti provides further examples to show that contrastive focus, just like
information focus, can be projected to domains as large as the whole verb
phrase or the whole clause. The English examples in (42) and (43), adapted
from Brunetti's Italian examples, illustrate this point.

(42)   a. Is someone knocking on the door?
       b. No, THEY ARE HAMMERING A NAIL.

(43)   a. Did John gain weight because he eats a lot of muffins?
       b. No, because HE DRINKS TOO MUCH BEER.

In both (42) and (43), we are clearly dealing with focus which is contrastive
(given the context sentences) and is projected to the whole verb phrase. Once
again, the stress facts would have been as indicated by the underlining, had the
sentences been uttered in the context of information focus.

To sum up, we have so far been able to show that contrastive focus, just like
information focus, can be larger than a word and project to the whole verb
phrase or clause, with the stress facts being identical in both cases.

In addition to the above difference with respect to the domain of
contrastive and non-contrastive focus, it has been suggested that only
emphatic/contrastive prominence can be associated with functional categories
(such as determiners), prepositions, and subparts of words (Chomsky 1971;
Jackendoff 1972; Zubizarreta 1998, among others). Some examples are given
in (44).

(44) a. I met THE candidate (not A candidate).
      b. I put the milk ON the fridge (not IN the fridge).
      c. They are going to IMport oil (not EXport oil).

The example in (45) (from Donati and Nespor 2003) shows the impossibility of associating informational focus with a focus smaller than a word.

(45) [John [just bought [a *[black]$_F$bird]$_F$]$_F$]$_F$.

Brunetti (2003) offers an interesting argument to show that the apparent unavailability of subparts of words being informationally focussed should not be taken as an inherent grammatical difference between the two. Instead, she claims that this restriction does not depend on the type of focus, but on purely pragmatic factors. She first notes that a wh-question/answer pair is the natural environment for non-contrastive/information focus to occur. A context where the answer to a wh-question would be a subpart of the word, on the other hand, is highly unusual, if not impossible. Consider (45). It is not possible to find a context question for (45) whose answer is *black*. In fact, *black* is part of the word *blackbird*, so its semantic content is not independent from the rest of the word. The only way *black* can express new information by itself is where the information given is metalinguistic. The context question for an answer with focus expressing metalinguistic information has to be an echo question with the wh-word replacing the subpart of the word under question. The Italian pair in (46) is provided by Brunetti, with the focussed part in bold.

(46) a. Hai   visto   un "cosa"-pardo?
          (you) have seen   a   what-pard
      b. Ho   visto   un **leo**pardo
          (I) have   seen   a   leopard

Once again, the contrastive equivalent of (46) would have identical behaviour with respect to stress. This is shown in (47). Thus, under this view, the difference in the acceptability of the exchanges in (46) and (47) is not due to an inherent difference between the two types of focus but rather the more natural status of the context in (47) compared to (46).

(47) a. Quel turista ha   visto un ghepardo
          that tourist has seen   a   cheetah
      b. No,   ha   visto un LEOpardo
          no, (he)   has seen   a   leopard

We have seen that the domain differences attributed to the two types of focus are illusory. We have also noted that, at least as far as sentential stress is concerned, the two focus types exhibit similar behaviour, with both contrastive and information focus receiving primary stress. The question remains whether there are any other phonetic differences between the two. It has been claimed in the literature that contrastive focus has a higher peak than information focus (e.g. Belletti 2002). It should be noted, however, that phonetic studies on focus peaks do not usually distinguish between contrastive and information focus (see Frascarelli 2000, in press), but always between broad and narrow focus (see sections 5.2, 5.6 and references cited therein). The problem is, as Brunetti (2003) correctly points out, that it is easier to find contexts in which broad focus has a non-contrastive interpretation and contexts where a narrow focus has a contrastive interpretation. It is this correlation between contrastive and narrow focus, on the one hand, and information and broad focus, on the other, that may have led to the conclusion that the two types of focus are different phonetically.

To sum up, we have provided reasons to treat contrastive and information focus as a unified phenomenon from a prosodic perspective. It is worth noting that this would lead to a much simpler system, where the stress caused by both foci will be handled by a single rule, namely, our Focus Stress Rule in (6), which predicts primary stress on the focussed constituent (in languages in which focus is marked prosodically), regardless of whether the focus is contrastive or informational. Thus, we can dispense with Zubizarreta's additional Emphatic/Contrastive Stress Rule. We are still left, however, with the question of how to deal with the fact that in Spanish and Italian only contrastive focus can be non-final in the sentence, which was essentially Zubizarreta's reason to want to have two rules determining the stress in the two cases, with only one, the FPR, being allowed to trigger p-movement. The facts are repeated in (48) and (49) with contrastive focus in capital letters and information focus in **bold**.

(48)   Information focus: <u>**John**</u> ate an apple

    a. ?Ha mangiato una mela **Gianni**.   (Italian)
       has eaten   an apple Gianni
    b. Comió una manzana **Juan**.   (Spanish)
       ate an apple Juan

(49)   Contrastive focus: <u>JOHN</u> ate an apple (not Peter)

    a. <u>GIANNI</u> ha mangiato una mela (non Piero).   (Italian)
    b. <u>JUAN</u> comió una manzana (no Pedro).   (Spanish)

Let us review Zubizarreta's explanation for the stress facts in (48) and (49). According to her, while the Focus Prominence Rule forces the stress on the (informationally) focused constituent, the subject, the Nuclear Stress Rule requires the stress to fall on the predicate. To resolve this conflict, Spanish and Italian have a prosodically motivated movement rule which moves all the post-focal elements to the beginning of the clause, resulting in the order in (48). Then the NSR applies and puts the stress on the sentence-final subject. As for (49), Zubizarreta takes the stress to be the result of a different rule, the Emphatic/Contrastive Stress Rule, which puts the main prominence on the contrastively-focussed constituents. Emphatic/Contrastive stress has a meta-grammatical function and is freely assigned, thus not leading to the same kind of conflict with the NSR.[20] It is worth pointing out here that it is not clear in Zubizarreta's system why we do not see the same kind of contrast in English-type languages. Recall that in the case of English, according to Zubizarreta, the same kind of conflict between the FPR and the NSR results in the post-focal material becoming metrically invisible. One would expect that if the E/CSR freely assigns stress and does not conflict with the NSR in Spanish and Italian, the same would be true of English. In other words, we should only get metrical invisibility with information focus and not with contrastive focus. This is contrary to fact. In English, the post-focal material is destressed regardless of the type of focus.

It is now time to examine how the system developed in this monograph can account for the facts in (48) and (49). As noted above, in our system, the stress facts follow from the same Focus Stress Rule regardless of the type of focus. Both informationally- and contrastively-focussed constituents receive the main prominence of the sentence in Spanish and Italian, as well as in English and French and any other language which marks focus prosodically. Nothing more needs to be said to account for the stress facts in (48) and (49).

While the stress facts in (48) and (49) are expected, a question remains as to the different word orders in informationally-focussed and contrastively-focussed sentences in Italian and Spanish. I would like to propose that the order differences follow from some syntactic properties of these languages, totally independent from prosodic factors. Consider first the informationally-focused cases in (48). I am assuming a refined CP structure à la Rizzi (1997), shown in (50).

(50)   Rizzi's (1997) refined CP structure

      $[_{ForceP} [_{TopP} [_{FocP} [_{TopP} [_{FinP} [_{IP} \cdots$

              split CP

---

[20] Zubizarreta notes that contrastive stress is partly metagrammatical and partly focus-related. It is metagrammatical in that it serves the function of denying part of the hearer's presupposition; it is focus-related in that it introduces a variable and a value for it (Zubizarreta 1998: 45). Meanwhile, she continues to collapse contrastive focus and emphatic focus.

I propose that the sentence-final position of the informationally-focussed element in these cases is the result of the post-focal topicalized elements having moved to a specifier of a TopP higher than the focussed subject.[21] Thus, under this view, the difference between Italian and Spanish, on the one hand, and English and French, on the other, is a syntactic one. While topics move out to a special position in Italian and Spanish, we do not see such a syntactic movement in English or French. This topic movement leads to the informationally-focussed constituent ending up in the sentence final position. The contrast between the informationally-focussed sentences in (48) and their contrastively-focussed counterparts in (49), on the other hand, can be attributed to a syntactic difference posited in the literature with respect to the position of the two types of focus. In a study of the differences between informational focus and contrastive focus (or identificational focus in her terms), Kiss (1998) proposes that while contrastively-focussed elements involve movement, informationally-focussed constituents do not.[22] Belleti (2001, 2002) proposes that there are two distinct types of focus in Italian, information focus and contrastive focus, with the latter being at a higher syntactic position than the former. Benincà and Poletto (in press) suggest that both types of focus involve movement in Italian but that informationally-focussed elements move to a lower syntactic position than contrastively-focussed ones. The idea shared in all these proposals is that the position of contrastive focus is higher than information focus. The contrast between (48) and (49), therefore, follows from this syntactic difference, something independent of prosodic factors as suggested by Zubizarreta. In (49), the contrastively-focussed constituent is above the topic, while the informationally-focussed constituent in (48) is below it.[23]

Let us note finally that Zubizarreta's p-movement suffers from a conceptual problem, namely, its incompatibility with the Y-model. Recall that p-movement, which according to Zubizarreta is triggered by prosodic needs (i.e. the conflict between the FPR and the NSR), feeds the NSR. The NSR, on the other hand, is dependent on syntactic structure. Thus, as Zubizarreta

---

[21] Under the view that informational focus does not involve movement (Kiss 1998), the focussed subject can be taken to remain in the Spec–IP position and the topicalized phrase in a position higher than that, for example the lower TopP. If informational focus involves movement (see Benincà and Poletto in press), the topicalized phrase has to be taken to move to a higher position.

[22] Kiss (1998) attributes other syntactic and semantic differences to the two types of focus. These details are not relevant for our purposes.

[23] Brunetti (2003) offers a unified analysis of information and contrastive foci, arguing that both of these types of focus can appear high and low. In the case of information focus, however, she claims that the post-focal elements are obligatorily elided. I do not intend to go into the details of her analysis. The crucial point is that if her proposal in this respect turns out to be correct, it is not incompatible with the stress system developed here. For us, as for Brunetti, the two types of focus follow the same stress rule. The exact account of the various order possibilities is beside the point.

points out, it has to apply before spell-out. She suggests that the NSR actually applies at the point of spell-out. p-movement, which feeds the NSR, therefore, has to be a syntactic operation. In fact, Zubizarreta provides additional evidence from the licensing of negative polarity items in Italian that this operation has to be syntactic (Zubizarreta 1998: 145–6).[24] It is precisely the syntactic nature of p-movement that is incompatible with the Y-model, which does not allow phonological considerations to trigger syntactic operations. According to our proposal, on the other hand, these movement operations, which lead to the word order differences, are syntactic, making their syntactic consequences unsurprising.

To summarize this section, Zubizarreta's prosodically motivated movement suffers from several empirical and conceptual problems. From an empirical perspective, it is based on a crucial prosodic distinction between contrastive and information focus which, as we have seen in this section, is hard to maintain. If, on the other hand, the two types of focus are treated in a unified manner from a prosodic perspective, the order variations can follow from syntactic differences between the two. The latter approach, unlike Zubizarreta's, is also compatible with the Y-model of grammar, adopted in one form or another in the generative literature.

We have seen so far that a focused constituent, defined as the non-presupposed part of a sentence, receives the main prominence of the sentence in languages with prosodic marking of focus. A problem arises with respect to the behaviour of wh-phrases in a language like English. By definition, the wh-phrase is the non-presupposed part of the sentence, which forms the basis of the use of the wh-question/answer test to determine focus structure. Thus, one would expect the wh-phrase to receive the main prominence of a sentence, a prediction which is not borne out in English. In the following section, this issue is explored in more detail and a solution for this long-standing puzzle is proposed.

5.5 Wh-questions: solving the puzzle

This section deals with sentential stress in wh-questions, with its main goal to find a solution for the puzzling stress behaviour of wh-phrases in some languages such as English (see e.g. Rochemont 1986; Zubizarreta 1998). If focus is defined as the non-presupposed part of the sentence, then, by definition,

---

[24] Zubizarreta shows that p-movement does not affect binding, but argues that this fact is empirically neutral with respect to the question of where p-movement applies. Suñer (2000), on the other hand, argues that p-movement in Romance affects binding relations, providing further support for its syntactic nature.

the focus of a wh-question is the wh-phrase. We have already seen that the focussed constituent receives the main prominence of a sentence in English. It is therefore surprising that the wh-phrase does not receive sentential stress, as shown in (51).

(51)   a.   What did Helen <u>review</u>?
       b.   *<u>What</u> did Helen review?

The fact that wh-phrases do not receive stress in English wh-questions cannot be attributed to a lexical property of wh-words. For instance, one cannot classify wh-words with other lexical items such as anaphoric pronouns which do not attract stress (e.g. *He <u>reviewed</u> it*). Evidence against this approach comes from the stress behaviour of wh-words in wh-in-situ in English. Unlike its moved counterpart, wh-in-situ in English bears sentential stress, as shown in (52).

(52)   Who reviewed <u>what</u>?

The puzzle is now complete for English: how is it that a moved wh-phrase does not receive primary stress, while its in-situ counterpart does? Before considering a solution to this puzzle, let us see how Zubizarreta (1998) deals with the problem. Pointing to similar facts, Zubizarreta suggests that the difference between moved and in-situ wh-phrases is in the way they are licensed. She proposes that while a fronted wh-phrase is licensed syntactically, by virtue of occupying the specifier position of a functional category with the feature [+wh], wh-in-situ is licensed prosodically. In other words, according to Zubizarreta, in the languages under discussion, a wh-phrase is licensed either syntactically or prosodically, but not both (p. 93). In order to account for the stress facts, Zubizarreta then revises her Focus Projection Rule (FPR) to exclude moved wh-phrases. This is shown in (53).

(53)   Zubizarreta's revised FPR
      Given two sister categories C_i (marked [+F]) and C_j (marked [−F]), C_i is more prominent than C_j, unless C_i is a wh-phrase and is syntactically licensed by the wh-head of C_j.

While the revised FPR in (53) ensures that wh-word is not more prominent than the rest of the sentence in (51), it cannot be the whole story. Recall, that according to Zubizarreta's analysis of the interaction between focus structure and sentential stress, defocalized (or [−F]) constituents are metrically invisible. In other words, one would expect the rest of the sentence to not undergo the NSR, thus leading to a sentence with no prominent accent whatsoever. To avoid this problem, Zubizarreta suggests that a [−F] constituent is analysed as metrically invisible only if the FPR applies to it. According to this view, the FPR does not apply to a sentence containing a moved wh-phrase, which saves the rest of the sentence from becoming metrically invisible as well. In sum, a wh-question avoids the FPR because it involves a moved wh-phrase and undergoes the NSR, resulting in the sentence-final stress facts in (51).

To evaluate Zubizarreta's proposal, we need to consider it more closely. It should first be noted that (53) is no more than a stipulation that the FPR should not apply to moved wh-phrases in English. It does point to any significant generalization about why English wh-questions should behave this way. It would be promising, for instance, if the mutual exclusivity of syntactic and prosodic licensing was a general fact about human language. As Zubizarreta points out herself, this is not true of other focussed elements in other languages. It has been observed that F-marked (or focussed) constituents move to the specifier of a focus head in some languages.[25] Meanwhile, these elements still receive the main prominence of the sentence. A Spanish example from Zubizarreta is given in (54) (see also section 5.4).

(54)   EL   VINO   trajo   Pedro.
       the wine   brought   Pedro
       'Pedro brought <u>THE WINE</u>.'

It remains a puzzle why syntactic movement does not eliminate the need for prosodic licensing in these cases. Here is Zubizarreta's explanation:

There is an important difference between the functional feature "focus" and the functional feature "wh". Whereas checking by the wh-feature is sufficient to license an F-marked phrase, checking by the "focus" feature is not. In the latter case the F-marked phrase must contain main phrasal prominence as well: it must be prosodically licensed (Zubizarreta 1998: 179, n. 51).

She further suggests that this difference is related to the distinction between the extrinsically grammatical (or discourse-related) nature of the focus feature and the intrinsically grammatical nature of the wh-feature. This additional explanation, however, does not seem to add any major insight either. The problem is compounded when we consider languages in which wh-phrases have been argued to undergo focus fronting. In these languages, wh-phrases have been shown to move to the specifier of a focus position where they also receive the main prominence of the sentence (see Horvath 1986 for Hungarian,

---

[25] Kayne (1998) argues that all focussed constituents in all languages undergo this type of movement. Thus, in *Mary saw <u>JOHN</u>*, John undergoes movement to a Spec–FocP followed by remnant movement of TP over it leading to the given order. I am leaving this option aside for now.

Aghem, and Basque; Tuller 1992 for Chadic; Bošković 1997 and Stjepanović 1999 for Serbo-Croatian; Ndayiragije 1999 for Kirundi; Kahnemuyipour 2001 for Persian, among others). Two examples are given in (55).[26]

(55) a. Ali <u>KOJAA</u> raft?   (Persian)
          Ali where   went
          'Where did Ali go?'

      b. <u>MIT</u> vettel?   (Hungarian: Ladd 1996: 172)
          what bought.2SG
          'What did you buy?'

The examples in (55) show that in languages in which the wh-phrase undergoes focus movement, but crucially not wh-movement (as standardly assumed) to Spec–CP, the wh-phrase receives sentential stress. We have already seen that wh-phrases also receive sentential stress in situ in English (see (52)). Other wh-in-situ languages which mark focus prosodically also have the wh-phrase stressed, as seen in the examples in (56) from Ladd (1996).

(56) a. Halil'e <u>NE</u> verdiniz?   (Turkish: Ladd 1996: 171)
          Halil-to what gave.2SG
          'What did you give to Halil?'

      b. Ram <u>KAKE</u> dekhlo?   (Bengali: Ladd 1996: 171)
          Ram whom saw
          'Who did Ram see?'

Based on the facts discussed so far, we can define a typology of wh-questions based on whether wh-phrases are stressed and/or whether they involve movement. This typology is illustrated in the diagram in (57).

(57) Typology of wh-questions based on stress and movement

Move Stress	+	−
+	focus-fronting	wh-in-situ
−	wh-movement	*

The diagram in (57) can be summarized as follows. In focus-fronting languages, wh-phrases undergo (focus) movement and receive stress. In wh-movement languages, wh-questions involve movement of the wh-phrase, but the wh-phrase is not stressed. Wh-in-situ phrases, on the other hand, do not undergo movement and receive stress in their base-generated position. I

[26] For arguments showing that the wh-phrase has moved to a preverbal focus position, the reader is referred to the cited references.

am not aware of any language with prosodic marking of focus which neither moves nor marks wh-phrases prosodically.

We can now consider whether Zubizarreta's approach can lead to a coherent explanation of these facts. Recall that according to her, wh-phrases are focussed (or F-marked) by definition. In the case of fronted wh-phrases in a language such as English, the F-marked constituent is licensed syntactically, and thus prosodic licensing is unnecessary. English wh-in-situ, on the other hand, is licensed prosodically, and therefore there is no need for it to be licensed syntactically. Zubizurreta does not explain why wh-phrases allow the two possibilities and why they do so in a mutually exclusive way; as discussed above, this amounts to a mere stipulation to account for the facts. Even more problematic is the case of languages in which wh-phrases undergo focus fronting. In these languages we have a combination of syntactic movement and prosody to license the F-marking of the wh-phrase. This raises the question of why one of the two licensing devices is not sufficient. These are questions that do not receive a convincing response in Zubizarreta's account. In what follows, I propose a structural explanation for these facts which does not suffer from the same type of problems.

Consider first the wh-in-situ and focus-fronting languages, exemplified in (55) and (56) above. The stress behaviour of wh-questions in these languages is expected. In both cases, a wh-element, which is by definition focussed, receives the main prominence of the sentence. The only difference is in their word order. In one type of language, wh-phrases stay in situ while in the other type they move to a focus position. This is reminiscent of the difference between information and contrastive focus discussed in section 5.4. Recall from the discussion of the two types of focus that both information and contrastive focus receive sentential stress in languages which mark focus prosodically, while their word order differs. The word-order difference, following Kiss (1998), was argued to be due to contrastive focus (as opposed to information focus) involving movement. The difference between wh-questions in wh-in-situ and focus-fronting languages can thus be stated in these terms. In both types of language, wh-phrases are focused and stressed, with their only difference being that in one type, wh-in-situ languages, the information focus strategy is used to form wh-questions, while in the other type, focus-fronting languages, the contrastive focus strategy is used for this purpose, leading to differences in word order but not in prosody.

We are now left with the main question we started this section with. Why is it that wh-phrases, which are focused by definition, do not receive sentential stress in English (and other wh-movement languages like the Romance languages)? Here, I suggest that it is the mere fact that these languages are wh-movement languages that is responsible for wh-phrases not receiving the main prominence of the sentence. In other words, what leads to the wh-phrase not receiving stress is the fact that, as standardly assumed, the wh-phrase moves to the Spec–CP position to satisfy the wh-feature in C. The movement of the wh-phrase out of the focussed position leads to the wh-phrase escaping focus stress. As a result of the movement to Spec–CP, the focussed position marked for focus stress is deemed phonologically null, and stress assignment is determined solely by the Sentential Stress Rule. Thus, for example, in (51a), repeated in (58), the Sentential Stress Rule predicts stress on the verb.

(58)   What did Helen <u>review</u>?

When, on the other hand, the wh-phrase is left in-situ in these languages, either in multiple wh-questions or in echo questions, the in-situ wh-phrase receives sentential stress. This is shown in the examples in (59).

(59)   a. Who reviewed <u>what</u>?
       b. (I didn't quite catch you!) <u>Who</u> reviewed the book?

We now have a full account for the typology in (57). In wh-in-situ and focus-fronting languages in which the wh-phrase remains in focus position, whether this position is the Merge position or a derived focus position, the wh-phrase receives sentential stress.[27] In wh-movement languages where the wh-phrase moves out of the focus position to satisfy an extra formal feature, the wh-phrase does not receive the main prominence of the sentences. Wh-movement thus emerges as another interesting case of an element escaping stress due to syntactic movement, akin to the movement of (Persian) specific objects discussed in chapter 4.

A question arises with respect to wh-movement in English: does the wh-phrase move directly from its Merge position to Spec–CP or does it move through an intermediate focus position? It has been proposed on syntactic grounds that wh-movement in English occurs via an intermediary focus position (see e.g. den Dikken 2003). In what follows, I use some striking stress facts about D-linked wh-questions, from Bresnan (1971), to support this proposal. We will consider the stress facts and then provide an account for them using the notion of the intermediary focus position for wh-movement.

The D-linked wh-question stress facts are illustrated in the contrast in (60). In the non-D-linked wh-question in (60b), the verb receives sentential stress

---

[27] I am referring only to languages which mark focus prosodically. A wh-in-situ language like Chinese, which does not seem to mark focus prosodically (Xu 2004), has nothing to contribute to our discussion. Moreover, whether languages with no wh-movement still involve a wh-feature which is checked covertly is irrelevant to our discussion as well. Only overt movement can interact with stress assignment given a Y-model of grammar.

in a manner discussed above. In the D-linked wh-question in (60b), however, the stress on *book* is a surprise.

(60)   a.   What did Helen <u>review</u>?
      b.   Which <u>book</u> did Helen review?

If we take the wh-phrase in (60b) to have moved to the Spec–CP position, we would expect it to evade sentential stress similarly to its non-D-linked counterpart. If, on the other hand, we separate the movement of the wh-word *which* from the noun *book*, we allow for an explanation of these facts.[28] The wh-word in (60b), under this analysis, escapes sentential stress in the same manner as the non-D-linked wh-phrase in (60a). The noun *book*, on the other hand, does not undergo wh-movement and receives stress either in its Merge position or in an intermediate focus position. The simplest view would be to take *book* to receive stress in its Merge object position based on the Sentential Stress Rule and to attribute its final surface position to PF movement. Under this view, the head noun is in the low object position in narrow syntax. One would, therefore, expect the object head noun to behave as if it were in the low object position from a syntactic point of view. Certain binding facts, however, indicate that, syntactically, the object noun has to be at least higher than the subject.[29] An illustrative example is given in (61).

(61)   a.   * Kate and Tom thought Helen reviewed books about each other.
      b.   Kate and Tom wonder which books about each other Helen reviewed.

Example (61a) is a violation of Condition A of the binding theory. In simple terms, the reciprocal *each other* is too far from the matrix subject *Kate and Tom* to be bound by it. Example (61b), on the other hand, shows that the wh-counterpart is grammatical, which in turn shows that the wh-phrase containing the reciprocal has to be interpreted at least above the embedded subject *Helen* to allow for the matrix subject *Kate and Tom* to bind it. This type of evidence indicates that in a D-linked wh-question, the noun

---

[28] The idea that in a wh-DP it is the wh-determiner that satisfies the wh-feature and the noun simply pied pipes with it is fairly standard (see e.g. Sportiche 2003). Empirical support for the separation of the wh-determiner and the head noun comes from languages in which these elements can surface in non-adjacent positions (see e.g. Corver 1990 for Polish and Russian; Baker 1996 for Mohawk; Androutsopoulou 1997 for Greek). An example from Polish is given in (i).

(i)   **Jaki**$_1$ wykręciłeś   [e$_1$ **numer**]   (Polish: Corver 1990: 330)
     which   you-dialed   number
     'Which number did you dial?'

[29] Thanks to Milan Rezac for bringing the binding facts to my attention.

has to move syntactically to a position (at least) higher than the subject, ruling out an analysis that would attribute its main stress to its Merge position, and its final surface position to PF movement after the stress has been assigned.

We are thus facing a dilemma. From a prosodic perspective, the object head noun has to be in a stress position. Meanwhile, given the syntactic binding facts, this position cannot be the internal argument Merge position, but rather a position at least higher than the subject. The intermediate focus position provides us with a way of meeting both requirements. I propose that in English the wh-phrase as a whole moves to a focus position higher than the subject to satisfy the formal focus requirement. This movement operation is followed by the movement of the wh-word to Spec–CP to satisfy the wh-requirement. Under this view, the stress on the head noun in a D-linked wh-question can be attributed to the fact that it remains in the focussed and thus stressed position. Moreover, assuming that this focus position is higher than the subject, the syntactic binding facts do not come as a surprise. The wh-word, on the other hand, moves to Spec–CP to satisfy the wh-feature and as a result evades focus stress. Implicit in this approach is the idea that while the focus property is a property of the whole DP, the wh-property is that of the wh-determiner. By dissociating the wh-determiner and its head noun, we have been able to capture the stress facts and the binding facts simultaneously.[30]

In this section, we have looked at an old puzzle with respect to the stress behaviour of wh-phrases in languages with wh-movement such as English. A solution to this problem was proposed based on the very nature of wh-questions in these languages. It was suggested that while in wh-in-situ and focus-fronting languages, the wh-phrase remains in the focus position, thus receiving stress, in wh-movement languages, it moves out of the focus position to satisfy the wh-requirement, thus evading sentential stress. To account for the additional fact that in D-linked wh-questions in English the head noun in the wh-DP receives main stress, it was suggested that the wh-phrase moves through a focus position higher than the subject, followed by the movement of the wh-word alone to Spec–CP. As a result the head noun, which remains in

---

[30] A question may arise as to why, in cases of auxiliary inversion, the auxiliary cannot intervene between the head noun, which is in a focus position, and the wh-word, which is in Spec–CP (e.g. *Which is book Kate reading?* vs. *Which book is Kate reading?*). One way to handle this problem is to assume that in English auxiliary inversion the auxiliary moves to a head lower than the focus position in a refined CP structure (see (50)), for instance to Fin as suggested by Rizzi (1997). Alternatively, one can attribute the obligatory adjacency of the head noun and the wh-determiner to some English-specific PF requirement (see n. 28). Under this view, the head noun is in an intermediate focus position at the point of stress assignment but joins the wh-determiner due to a late PF requirement.

the focus position, receives primary stress.[31] Some comments are in order with respect to the interaction between movement and sentential stress. In this section, we argued that wh-questions emerge as a case where an element evades sentential stress due to syntactic movement. In this respect, wh-questions behave like (specific) objects in Persian and some other languages, where the movement of the object, as was argued in chapter 4, leads to them not receiving sentential stress. Topicalized elements were also used to indicate that stress cannot be assigned to the base-generated position of a syntactic object, contra Bresnan (1971) and Legate (2003). Otherwise, one would expect a topicalized object to receive sentential stress due to its being in a stressed position at merge. Topicalization, therefore, presents itself as another case where an element moves out of a stressed position, evading sentential stress. An English example is given in (62), where stress falls on the verb rather than the topicalized object.

(62)   Beans, I <u>like</u>.

It is worth noting, however, that not all syntactic movements affect the stress pattern of a sentence. In fact, we can formulate a typology of movement with respect to its interaction with stress. We have already seen cases in which movement out of a stressed position results in an element, which would have received stress in its Merge position, evading stress. Meanwhile, there are also those cases where an element moves into a stressed position. The movement of the object to the Spec–AspP (see ch. 4), which results in it receiving stress, can be seen as one such case. There are those movements, on the other hand, that do not affect the stress pattern of the sentence at all as they involve movement of an element from an unstressed position to another unstressed position. I use the case of topicalization in Persian to illustrate the point. The examples in (63) show that while the non-specific object receives stress in the neutral case (63a), when it is topicalized (63b) it does not receive stress. This, like the English example in (62), is a case where movement affects stress. In (64a), on the other hand, the non-specific object is not in a stressed position in the first place, the highest element in the SPELLEE being the measure adverb *a lot*. Example (64b) shows that the movement of the topicalized object does not

---

[31] The relationship between the typology of wh-questions and sentential stress has interesting implications for determining the type of a language with respect to wh-questions. If a language marks focus prosodically and fronts the wh-word, this fronted position has to be a focus position if the wh-word is stressed and it has to be a special wh-position (like Spec–CP) if it is not stressed. This idea is challenged by proposals which take the movement of the first wh-phrase in a multiple wh-fronting language to be wh-movement and the rest focus fronting (e.g. Bošković, Ž. 1997) or those who take all the movements to be wh-movement (Alboiu 2002). One would expect all but the first wh-phrase to be stressed under the former view and none to be stressed under the latter view. This prediction does not seem to be borne out.

affect stress as it involves movement from an unstressed position to another unstressed position. This latter example serves an extra purpose: it highlights the fact that topicalization in Persian does involve movement.[32]

(63) a. Ali <u>sib</u>   xord.
         Ali apple   ate
         'Ali ate apples.'
      b. Ali sib   <u>xord</u>.
         Ali apple   ate
         'Apples, Ali ate.'

(64) a. Ali <u>xeyli</u> sib   xord.
         Ali a lot   apple   ate
         'Ali ate apples a lot'
      b. Ali sib   <u>xeyli</u> xord.
         Ali apple a lot   ate
         'Apples, Ali ate a lot.'

In our discussion of the interactions between information structure and sentential stress, we have treated focus as a syntactic property interpreted in the semantic and phonological components, realized by prosodic prominence in some languages. The Focus Stress Rule proposed in this section takes the focus structure as input and incorporates its effect in the calculation of sentential stress for the whole clause in a manner detailed above. The direction is crucially from focus to sentential stress/accent. This approach stands in contrast to some other frameworks, such as the Focus Projection Algorithm (see Selkirk 1984, 1995; Rochemont 1986, 1998), which take sentential stress/accent as the input to an elaborate algorithm that derives the focus structure of a sentence. The Focus Projection Algorithm is the topic of the following section.

5.6 The Focus Projection Algorithm

It has been proposed in this chapter that sentential stress is determined as a result of an interplay between two rules, the default Sentential Stress Rule and the Focus Stress Rule. The idea that a default rule is needed to determine neutral stress, realized in our Sentential Stress Rule, goes back at least to Newman (1946), but found its definitive expression in Chomsky and Halle's (1968) Nuclear Stress Rule. The relevance of information structure for sentence

---

[32] PF movement, if it exists, should not interact with stress, according to the theory developed in this monograph. In other words, as far as stress is concerned, syntactic movement that does not affect stress is indistinguishable from PF movement. If, on the other hand, some movement interacts with stress assignment, it has to be syntactic.

stress/accent, reflected in our Focus Stress Rule, has also been noted by many linguists (see e.g. Daneš 1967; Halliday 1967; Bresnan 1971, 1972; Chomsky 1971; Jackendoff 1972; Chafe 1973, 1976; Halliday and Hasan 1976). Meanwhile, this interaction between information structure and sentential stress has led some scholars to reject a default sentential stress rule altogether. Bolinger (1958, 1972), for instance, argues adamantly against the need for a rule to determine sentential stress in neutral contexts. According to Bolinger, what speakers decide to highlight is not a matter of grammar but a matter of what they are trying to say in a specific context. His view is clearly summed up in the title of his 1972 paper, "Accent is predictable (if you are a mind-reader)". Other scholars have taken the sentential stress/accent as the input to an algorithm which derives the focus structure of a sentence, hereafter called the focus projection algorithm. Such an approach stands in sharp contrast to the system developed in this monograph. According to the framework developed here (in line with Chomsky 1971, 1976; Jackendoff 1972), the focus structure of a sentence is input to semantic and phonological interpretation. Therefore, the Focus Stress Rule takes the focus structure as input and incorporates its effect in the calculation of sentential stress for the whole clause. The direction is crucially from focus to sentential stress/accent. In a "focus projection" framework, on the other hand, the sentence stress/accent is a given and the focus structure is derived following an elaborate algorithm. It is worth noting that this assumption is incompatible with the Y-model adopted in one form or another in the generative tradition (see Chomsky and Lasnik 1977; Chomsky 1981, and subsequent authors). Recall that the Y-model of grammar disallows direct interaction between the phonological component (PF or PHON) and the semantic component (LF or SEM). PF and LF are connected only via the computational component, or syntax (see ch. 1). The system developed in this monograph, on the other hand, is totally compatible with the Y-model of grammar in that focus is part of the computational system with semantic and phonological interpretation.[33]

The focus projection algorithm has been explored in works by Selkirk and Rochemont in the past two decades (see Selkirk 1984, 1995; Rochemont 1986, 1998). In this section, I discuss Selkirk (1995) in some detail, provide several arguments against this type of approach, and show how our system

---

[33] This type of direct PF–LF interaction is especially problematic in a generative framework in which (most of) these focus projection theories are framed—as is the present monograph. If such interactions are allowed, then it is really surprising to see them realized in such a restricted fashion. Why should the interaction between PF and LF be limited to information structure and not extended to a much wider range of phenomena? (For a different view of grammar which takes the semantic and phonological components to be generative in addition to the syntactic component, see Jackendoff 1997, 2002.)

fares better with the data. It is worth noting once again that the main goal here is to account for the prosodic consequences of focus rather than its syntactic/semantic implications. The Focus Projection Algorithm is discussed and compared with the proposed system insofar as facts regarding sentential stress/accent are concerned. Detailed discussions of issues such as the scope or representation of focus are beyond the scope of this monograph.

I start the discussion of Selkirk's (1995) focus projection algorithm with a brief review of its basic principles using some illustrative examples. The theory of focus projection consists of a set of principles for the licensing of F-marking which take sentential accent as input and derive the focus structure of the sentence accordingly. The Basic Focus Rule, given in (65), states that the assignment of a pitch accent to a word entails the F-marking of the word.

(65)   Basic Focus Rule   (Selkirk 1995: 555)
        An accented word is F-marked.

In addition to the Basic Focus Rule, there are two principles which license the projection of the F-marking of a word to higher constituents. These principles, grouped under the heading of Focus Projection, are given in (66).

(66)   Focus Projection

        (a) F-marking of the head of a phrase licenses the F-marking of the phrase.
        (b) F-marking of the internal argument of a head licenses the F-marking of the head.

To illustrate how the algorithm works, consider an example from Selkirk (1995). The sentence *Mary bought a book about <u>bats</u>*, with accent marked by underlining in conformity with the conventions used in this monograph, is an appropriate answer to the set of wh-questions listed in (67). The corresponding focus structures and thus the F-markings have been provided in front of each wh-question (see 5.2).

(67)
a. What did Mary buy a book about?   Mary bought a book about [<u>bats</u>]$_F$.
b. What kind of book did Mary buy?   Mary bought a book [about <u>bats</u>]$_F$.
c. What did Mary buy?   Mary bought [a book about <u>bats</u>]$_F$.
d. What did Mary do?   Mary [bought a book about <u>bats</u>]$_F$.
e. What's been happening?   [Mary bought a book about <u>bats</u>]$_F$.

Crucially, an accent on *Mary* is not an appropriate answer to any of the questions in (67), but only to the question in (68), with the corresponding F-marking.

(68)   Who bought a book about bats?   [Mary]$_F$ bought a book about bats.

A question arises as to why a pitch accent on the sentence-final word allows for the wide range of focus structures in (67), while one on the subject does not make the same range of options available. We have already seen how the facts in (67) and (68) are accounted for in the system developed in this chapter. Here is how Selkirk's focus projection algorithm accounts for these facts. Recall that in this system the accent is a given. According to the Basic Focus Rule in (65), the accented word *bats* is F-marked. Selkirk further assumes that the focus of a sentence (FOC) is defined as an F-marked constituent not dominated by any other F-marked constituent. Thus, if F-marking stops at *bats*, the result is the sentence that would be an answer to the question in (67a). The Focus Projection principles in (66), however, allow for the projection of the F-marking on *bats* to higher constituents. So, for instance, the F-marking of the internal argument NP/DP *bats*, licenses the F-marking of its head, the preposition *about*. The F-marking of the head *about* licenses the F-marking of the prepositional phrase. The F-marking of the prepositional phrase, a complement of the noun *book*, licenses the F-marking of the head *book*, and so on. The F-markings and the corresponding FOCs are shown in (69).

(69)   Mary bought a book about <u>bats</u>.

   (a)   Mary bought a book about $_{FOC}[$[<u>bats</u>]$_F$]$_{FOC}$.

   (b)   Mary bought a book $_{FOC}[$[[about]$_F$[<u>bats</u>]$_F$]$_F$]$_{FOC}$.

   (c)   Mary bought $_{FOC}[$a [book]$_F$ [[about]$_F$ [<u>bats</u>]$_F$]$_F$]$_{FOC}$.

   (d)   Mary $_{FOC}[$[[bought]$_F$ [a [book]$_F$ [[about]$_F$ [<u>bats</u>]$_F$]$_F$]$_F$]$_{FOC}$.

   (e) $_{FOC}[$[Mary [[bought]$_F$ [a [book]$_F$ [[about]$_F$ [<u>bats</u>]$_F$]$_F$]$_F$]$_F$]$_{FOC}$.

Crucially, according to the focus projection principles in (66), the F-marking of the subject *Mary*, unlike an internal argument, cannot extend beyond itself. This is shown in (70).[34]

(70) $_{FOC}[$[<u>Mary</u>]$_F$]$_{FOC}$ bought a book about bats.

It should be noted that the F-marking used in section 5.2 is somewhat different from Selkirk's usage of the notation. The closest equivalent to our F-marking, which marks a focussed constituent, in Selkirk's system is FOC. There is, in fact, a small difference between the two notions, which we are

---

[34] Selkirk sets aside functional projections like IP and DP for the sake of convenience. Otherwise, the correct characterization is that the F-marking of an NP projects to its head D first and so on. Such differences in detail would not affect the main proposal in any significant way.

abstracting away from here. While, for us, F-marking or focus represents and can contain only new information, for Selkirk, FOC can include new as well as old information.[35]

We have seen how Selkirk's focus projection algorithm handles the relation between sentence accent/stress using a basic sentence uttered in different contexts. In the remainder of this section, some important features of Selkirk's system will be discussed in more detail and arguments against different aspects of her proposal will be presented.

One of the characteristics of Selkirk's Focus Projection Algorithm is that it makes a sharp distinction between arguments and adjuncts. Whereas arguments project focus, adjuncts do not (see also Gussenhoven 1984; Rochemont 1998). This distinction, according to the proponents of the Focus Projection Algorithm, can account for the impossibility of (71a) as opposed to (71b) in an out-of-the-blue context (pair from Godjevac 2000). In (71a), the prepositional phrase is an adjunct and does not allow focus projection to higher constituents, whereas the one in (71b) is an internal argument and allows for such focus projection.

(71) a. # John is smoking in a <u>tent</u>.
      b. John is living in a <u>tent</u>.

While not allowing non-arguments to project focus to higher constituents may provide an account for the contrast in (71), it is, in fact, making a stronger claim. It essentially predicts that we should not have the main accent of a sentence on an adjunct in an out-of-the-blue context. This prediction does not seem to be borne out in Persian (and Eastern Armenian), where the main stress of the sentence falls on the manner adverb in an out-of-the-blue context (see ch. 4 for a detailed discussion). It is not clear how the accent/focus on the manner adverb in (72) can be projected to the whole clause based on the Focus Projection Algorithm.

(72) Ali <u>xub</u> futbaal baazi mi-kon-e.
     Ali well soccer play DUR-do-3SG
     'Ali plays soccer well.'

Another feature of the Focus Projection Algorithm is its treatment of passive and unaccusative sentences. As discussed at some length in chapters 2 to 4, the subjects of unaccusative (as opposed to unergative) and passive verbs receive primary stress in the out-of-the-blue context. The stress behaviour of passives and unaccusatives was taken as one of the motivations for the

---

[35] For a discussion of how Selkirk's focus structure translates into the given–new information structure of a sentence, the reader is referred to the discussion in Selkirk (1995).

system proposed in this monograph for the assignment of sentential stress. According to our proposal, the sentential stress on the subject in these sentences follows from the fact that unaccusative and passive verb phrases do not constitute phases. As a result, the only phasal head in the clause is C, with the highest element in the SPELLEE being the subject. Some English examples are repeated in (73).

(73) a. <u>My bike</u> was stolen.
      b. <u>Johnson</u> died.
      c. <u>The sky</u> is falling.
      d. <u>The sun</u> came out.
      e. <u>The baby's</u> crying.

Let us now consider how passives and unaccusatives are treated in the Focus Projection Algorithm. Selkirk introduces them as counterexamples to the phrase-based theories of sentential stress (e.g. Cinque 1993) and points out that they can be easily accounted for with a minor revision to her theory of focus projection. To account for these facts, she introduces an amendment to her Focus Projection Algorithm allowing the F-marking of a moved constituent to license the F-marking of its trace. This is stated in (74).

(74) Selkirk's trace-driven focus projection.   (Selkirk 1995: 561)
      F-marking of the antecedent of a trace left by NP- or wh-movement
      licenses the F-marking of the trace.

In passive and unaccusative sentences, the examples in (73), the subject starts off as the internal argument of the verb. Thus, given the additional principle of focus projection in (74), F-marking (via accent) of the subject licenses the F-marking of the trace. The trace as the internal argument of the verb, in turn, licenses the F-marking of the VP and consequently the F-marking of the whole sentence.

Before we consider cases of wh-movement, it is worth noting that while Selkirk's additional principle of focus projection explains why accent on the subject in passives and unaccusatives can be projected to the whole sentence, it does not explain why we get accent on the subject, rather than the verb, in the out-of-the-blue context. It is true that the accent or F-marking on the subject can be projected to the whole clause with the amendment in (74), but an accent or F-marking on the verb can also be projected to the whole sentence following the focus projection principles in (66). Thus, Selkirk's account, at best, explains why we *can* get accent on the subject, but not why we get it *obligatorily* in an out-of-the-blue context. It remains a question, therefore, why accent on the verb would lead to a narrow focus interpretation in unaccusatives and passives (see ch. 4 and references cited therein).

Turning to wh-movement, according to Selkirk's trace-driven focus projection, wh-moved elements can also license F-marking of their traces. Selkirk uses this to account for the stress behaviour of D-linked wh-questions discussed in the previous section. As we saw in section 5.5, in a D-linked wh-question the sentential stress/accent falls on the head noun rather than on the sentence-final verb as predicted by the traditional Nuclear Stress Rule or our default sentential stress rule. This is repeated in (75).

(75)   What <u>books</u> has Helen reviewed?

The idea here is that the accent on *books* can be projected to the whole sentence via its trace, which is the internal argument of the verb, in a manner similar to the cases of NP-movement discussed above.

The trace-driven Focus Projection Algorithm, however, suffers from a type of problem similar to the one raised in chapter 3 for Legate's (2003) system, where she took the Cinque-style nuclear stress rule to apply to the Merge position of the subject and allowed it to have its stress inherited by the higher copy. The question arises why such licensing of F-marking from a syntactic object to its trace does not extend to (non D-linked) wh- or topicalized elements. In other words, why do we not have sentential stress/accent on the wh-word or the topicalized element, as shown in (76)?

(76)   a. *<u>Who</u> did John kiss? vs. Who did John <u>kiss</u>?
       b. *<u>Beans</u>, I like.   vs. Beans, I <u>like</u>.
                                          (under the topicalized reading)

The trace-driven focus projection principle in (74) should allow accent on the wh-word or the topicalized element to project to the whole sentence, contrary to the facts shown in (76).

In addition, Selkirk's trace-driven focus projection runs into trouble in the face of the Persian cases discussed in chapter 4 (also found in Eastern Armenian, German, Dutch, etc.), where the specific object moves out of the vP domain to a higher position, thus escaping sentential stress. It is not clear in Selkirk's system why an accent on the specific object is not able to project to the whole sentence via F-marking of its lower trace. The impossibility of the projection of the accent on the specific object is illustrated by the pair in (77). Stress on the specific object is only possible in a narrow-focus reading, where the context is "What did Ali eat?", rather than "What happened?". The out-of-the-blue response is given in (77b).

(77)   Context: What happened?

    a. *Ali <u>keyk-o</u>$_i$ [$_{vP}$ t$_i$ xord].

    b. Ali   keyk-o$_i$ [$_{vP}$ t$_i$ <u>xord</u>].
      Ali   cake-ACC   ate
      'Ali ate the cake.'

Rochemont (1998) suggests that trace-driven focus projection is limited to traces of A-movement.[36] This additional stipulation could resolve the problem for the (non D-linked) wh-and topicalized examples in (76), and perhaps to the case of Persian specific objects in (77), if we take the latter to be an instance of A'-movement. Meanwhile, with this added stipulation, the account for the D-linked wh-question in (75) will be lost. It remains a puzzle why D-linked wh-movement allows for the trace-driven focus projection, while non-D-linked wh-movement does not. Neither Selkirk nor Rochemont address this question. The reader is referred to the previous section for an account of the stress facts in D-linked and non-D-linked wh-questions which does not run into similar problems.

Another area where Selkirk uses trace-driven focus projection is in her account of the contrast between individual-level and stage-level predicates with respect to stress/accent. In the syntactic literature, a distinction is often made between individual-level and stage-level predicates. While individual-level predicates such as *convenient* indicate a permanent property, stage-level predicates such as *available* indicate a temporary one (see Carlson 1977 and subsequent authors). Citing Gussenhoven (1984, 1992), Selkirk points to the accentual differences between a sentence with an individual-level predicate as opposed to one with a stage-level predicate. This contrast is shown in (78), which indicates that accent on the subject can project focus to the whole sentence only with a stage-level predicate (78a) and not with an individual-level predicate (78b).[37]

(78)   a. <u>Your eyes</u> are red.
     b. <u>Your eyes</u> are <u>blue.</u>   not   *<u>Your eyes</u> are blue.

Selkirk uses Diesing's (1992) syntactic analysis of individual-level and stage-level predicates to account for the contrast in (78). Diesing proposes a structure with the subject raising from a VP-internal position (leaving a trace) for stage-level predicates exemplified in (78a) and a control structure with

---

[36] Rochemont's proposal is based on his analysis of Heavy NP Shift, details of which are beyond the scope of this monograph.

[37] Following Selkirk, I have not indicated primary and secondary accent/stress in (78b). It should be noted, however, that the prominence on the adjective is higher than that of the subject.

a VP-internal PRO for individual-level predicates exemplified in (78b). The corresponding structures are shown schematically in (79).

(79) a. [$_{IP}$ NP$_i$ ... [$_{VP}$ t$_i$ [$_{V'}$ ...]]]   Stage-level predicates

   b. [$_{IP}$ NP$_i$ ... [$_{VP}$ PRO$_i$ [$_{V'}$ ...]]]   Individual-level predicates

Selkirk argues that, given this syntactic difference, the stress facts follow from the Focus Projection Algorithm straightforwardly. In the stage-level predicate in (78a) and (79a), the focus on the accented subject can project to the whole sentence via its VP-internal trace, whereas in the individual-level predicate in (78b) and (79b), focus cannot be projected via the VP-internal PRO, and thus the predicate needs to be accented.

Godjevac (2000) points to a serious problem with Selkirk's line of argumentation. Recall that according to Selkirk's Focus Projection Algorithm, focus can only project from a VP-internal argument and not from a VP-external one. The trace of the subject in (79a), however, is in the specifier of VP (i.e. an external argument position) according to Diesing's analysis. Therefore, the focus on the trace cannot be projected to the VP or the whole sentence in Selkirk's system, and the accentual difference between stage-level and individual-level predicates remains an unsolved puzzle. To make Selkirk's story work, we would need the subject of the stage-level predicate in (78a) to start off as the internal argument of the predicate. In other words, we would need the adjective to behave like an unaccusative verb. This goes against Diesing's structure for these constructions and standard assumptions about adjectives which take them to be characteristically unergative (see, e.g., Burzio 1986; Levin and Rappaport Hovav 1986, among others).[38] If, on the other hand, one attempts to save Selkirk's explanation by suggesting that focus can also be projected from a VP-external argument position, then one of the main motivations of the focus projection algorithm is lost—namely, the fact that F-marking on the subject cannot be projected to the whole clause (see (70) above).

It is now time to examine whether our phase-based theory of sentential stress may fare better with these facts.[39] Recall that, according to the theory

---

[38] For a different view of adjectives, see Toman (1986) and Koster (1987). Cinque (1990) argues for a class of unaccusative adjectives (what he calls ergative), but there does not seem to be any correspondence with the individual-level/stage-level distinction discussed here. I continue to assume the structures provided by Diesing, where the subject starts off as the external argument.

[39] Legate (2003) offers a phase-based solution which suffers from the same problem as Selkirk's (1995). Recall that Legate's theory was based on a Cinque-style system where the "most deeply embedded" element in a construction receives stress. Therefore, for the subject in the stage-level predicate construction to inherit stress from its lower copy, the lower copy has to be the most deeply embedded element, that is, the internal argument of the adjective, which runs into the same problem as Selkirk's account.

developed in this monograph, the highest element in the spelled out constituent or SPELLEE receives stress. In other words, if we were able to show
that the structure for stage-level predicates in (79a) involves a single clausal
phase, whereas the individual-level one in (79b) involves two phases—one at
the verb phrase and another one at the clausal level—the stress facts would
follow straightforwardly. The subject in (79a) would be the highest element
in the only SPELLEE, thus receiving stress. In (79b), on the other hand, we
would be dealing with two SPELLEEs, thus predicting stress on the predicate
and the subject, with the lower one on the predicate being more prominent.
Below I provide a line of argument which suggests that positing an extra level
of phasal boundary in (79b) is plausible. This argument relies on Diesing's
analysis of these constructions and is based on the status of PRO, or the idea
that the existence of PRO in (79b) may induce an extra phasal boundary. In
other words, I propose that the difference in the phasal structures of (79a) and
(79b) is due to the latter having a control structure, as elaborated below.[40]

To better understand this proposal, we need to look at Diesing's (1992)
analysis more closely. According to Diesing, in the stage-level predicate construction, the subject is base-generated in Spec–VP, receives a theta role from
V and moves to Spec–IP for case. In the individual-level predicate construction, on the other hand, the subject is base-generated in Spec–IP, where it
receives its theta role from I. In addition, in the latter construction, there
is a PRO in the Spec–VP which is theta-marked by V.[41] Diesing notes that
the existence of PRO in Spec–VP raises a problem with respect to the PRO
theorem, which requires that PRO be ungoverned. To maintain both the PRO
theorem and her analysis, she suggests that PRO may be forced to move to
a position outside VP. One possible candidate, according to Diesing, is the
specifier of Pesetsky's μ-phrase (the precursor to vP). If, in fact, the difference
between (79a) and (79b), as Diesing suggests, is that only the latter involves an
extra verbal layer vP, using the more recent terminology, then the difference
in phasal structure between the two is not unexpected.[42] Under this view, the
verb *be* in general does not induce a phasal boundary. It is only when it is used
in an individual-level predicate construction, which, according to Diesing,

---

[40] The status of PRO is questionable from a Minimalist perspective. I do not intend to pursue here
the question of how the analyses involving PRO should be reformulated in the Minimalist framework.
It is conceivable, however, that the ensuing discussion can be recast under a movement theory of
control which dispenses with PRO (see e.g. Hornstein 2001; Boeckx and Hornstein 2004), as long as
the "control" structure involves a light v layer and thus an additional phasal head.

[41] I am abstracting away from the syntactic and semantic reasons as to why such structures should
be preferred. For details, see Diesing (1992) and Kratzer (1995).

[42] Whether PRO is base-generated in Spec–vP or obligatorily moves to such a position as Diesing
suggests is not crucial here. What matters is the existence of this extra level of structure.

involves a control structure, that the existence of PRO in the verbal domain forces an additional verbal layer, thus inducing an extra phasal boundary. Once it is established that the individual-type predicate construction involves two phases, the stress facts follow straightforwardly in a manner explained above and elaborated in chapter 4. In short, in the stage-level example in (78a) we are dealing with a single phasal domain, with the subject—the highest element in the SPELLEE—receiving sentential stress. In the individual-level example in (78b), on the other hand, we are dealing with two phases and thus two stress domains, with the adjective receiving primary stress as the highest element in the lower SPELLEE and the subject receiving secondary stress as the highest element in the higher SPELLEE.[43]

In addition to the above issues, there are some other cross-linguistic facts which seem to favour the kind of theory developed in this monograph, which is a theory based on a system of two interacting components with one determining the default sentential stress and the other the focal accent/stress, as opposed to the single-component system proposed by the proponents of the Focus Projection Algorithm which takes stress/accent as an input to the system that determines the focus structure of a sentence. It has been observed, for example, that focus can be realized by different means in different languages. While in many languages focus has been tied to phonological marking of the kind discussed in this chapter, in some other languages focus is marked morphologically or syntactically.[44] Morphological marking of focus has been proposed for Navajo (Vallduví and Engdahl 1996, citing Schauber 1978) and a number of Bantu languages (Watters 1979; Odden 1984; Hyman and Watters 1984), and syntactic marking of focus for Catalan (Vallduví 1992; Vallduví and Engdahl 1996), Spanish (Zubizarreta 1998), Hungarian (Horvath 1986), Hindi (Kidwai 2000), Mandarin (Xu 2004), etc.[45] The different cross-linguistic realizations of focus can be captured more easily in a theory where focus is part of the computational component which happens to be realized differently in different languages, by morphological marking, syntactic movement or prosodic

---

[43] Following Stump (1985), Diesing (1992) assumes that the source of the syntactic difference between the individual-type and stage-level type predicate constructions lies in the existence of two verbs *be* (see Moltmann 1989 for a different view). One could then attribute the difference in the phasal structures of the two constructions to the individual-level *be* (as opposed to the stage-level one) inducing a phasal boundary. I do not pursue this option here.

[44] Syntactic marking can be accompanied by phonological marking, as seen in the Romance languages discussed in this chapter.

[45] Even in languages that mark focus phonologically, the phonological marking is not necessarily of the same type (see Godjevac 2000 and references cited there). This raises the same kind of question for the focus projection theory which takes "pitch accent" to be the input to their system. In order to extend their theory to these other languages, they would have to have a different "Basic Focus Rule" for every language depending on what, other than pitch accent, marks focus.

prominence. On the other hand, a theory which takes the accent/stress as a given and uses a principle such as the Basic Focus Rule in (65) to derive focus structure would need a different focus rule for every single type of language. The problem would in fact be compounded if the languages which mark focus by non-phonological means still show prominence on a certain element in the clause (in the out-of-the-blue context) irrespective of the focus structure. This kind of evidence would strongly support a theory which has a separate component to account for neutral stress along the lines of the one developed here. Whether the languages with non-phonological marking of focus exhibit stress in out-of-the-blue contexts is a question I leave for future research.[46]

We have already seen in the previous sections that languages which mark focus prosodically still exhibit secondary stress on the element predicted to receive stress by the default sentential stress rule. In fact, even in contexts where the whole clause is given, one element receives more prominence than the others, which is predicted correctly by the default sentential-stress rule. An example is given in (80). In this sentence, the whole italicized clause is given. No element in this clause is F-marked, therefore the stress on the object requires a different explanation, provided readily by the default sentential-stress rule. This type of evidence provides support for the default sentential stress rule and thus a two-component system of the kind proposed in this monograph.

(80)   (Context: John ate his lunch.)
        If John ate his lunch, (he can have dessert now).

Finally, phonetic differences have been reported in some languages between the accent on narrowly -as opposed to broadly-focussed elements. While the evidence for English is inconclusive, with most linguists indicating no difference between the two (e.g. Chomsky 1971; Jackendoff 1972; Ladd 1996; but see Selkirk 2002), different accents for broad and narrow focus have been reported in a number of other languages: Bengali (Hayes and Lahiri 1991); Central Basque (Irurtzun 2003); European Portuguese (Frota 1995); Finnish (Välimaa-Blum 1993); Greek (Baltazani 2002); (some dialects of) Italian (Grice et al. 2004; Brunetti 2003, and references cited

---

[46] Xu (2004) suggests that in a neutral sentence in Mandarin, no word is more prominent than any other. He does qualify his statement, however, by pointing out that it is based solely on impressionistic judgements and not confirmed by phonetic analyses. It is worth noting, however, that while the existence of languages which mark neutral stress phonologically irrespective of focus marking provides support for the two-component system developed here, the existence of Mandarin-type languages, if Xu's impressionistic judgment is in fact correct, does not provide evidence in support of a one-component system like the focus projection theory. It simply makes no contribution to this debate.

there) (see also 5.2).[47] Such differences are placed more naturally in a theory with two interacting systems for the assignment of neutral (or broad-focus) stress and focal (or narrow-focus) stress, such as the one developed in this monograph, as opposed to a single-component system such as Selkirk's Focus Projection Algorithm. In a two-component system, the differences can be attributed to the interpretation of the two different rules. A single-component system, on the other hand, builds on the assumption that narrow and broad focus accents are essentially the same and makes it its goal to explain why the accent can be projected to different levels of focus. It therefore has a hard time handling such phonetic differences between the two types of accent.

5.7 Conclusion

In this chapter, we have looked at the interaction between information structure and sentential stress in languages which mark focus prosodically. To account for these relations, an additional component was introduced to our system of stress assignment. The role of this additional component, the Focus Stress Rule, is to ensure that the main prominence of the sentence falls on a focussed constituent when there is one. The Focus Stress Rule, like the Sentential Stress Rule, applies in a phase-based manner. It was shown that sentential stress is determined in an interplay between the Focus Stress Rule and the Sentential Stress Rule. While both rules apply to every sentence independently, in the phonetic realization of their application, an element marked by the Focus Stress Rule receives higher prominence than one marked by the default Sentential Stress Rule. The application of the latter rule results in secondary stress in sentences with narrowly focussed phrases. While we followed tradition and used the wh-question/answer test to determine focus structure, some issues were raised with respect to the application of this test. It was argued, in particular, that sometimes this test may not be adequate and other contextual factors need to be brought into the picture. The test should therefore be seen as a means of representing rather than replacing the context of an utterance.

We then turned to Zubizarreta's (1998) treatment of the interaction between focus structure and sentential stress, concentrating on her proposal with respect to prosodically motivated movement in Spanish and Italian. The theory developed in this monograph is framed in the Y-model of grammar adopted in one way or another in the generative tradition. According to this

---

[47] For the exact characterization of these differences, the reader is referred to the cited works. Such details are not crucial to the point being made here.

model, the syntactic component feeds into the phonological and semantic components. Focus is a formal property with realizations in both the semantic and the phonological components, LF and PF. Focus is realized prosodically in some languages. In this framework, syntactic operations cannot be motivated by prosodic considerations, contrary to Zubizarreta's (1998) p-movement. Several arguments against her proposal and an alternative way of accounting for the facts were presented in this chapter. We also looked at the apparently problematic behaviour of wh-questions with respect to stress in languages with wh-movement. It was suggested that wh-phrases do not receive stress in these languages due to the fact that wh-words move out of the stress position to satisfy a wh-feature. Wh-questions, therefore, emerged as another interesting case where an element evades sentential stress due to syntactic movement.

Finally, we considered theories which take sentential accent as input to an algorithm which derives the focus structure. In particular, we discussed Selkirk's (1995) influential focus projection theory in some detail. A wide range of data, including the argument/adjunct contrast, individual/stage-level predicates, and passive and unaccusative sentences were discussed. It was shown that, unlike its predecessors, the theory of sentential stress developed in this monograph fares better with the empirical facts than Selkirk's theory. Additional conceptual and empirical problems were raised for the focus projection algorithm.

In the first four chapters of this monograph we developed a theory of stress assignment to account for sentential stress in sentences uttered out of the blue. In this chapter we added another component to the system to handle the interactions between sentential stress and information structure. We have seen at some length how these proposals pave the way for an account of some unexplained facts in a range of languages. In the following chapter, we conclude the monograph by summarizing the main proposals and discussing some of their implications and remaining questions for future research.

6

Conclusions and implications

6.1 Introduction

In this monograph we have explored the nature of sentential stress, its manner of assignment, and its interaction with information structure. The monograph has thus dealt with two interdependent issues: the assignment of sentential stress in focus-neutral sentences and the interaction between information structure and sentential stress in sentences uttered in non-neutral contexts. Proposals were made to account for the facts in both areas. In this concluding chapter, I briefly review these proposals, investigate their consequences and implications, and discuss some potential areas for future research.

6.2 Summary of proposals

With respect to the assignment of sentential stress, it was proposed that sentential stress is determined syntactically and that cross-linguistic differences in this respect follow from syntactic variation. It was shown that phonological accounts of sentential stress suffer from an overgeneration problem and fail to account for certain stress facts. This monograph therefore sided with other syntactic accounts of sentential stress, namely Cinque (1993) and Zubizarreta (1998), in dispensing with the need for a parameterized directional phonological rule to account for the position of sentential stress in focus-neutral sentences. It was shown, however, that the previous syntactic accounts of sentential stress suffered from several conceptual and empirical problems.

On the conceptual side, it was argued that Cinque's (1993) theory of nuclear stress falls apart once the head parameter is dispensed with (Kayne 1994). Moreover, to account for stress on the subject when the subject is more complex than the predicate, Cinque had to resort to "information structure", an implausible move for a null theory of sentential stress. Several empirical problems with Cinque's theory were also presented, mainly based on the behaviour of sentential stress in Persian, but also Eastern Armenian and some German examples, where stress falls on the leftmost element within a certain stress domain rather than the constituent to the immediate left of the verb as

predicted by Cinque's system. Unaccusative and passive sentences with stress
on the subject posed further problems to Cinque's theory. Legate's (2003)
revision of Cinque's system, on the other hand, was able to account for the
unaccusative/passive facts which it was originally proposed for, but ran into
trouble in the face of wh- and topicalized sentences. Moreover, it offered no
improvement over Cinque's system with respect to the Persian and German
data discussed in detail in chapter 3.

As for Zubizarreta's (1998) modular system of the nuclear stress rule, it was
shown that her theory exhibits a certain degree of internal redundancy and
also fails to account for secondary stress. On the empirical side, a range of
problems from Persian and German were presented which call into question
any attempt, such as Zubizarreta's, that relies on the selectional ordering of
constituents in determining sentential stress. It was suggested that with the
correct characterization of the sentential stress rule, a purely syntactic system which is sensitive only to hierarchical structure can account for these
stress facts.

To overcome the conceptual and empirical problems raised for phonological and previous syntactic accounts of sentential stress, a new system based on
the notion of phases and multiple spell-out was introduced. It was proposed
that sentential stress is assigned to the highest element in the spelled out
constituent referred to as the SPELLEE. The phase-based system of stress
assignment is shown schematically in (1).

(1)

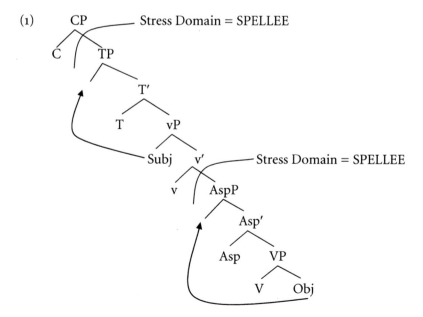

It was shown that this new formulation of the sentential stress rule provides a systematic way of accounting for a wide range of cross-linguistic facts. In particular, from an empirical point of view, the SOV facts exemplified in this book by Persian, German V-final sentences, and Eastern Armenian, where stress is neither on the element immediately preceding the verb (as predicted by Cinque 1993) nor on the lowest selectionally ordered element (as predicted by Zubizarreta 1998), received a straightforward account in the proposed system. The proposed system also provided a simple way of accounting for the curious passive/unaccusative stress facts in English, German, and Persian. Under the standard assumption that unaccusative and passive verb phrases do not induce phasal boundaries, the only phasal head is C, with its complement, or SPELLEE, being the TP. The stress on the highest element in the TP, or the subject, is thus expected.[1]

To account for the stress behaviour of specific objects in Persian, it was proposed that, following standard syntactic assumptions, the specific object moves out of the stress domain and thus avoids sentential stress. This points to an important characteristic of the proposed system. Like Cinque (1993) and Zubizarreta (1998), but unlike Bresnan (1971, 1972) and Legate (2003), the system proposed here is insensitive to "deep" structure and relies solely on "surface" syntactic structure.

With certain assumptions about the syntax of adverbials (including circumstantial PPs) and the details of how the system of stress assignment operates, we accounted for the apparent rightward (sentence-final) stress in English. To the extent that the proposed system was successful in accounting for these stress facts, it provides further support for the proposals with respect to the syntax of these adverbials (Cinque 1999, 2002, 2004). The difference in the stress behaviour of manner adverbs in Persian and Eastern Armenian, on the one hand, and English and German, on the other, was attributed to a structural difference between the two types of language with respect to where the manner adverb is merged. It was suggested that while manner adverbs respect the universal order of elements in a relative manner, in Persian and Eastern Armenian they are merged inside the SPELLEE/stress domain, while in English and German they are merged outside the SPELLEE/stress domain. Moreover, given the nature of multiple spell-out, the proposed stress system predicts that stress should be assigned iteratively. It was shown that this property of the system is supported by the facts with respect to secondary stress.

[1] In chapter 4 we discussed some complications that arise when adverbials are added to the sentence. The reader is referred to the discussion in that chapter for a detailed exposition of the problem and a possible solution.

The types of explanation outlined above underline an important property of the system proposed in this monograph: it is sensitive only to hierarchical structure. Neither a phonological rule nor other syntactic considerations (such as selectional requirements) play into determining the position of sentential stress in this system. In addition, to the extent that this monograph has been successful in providing an account for the above facts, it offers further support for the notion of phases and multiple spell-out, originally proposed on totally independent grounds.

As for the interactions between sentential stress and information structure in languages which mark focus prosodically, an additional component was introduced to our system of stress assignment. The role of this additional component, which we referred to as the Focus Stress Rule, is to ensure that the main prominence of the sentence falls on a focused constituent. Sentential stress is determined in an interplay between the default Sentential Stress Rule and the Focus Stress Rule, both of which apply in a phase-based manner. These rules apply independently to a clause and mark (different) constituents for sentential and focus stress. An element marked for focus stress crucially receives higher prominence than one that is marked for default sentential stress, while the latter is still marked by secondary stress, a fact captured straightforwardly in the proposed system. The application of these rules to a clause will lead to the different surface realizations of stress found in languages that mark focus prosodically (for details, see ch. 5).

One crucial property of the system developed in this monograph is that, unlike some other theories dealing with the interactions between information structure and prosody, it is framed in the Y-model of grammar adopted in one way or another in the generative tradition. According to this model, the syntactic component feeds into the phonological and semantic components. Focus is a syntactic property with realizations in both the semantic and the phonological components LF and PF. Focus is realized prosodically in some languages. In this framework, syntactic operations cannot be motivated by prosodic considerations, as suggested, for instance, by Zubizarreta's (1998) p-movement. Several arguments against her proposal and an alternative way of accounting for the facts were presented in this monograph.

We also looked at the apparently problematic behaviour of wh-questions with respect to stress in languages with wh-movement. Given the definition of focus, it is expected that the wh-elements receive stress as the non-presupposed part of the sentence, contrary to the facts in wh-movement languages. It was suggested that wh-phrases do not receive stress in these languages due to the fact that wh-words move out of the stress position to satisfy a wh-feature. Wh-questions, therefore, emerge as another case where an element evades sentential stress due to syntactic movement. It is worth noting, however, that not all syntactic movements affect the stress pattern of a sentence. A typology of movement with respect to its interaction with stress was formulated. On the one hand, we have cases in which movement out of a stressed position results in an element, which would have received stress in its Merge position, evading stress (e.g. movement of the specific object in Persian; wh-movement). Meanwhile, there are also those cases where an element moves into a stressed position. The movement of the object to the Spec–AspP (see ch. 4) which results in it receiving stress can be seen as one such case. There are also those movements, on the other hand, that do not affect the stress pattern of the sentence at all, such as topicalization out of a position which would not be a stress position in the first place (see ch. 5).[2]

We also considered theories which have attempted to dispense with a phrasal stress rule in favour of accounts which take sentential accent as input to an algorithm which derives the focus structure. In particular, we discussed Selkirk's (1995) influential focus projection theory in some detail. A wide range of data, including the argument/adjunct contrast, individual vs. stage-level predicates and passive and unaccusative sentences were discussed; several empirical arguments against Selkirk's approach were presented. It was shown that, unlike its predecessors, the theory of sentential stress developed in this monograph fares better with the empirical facts than the Focus Projection Algorithm.

In the remainder of this chapter we will look at some consequences of the proposals made here and some potential areas for future research.

6.3 Implications and remaining questions

In this section we will look at some implications of the proposed system for the assignment of sentential stress. We will also consider some potential areas for future research which arise from the ideas put forth in this monograph.

6.3.1 *Sentential stress as means of evaluation*

An interesting consequence of the thesis that sentential stress is assigned in a purely syntactic manner is that it can be used as a yardstick to evaluate different proposed structures for syntactic constructions across languages. Of the proposed structures, the one that would produce the correct result

---

[2] PF movement, if it exists, should not interact with stress according to the theory developed in this monograph. In other words, as far as stress is concerned, syntactic movement that does not affect stress is indistinguishable from PF movement. If, on the other hand, some movement interacts with stress assignment, it has to be syntactic.

with respect to stress when subjected to the Sentential Stress Rule should be preferred. To illustrate this point, let us take the case of specific and non-specific objects in Persian. There are two different accounts of the position of the specific object in Persian. While Browning and Karimi (1994) (as well as Ghomeshi 1996; Megerdoomian 2002) propose that the specific object is in a higher VP-external position, Karimi (2003) proposes both the specific and non-specific objects to be in a VP-internal position. If the system of stress assignment proposed in this monograph is on the right track, it provides further support for Browning and Karimi's position (for more details see ch. 4).³ Once we have taken sentential stress to be determined on a purely syntactic basis, regardless of the exact formulation of the sentential stress rule, we have implicitly agreed that it has something to tell us about the syntactic structure of a clause. This type of correspondence between syntactic structure and sentential stress has not received the attention it deserves.

6.3.2 *Phases and other phonological phenomena*

Though we have provided a syntactic account of sentential stress, it is worth noting that this does not necessarily entail that all other phonological phenomena that rely on syntax—typically accounted for within a 'Phrasal Phonology' framework—can be reworked in purely syntactic terms. In fact, there are some reasons to believe that stress is distinct from other phonological processes in terms of the way it relates to syntax (the interaction of sentential stress and information structure, scope, etc.). The debate between an indirect approach to the phonology/syntax interaction, as in phrasal phonology, and a direct one in which phonological rules can refer to syntactic structures directly is not a new one (see e.g. Cooper and Paccia-Cooper 1980; Kaisse 1985; Odden 1987, 1990; Rizzi and Savoia 1992, for a direct approach; Selkirk 1980a, 1981; Nespor and Vogel 1986; and Hayes 1989, for arguments against a direct approach). With the recent advances in syntactic theory and the introduction of phases and multiple spell-out, the debate has taken a new perspective. In a theory in which syntactic structure is sent off to PF in phases, the question is now whether phases can replace the prosodic domains used in phrasal phonology (see e.g. McGinnis 2001; Seidl 2001; Collins 2002). In this monograph I have focussed on sentential stress. I leave the possibility of extending this approach to other phonological phenomena for future research.

---

³ I am not advancing the strong claim that sentential stress should be the sole deciding factor in such situations. Meanwhile, if sentential stress is taken to be a syntactic phenomenon, at the very least it should enter the debate as one of several deciding criteria.

6.3.3 *Phases and other syntactic phenomena*

Phases have been proposed here to be the relevant domains for the computation of sentential stress. This proposal has interesting consequences for the larger question of whether phases are the (only) relevant domains for (other) syntactic phenomena. The most interesting result would be if the domains for different syntactic computations converged on phases. A striking case of this type of isomorphism is found in Persian, where the domains for sentential stress and verbal agreement seem to coincide. Persian has a (periphrastic) progressive construction illustrated in (2). In this construction, the auxiliary and the verb behave as if they belong to two different stress domains, thus leading to the main stress on the verb and secondary stress on the auxiliary. Interestingly, the verb and the auxiliary both show agreement with the first person singular subject. We thus have isomorphism between the sentential stress and verbal agreement domains, that is, two stress domains corresponding to two agreement domains.

(2) [daar-am] [mi-xor-am].
         2   1
      have-1SG   DUR-eat-1SG
      'I am eating.'

An example from a different Persian construction also involving an auxiliary and a main verb makes the claim more robust. In the (formal) future construction in (3), the auxiliary rather than the verb receives primary stress. In other words, the auxiliary is inside the single stress domain. Interestingly, we see agreement only on the auxiliary, once again indicating isomorphism between stress and agreement domains—in other words, one stress domain corresponding to one agreement domain.

(3) [xaah-am xord].
      want-1SG ate
      'I shall eat.'

This correspondence between the domains of sentential stress and verbal agreement has interesting consequences for the relevance of phases for different syntactic computations, an issue I leave open for future research.

6.4 Concluding remarks

I have developed a system for the assignment of sentential stress based on the notion of phases and multiple spell-out. The generalizations have been based on a relatively wide range of cases in a limited set of languages, namely Persian,

English, German, Eastern Armenian, and some Romance languages. Examination of a much wider range of data from a wider range of typologically different languages will reveal whether the system proposed here is sufficient or whether further parameterization is required. Due to the syntactic nature of the system proposed in this monograph, its application to other languages depends largely on the understanding of and assumptions about the syntax of those languages. While the preliminary findings look promising, like any other work of this type, this monograph is subject to the test of time.

References

Adger, D. 2002. Syntax and prosody in Scottish Gaelic. Paper presented at the VSO Workshop, Stuttgart.

—— 2003. Stress and Phasal Syntax. *Linguistic Analysis* 33(3–4): 238–66.

Alboiu, G. 2002. *The Features of Movement in Romanian*. Bucharest University Press.

Alexiadou, A. and E. Anagnostopoulou. 2001. Syntactic adjacency as a condition on phases. Paper presented at GLOW 24, Braga, Portugal.

Androutsopoulou, A. 1997. Split-DPs, focus and scrambling in Modern Greek. *Proceedings of WCCFL* 16: 1–16.

Aoun, J. and Y.-H. A. Li. 1989. Scope and constituency. *Linguistic Inquiry* 20: 141–72.

Arregi, K. 2003. Nuclear stress and syntactic structures. Paper presented at the 1st North American Syntax Conference, Concordia University.

Baker, M. 1996. *The Polysynthesis Parameter*. Oxford: Oxford University Press.

Baltazani, M. 2002. Quantifier scope and the role of intonation in Greek. Doctoral dissertation, UCLA.

Barbiers, S. 1995. The syntax of interpretation. Doctoral dissertation, University of Leiden.

Barss, A. and H. Lasnik. 1986. A note on anaphora and double objects. *Linguistic Inquiry* 17: 347–54.

Belletti, A. 2001. Inversion as focalization. In A. Hulk and J. Y. Pollock, eds., *Subject Inversion in Romance and the Theory of Universal Grammar*. Oxford: Oxford University Press, 60–90.

—— 2002. Aspects of the low IP area. In L. Rizzi, ed., *The Structure of IP and CP: the Cartography of Syntactic Structures 2*. Oxford: Oxford University Press, 16–52.

Benincà, P. and C. Poletto. In press. Topic, focus and V2: defining the CP sublayers. In A. Belletti and L. Rizzi, eds., *Proceedings of the Workshop on the Cartography of Syntactic Positions and Semantic types*. Certosa di Pontignano, November 1999.

Boeckx, C. and N. Hornstein. 2004. Movement under control. *Linguistic Inquiry* 35: 431–52.

Bolinger, D. 1958. A theory of pitch accent in English. *Word* 14: 109–49.

—— 1961. Ambiguities in pitch accent. *Word* 17: 309–17.

—— 1972. Accent is predictable (if you're a mind reader). *Language* 48: 633–44.

Bonet, E. 1990. Subjects in Catalan. *MIT Working Papers in Linguistics* 13: 1–26.

Borer, H. 1994. The projection of arguments. In E. Benedicto and J. Runner, eds., *University of Massachusetts Occasional Papers in Linguistics 17: Functional Projections*. GSLA, University of Massachusetts, Amherst.

Bošković, Ž. 1997. Superiority effects with multiple wh-fronting in Serbo-Croatian. *Lingua* 102: 1–20.

Bresnan, J. 1971. Sentence stress and syntactic transformations. *Language* 47(2): 257–81.

———— 1972. Stress and syntax: a reply. *Language* 48(2): 326–42.

Brody, M. 1997. Mirror theory. MS., University College London.

Browning, M. A. and E. Karimi. 1994. Scrambling to object position in Persian. In N. Corver and H. van Riemsdijk, eds., *Studies in Scrambling*. Berlin: Mouton de Gruyter, 61–100.

Brunetti, L. 2003. A unification of focus. Doctoral dissertation, University of Florence.

Büring, D. 1997. The Meaning of Topic and Focus–the 59th Street Bridge Accent. London: Routledge.

Burzio, L. 1986. *Italian Syntax: a Government-Binding approach*. Dordrecht: Reidel.

Butler, J. 2003. Phase structure is event structure. Paper presented at the "Phases and the EPP" workshop, MIT.

Carlson, G. 1977. Reference to kinds in English. Doctoral dissertation, University of Massachusetts, Amherst.

Chafe, W. 1973. Language and memory. *Language* 49: 261–81.

———— 1976. Givenness, contrastiveness, definiteness, subjects, topics, and points of view. In C. Li, ed., *Subject and Topic*. New York: Academic Press, 25–56.

Chomsky, N. 1971. Deep structure, surface structure and semantic interpretation. In D. Steinberg and L. Jakobovits, eds., *Semantics: an Interdisciplinary Reader in Philosophy, Linguistics and Psychology*. Cambridge: Cambridge University Press, 183–216.

———— 1976. Conditions on rules of grammar. *Linguistic Analysis* 2: 303–51.

———— 1981. *Lectures on Government and Binding*. Dordrecht: Foris.

———— 1993. A minimalist program for linguistic theory. In K. Hale and S. Keyser, eds., *The View from Building 20: Essays in Linguistics in Honor of Sylvain Bromberger*. Cambridge: MIT Press, 1–52.

———— 1995. *The Minimalist Program*. Cambridge: MIT Press.

———— 2000. Minimalist inquiries: the framework. In R. Martin, D. Michaels, and J. Uriagereka, eds., *Step by Step: Essays on Minimalist Syntax in Honor of Howard Lasnik*. Cambridge: MIT Press, 89–155.

———— 2001. Derivation by phase. In M. Kenstowicz, ed., *Ken Hale: A Life in Language*. Cambridge: MIT Press, 1–52.

———— and M. Halle. 1968. *The Sound Pattern of English*. New York: Harper and Row.

———— and H. Lasnik. 1977. Filters and control. *Linguistic Inquiry* 8: 425–504.

Cinque, G. 1990. Ergative adjectives and the Lexicalist Hypothesis. *Natural Language and Linguistic Theory* 8: 1–40.

———— 1993. A null theory of phrase and compound stress. *Linguistic Inquiry* 24: 239–97.

———— 1996. The antisymmetric programme: theoretical and typological implications. *Journal of Linguistics* 32: 447–64.

———— 1999. *Adverbs and Functional Heads: a Cross-linguistic Perspective*. New York: Oxford University Press.

———— 2000. On Greenberg's Universal 20 and the Semitic DP. *The University of Venice Working Papers in Linguistics* 10(2): 45–61.

Cinque, G. 2002. Complement and adverbial PPs: implications for clause structure. Paper presented at CONSOLE XI. Universit di Padova.

—— 2004. Issues in adverbial syntax. *Lingua* 114: 683–710.

Collins, C. 2002. Eliminating labels. In S. Epstein and D. Seely, eds., *Derivation and explanation in the Minimalist Program*. Oxford: Blackwell, 42–64.

Contréras, H. 1976. *A Theory of Word Order with Special Reference to Spanish*. Amsterdam: North-Holland.

Cooper, W. E. and J. Paccia-Cooper. 1980. *Syntax and Speech*. Cambridge: Harvard University Press.

Corver, N. 1990. The syntax of left branch extraction. Doctoral dissertation, University of Tilburg.

Cowper, E. and D. C. Hall. 2001. Overriding the phase. Paper presented at the Canadian Linguistic Association annual meeting, Quebec.

Culicover, P. and M. Rochemont. 1983. Stress and focus in English. *Language* 59: 123–165.

Dabir-Moghaddam, M. 1982. Passives in Persian. *Studies in the Linguistic Sciences* 12(1): 63–90.

—— 1992. On the (in)dependence of syntax and pragmatics: evidence from the postposition *-rā* in Persian. In D. Stein, ed., *Cooperating with Written Texts: the Pragmatics and Comprehension of Written Texts*. Berlin: Mouton de Gruyter, 549–73.

Daneš, F. 1967. Order of elements and sentence intonation. *To Honour Roman Jakobson: Essays on the Occasion of his Seventieth Birthday*. The Hague: Mouton, 400–512.

Dezsö, L. 1974. Topics in syntactic typology. In M. Romportl, V. Skalicka, L. Popela, and B. Palek, eds., *Linguistica Generalia*. Vol. 1: Studies in Linguistic Typology. Prague: Charles University, 191–210.

—— 1977. Toward a typology of theme and rheme: SOV languages. In M.-E. Conte, A. Ramat, and P. Ramat, eds., *Wortstellung und Bedeutung*. Tübingen: Niemeyer, 3–11.

Dezsö, L. 1982. *Studies in Syntactic Typology and Contrastive Grammar*. The Hague: Mouton.

Diesing, M. 1992. *Indefinites*. Cambridge: MIT Press.

Dikken, M. den. 2003. On the morphosyntax of wh-movement. In C. Boeckx and K. Grohmann, eds., *Multiple wh-fronting*. Linguistics Today 64. Amsterdam: John Benjamins, 77–98.

Dixon, R. M. W. 1977a. *A Grammar of Yidiɲ*. Cambridge: Cambridge University Press.

—— 1977b. Some phonological rules of Yidiɲ. *Linguistic Inquiry* 8: 1–34.

Domínguez, L. 2004. Intonation and word order in focus constructions in Spanish. Paper presented at the Linguistic Society of America annual meeting, Boston.

Donati, C., and M. Nespor. 2003. From focus to syntax. In A. Goskel and S. Ozsoy, eds., *Lingua* 113: 1119–42.

Donegan, P. and D. Stampe. 1983. Rhythm and the holistic organization of language structure. In *The Interplay of Phonology, Morphology and Syntax*. Chicago: Chicago Linguistic Society, University of Chicago, 337–353.

Enç, M. 1991. The semantics of specificity. *Linguistic Inquiry* 22: 1–25.

Ernst, T. 2001. *The Syntax of Adjuncts*. Cambridge: Cambridge University Press.

Erteschik-Shir, Nomi. 1998. The syntax-focus structure interface. In P. Culicover and L. McNally, eds., *The Limits of Syntax. Syntax and Semantics*, vol. 29: 211–40.

Everaert, M. 1992. Auxiliary selection in idiomatic constructions. Ms., Utrecht University, Utrecht, the Netherlands.

Frascarelli, M. 2000. *The Syntax-Phonology Interface in Focus and Topic Constructions in Italian*. Dordrecht: Kluwer.

—— In press. L'interpretazione del focus e la portata degli operatori sintattici. In *Atti del Convegno Nazionale Il Parlato Italiano*.

Frota, S. 1995. On the prosody of intonation of focus in European Portuguese. Ms., University of Lisbon.

Ghomeshi, J. 1996. Projection and inflection: a study of Persian phrase structure. Doctoral dissertation, University of Toronto.

Godjevac, S. 2000. Intonation, word order, and focus projection in Serbo-Croatian. Doctoral dissertation, Ohio State University.

Grice, M., M. D'Imperio, M. Savino, and C. Avesani. 2004. Strategies for intonation labelling across varieties of Italian. In S.-A. Jun, ed., *Prosodic Typology*. Oxford: Oxford University Press, 629–83.

Grimshaw, J. 1987. Unaccusatives—an overview. In J. McDonough and B. Plunkett, eds., *Proceedings of NELS* 17. GLSA, University of Massachusetts, Amherst, 244–59.

Grohmann, K. 2003. *Prolific Domains: on the Anti-locality of Movement Dependencies*. Amsterdam: John Benjamins.

Gussenhoven, C. 1984. *On the Grammar and Semantics of Sentence Accents*. Dordrecht: Foris.

—— 1992. Sentence accents and argument structure. In I. M. Roca, ed., *Thematic Structure: its Role in Grammar*. Berlin and New York: Foris, 79–106.

—— and S. J. Keyser. 1993. On argument structure and the lexical representation of syntactic relations. In K. Hale and S. Keyser, eds., *The View from Building 20: Essays in Linguistics in Honor of Sylvain Bromberger*. Cambridge: MIT Press.

—— and J.-R. Vergnaud. 1987. *An Essay on Stress*. Cambridge: MIT Press.

Halliday, M. A. K. 1967. Notes on transitivity and theme in English (part II). *Journal of Linguistics* 3: 199–244.

—— and R. Hasan. 1976. *Cohesion in English*. London: Longman.

Harley, H. 1995. Subjects, events and licensing. Doctoral dissertation, MIT.

Hayes, B. 1989. The prosodic hierarchy in meter. In P. Kiparsky and G. Youmans, eds., *Rhythm and Meter*. Orlando: Academic Press, 201–60.

—— 1995. *Metrical Stress Theory: Principles and Case Studies*. Chicago: University of Chicago Press.

Hayes, B. and A. Lahiri. 1991. Bengali Intonational Phonology. *Natural Language and Linguistic Theory* 9: 47–96.

Holmberg, A. 1986. Word order and syntactic features in the Scandinavian languages. Doctoral dissertation, University of Stockholm.

Hoop, H. de. 1996. *Case Configuration and Noun Phrase Interpretation*. New York: Garland Publishing.

Hornstein, N. 2001. *Move! A Minimalist Theory of Construal*. Oxford: Blackwell.

Horvath, J. 1986. *Focus in the Theory of Grammar and the Syntax of Hungarian*. Dordrecht: Foris.

Hsiao, F. 2002. Tonal domains are stress domains in Taiwanese: evidence from focus. *MIT Working Papers in Linguistics* 42: 109–40.

Hyman, L. M. and J. R. Watters. 1984. Auxiliary focus. *Studies in African Linguistics* 15: 233–73.

Irurtzun, A. 2003. The intonational phonology of Errenteria Basque. Paper presented at the 1st Phonetics and Phonology in Iberia Conference, Lisbon.

Jackendoff, R. 1972. *Semantic Interpretation in Generative Grammar*. Cambridge: MIT Press.

—— 1997. *The Architecture of the Language Faculty*. Cambridge: MIT Press.

—— 2002. *Foundations of Language*. Oxford: Oxford University Press.

Jacobs, J. 1991. Focus ambiguities. *Journal of Semantics* 8: 1–36.

Jelinek, E. and A. Carnie. 2003. Argument hierarchies and the mapping principle. In A. Carnie, H. Harley, and M Willie, eds., *Formal Approaches to Function*. Amsterdam: John Benjamins, 265–296.

Johnson, K. 1991. Object positions. *Natural Language and Linguistic Theory* 9: 577–636.

Kadmon, N. 2001. *Formal Pragmatics*. Malden, Mass.: Blackwell.

Kahnemuyipour, A. 2001. On wh-questions in Persian. *Canadian Journal of Linguistics* 46(1–2): 41–61.

—— 2003. Syntactic categories and Persian stress. *Natural Language and Linguistic Theory* 21(2): 333–79.

—— and D. Massam. 2006. Patterns in phrasal movement: The Niuean DP. In H.-M. Gärtner, P. Law, and J. Sabel, eds., *Clause Structure and Adjuncts in Austronesian Languages*. Berlin: Mouton de Gruyter, 125–49.

Kaisse, E. 1985. *Connected Speech*. San Diego: Academic Press.

Kálmán, L. 1985. Word order in neutral sentences. In I. Kenesei, ed., *Approaches to Hungarian 1*. Szeged: JATE Press, 13–23.

Karimi, S. 1990. Obliqueness, specificity, and discourse functions: *râ* in Persian. *Linguistic Analysis* 20: 139–191.

—— 1996. Case and specificity: Persian *râ* revisited. *Linguistic Analysis* 26: 174–94.

—— 2003. On object positions, specificity, and scrambling in Persian. In S. Karimi, ed., *Word Order and Scrambling*. London: Blackwell, 91–124.

Karimi-Doostan, M.-R. 1997. Light verb constructions in Persian. Doctoral dissertation, University of Essex.

Kayne, R. S. 1994. *The Antisymmetry of Syntax*. Cambridge, Mass. MIT Press.

Kayne, R. 1998. Overt vs. covert movement. *Syntax* 1: 128–91.

Kenesei, I. 1986. On the logic of word order in Hungarian. In W. Abraham and S. de Meij, eds., *Topic, Focus, and Configurationality*. Amsterdam: John Benjamins, 143–59.

Kidwai, A. 2000. *XP-adjunction in Universal Grammar*. New York: Oxford University Press.

Kim, A. H.-O. 1988. Preverbal focussing and type XXIII languages. In M. Hammond, E. Moravcsik, and J. R. Wirth, eds., *Studies in Syntactic Typology*. Amsterdam: Benjamins, 147–69.

Kiparsky, P. 1966. Über den deutschen Akzent. *Studia Grammatica* 7: 69–98.

Kiss, K. E. 1998. Identificational focus and information focus. *Language* 74: 245–73.

—— 2002. *The Syntax of Hungarian*. Oxford: Oxford University Press.

Koizumi, M. 1995. Phrase structure in Minimalist syntax. Doctoral dissertation, MIT.

Koopman, H. and D. Sportiche. 1991. The position of subjects. *Lingua* 85: 211–58.

Koster, J. 1987. Domains and Dynasties. Dordrecht: Foris.

Kratzer, A. 1991. The representation of focus. In A. von Stechow and D. Wunderlich, eds., *Semantics: an International Handbook of Contemporary Research*. Berlin: Walter de Gruyter, 831–4.

—— 1994. On external arguments. In E. Benedicto and J. Runner, eds., *Occasional Papers in Linguistics* 17. Amherst: GLSA, University of Massachussetts, 103–30.

—— 1995. Stage level and individual level predicates. In G. Carlson and J. Pelletier, eds., *The Generic Book*. Cambridge: Cambridge University Press, 176–223.

—— and L. Selkirk. 2007. Phase theory and prosodic spellout: the case of verbs. *the Linguistic Review* 24: 93–135.

Krifka, M. 1984. Fokus, Topik, syntaktische Struktur und semantische Interpretation. Ms., Universität Tübingen.

Ladd, D. R. 1996. *Intonational Phonology*. New York: Cambridge University Press.

Lakoff, G. 1968. *Pronouns and Reference*. Bloomington: Indiana University Linguistics Club.

—— 1972. The global nature of the nuclear stress rule. *Language* 48(2): 285–303.

Lambrecht, K. 1994. *Information Structure and Sentence form: Topic, Focus and the Mental Representations of Discourse Referents*. New York: Cambridge University Press.

Larson, R. 1988. On the double object construction. *Linguistic Inquiry* 19: 335–91.

—— 1990. Double objects revisited: reply to Jackendoff. *Linguistic Inquiry* 21: 589–632.

Lazard, G. 1992. *A Grammar of Contemporary Persian*. Transl. from French by Shirley Lyons. Costa Mesa, Cal: Mazda Publishers.

Legate. J. A. 2003. Some interface properties of the phase. *Linguistic Inquiry* 34(3): 506–16.

Levin, B. and M. Rappaport Hovav. 1986. The formation of adjectival passives. *Linguistic Inquiry* 17: 623–61.

—— and M. Rappaport Hovav. 1988. Non-event -er nominals: a probe into argument structure. *Linguistics* 26: 1067–83.

—— and M. Rappaport Hovav. 1995. *Unaccusativity at the Syntax-Lexical Semantics Interface*. Cambridge, Mass.: MIT Press.

Liberman, M. 1975. The intonational system of English. Doctoral dissertation, MIT.

McCarthy, J. and A. Prince. 1993. Generalized alignment. In G. Booij and J. van Marle, eds., *Yearbook of Morphology*. Dordrecht: Kluwer, 79–153.

McGinnis, M. 2001. Phases and the syntax of applicatives. In M. Kim and U. Strauss eds., *Proceedings of NELS*, vol. 31. Amherst, Mass.: GLSA.

Mahajan, A. 1990. The A/A-bar distinction and movement theory. Doctoral dissertation, MIT.

Manzini, M. R. 1995. Adjuncts and the theory of phrase structure. Ms., University of Florence.

Marácz, L. 1989. Asymmetries in Hungarian. Doctoral dissertation, University of Groningen.

Megerdoomian, K. 2001. Event structure and complex predicates in Persian. *Canadian Journal of Linguistics* 46(1–2): 97–125.

—— 2002. Beyond words and phrases: a unified theory of predicate composition. Doctoral dissertation, University of Southern California.

—— 2007. The auxiliary clitic and sentential stress in Eastern Armenian. Paper presented at GURT 2007, Georgetown University: Washington, D.C.

Moltmann, F. 1989. Adjectives and argument structure in German. Ms., MIT.

Moyne, J. A. 1974. The so-called passive in Persian. *Foundations of Language* 12: 249–67.

Ndayiragije, J. 1999. Checking economy. *Linguistic Inquiry* 30: 399–444.

Neeleman, A. and T. Reinhart. 1998. Scrambling and the PF interface. In M. Butt and W. Geuder, eds., *The Projection of Arguments: Lexical and Compositional Factors*. Stanford: CSLI Publications, 309–53.

Nespor, M. 1999. Stress domains. In H. van der Hulst, ed., *Word Prosodic Systems in the Languages of Europe*. Berlin: Mouton de Gruyter, 117–59.

—— and I. Vogel. 1982. Prosodic domains of external sandhi rules. In H. van der Hulst and N. Smith, eds., *The Structure of Phonological Representations*, Part I. Dordrecht: Foris, 225–55.

—— —— 1986. *Prosodic Phonology*. Dordrecht: Foris.

—— —— 1989. On clashes and lapses. *Phonology* 6(1): 69–116.

Newman, S. S. 1946. On the stress system of English. *Word* 2: 171–87.

Nilsen, Ø. 2000. *The Syntax of Circumstantial Adverbials*. Oslu: Novus.

Odden, D. 1984. Formal correlates of focusing in Kimatuumbi. *Studies in African Linguistics* 15: 275–99.

—— 1987. Kimatuumbi Phrasal Phonology. *Phonology Yearbook* 4: 13–26.

—— 1990. Syntax, lexical rules and postlexical rules in Kimatuumbi. In S. Inkelas and D. Zec, eds., *The Phonology-Syntax Connection*. Chicago: Chicago University Press, 259–77.

Paul, H. 1970 (1888). *Principien der Sprachgeschichte/Principles of the History of Language*. Trans. by H. A. Strong. College Park: McGrath Publishing Co.

Pearce, E. 2002. DP structure and DP movement in Maori. Paper presented at COOL5, University of Canberra, Australia. Ms., Victoria University of Wellington: New Zealand.

Peperkamp, S. 1997. *Prosodic Words*. The Hague: Holland Academic Graphics.

Perlmutter, D. 1978. Impersonal passives and the unaccusative hypothesis. In *Proceedings of the 4th Annual Meeting of Berkeley Linguistics Society* 157–89.

Pesetsky, D. 1995. *Zero Syntax: Experiencers and Cascades*. Cambridge, Mass.: MIT Press.

—— and E. Torrego. 2001. T-to-C movement: causes and consequences. In M. Kenntowicz, ed., *Ken Hale: A Life in Language*. Cambridge: MIT Press, 355–426.

Pinto, M. 1994. Subjects in Italian: distribution and interpretation. In R. Bok-Bennema and C. Cremers, eds., *Linguistics in the Netherlands*. Amsterdam: John Benjamins, 175–86.

Pollock, J.-Y. 1989. Verb movement, universal grammar and the structure of IP. *Linguistic Inquiry* 20: 365–424.

—— 1997. Notes on clause structure. In L. Haegeman, ed., *Elements of Grammar*. Dordrecht: Kluwer, 237–79.

Prince, A. and P. Smolensky. 1993. Optimality: constraint interaction in generative grammar. Technical Report 2, Rutgers Center for Cognitive Sciences.

Rackowski, A. and L. Travis. 2000. V-initial languages: X or XP movement and adverb placement. In A. Carnie and E. Guilfoyle, eds., *The Syntax of Verb Initial Languages*. Oxford: Oxford University Press, 117–41.

Reinhart, T. 1983. *Anaphora and Semantic Interpretation*. London: Croom Helm.

—— 1995. Interface strategies. *OTS Working Papers in Linguistics*, Utrecht University: Utrecht.

—— 1996. Interface economy: focus and markedness. In C. Wilder, H. M. Gaertner and M. Bierwisch, eds., *The Role of Economy Principles in Linguistic Theory*. Berlin: Akademie Verlag, 146–69.

Richards, N. 2002. Very local A′ movement in a root-first derivation. In S. Epstein and D. Seely, eds., *Derivation and Explanation in the Minimalist Program*. Blackwell, 227–48.

Ritter, E. and S. T. Rosen. 2001. The interpretive value of object splits. *Language Sciences* 23: 425–51.

Rizzi, L. 1997. The fine structure of the left periphery. In L. Haegeman, ed., *Elements of Grammar: Handbook in Generative Syntax*. Dordrecht: Kluwer, 281–337.

—— and L. M. Savoia. 1992. Conditions on/u/propagation in Southern Italian dialects: a locality parameter for phonosyntactic processes. In A. Belletti, ed., *Syntactic Theory and the Dialects of Italy*. Turin: Rosenberg and Sellier, 252–318.

Rochemont, M. 1986. *Focus in Generative Grammar*. Amsterdam: John Benjamins.

—— 1998. Phonological focus and structural focus. In P. Culicover and L. McNally, eds., *The Limits of Syntax. Syntax and Semantics*, vol. 29: 337–63.

Rooth, M. 1985. Association with Focus. Doctoral dissertation, University of Massachusetts: Amherst.

—— 1992. A theory of focus interpretation. *Natural Language Semantics* 1: 75–116.

—— 1995. Focus. In S. Lapin, ed., *The Handbook of Semantic Theory*. Cambridge: Blackwell, 271–97.

Samek-Lodovici, V. 2005. Prosody-syntax interaction in the expression of Focus. *Natural Language and Linguistic Theory* 23: 687–755.

Schauber, E. 1978. Focus and presupposition: a comparison of English intonation and Navajo particle placement. In D. J. Napoli, ed., *Elements of Tone, Stress and Intonation*. Washington D.C.: Georgetown University Press, 144–73.

Schmerling, S. 1976. *Aspects of English Sentence Stress*. Austin: University of Texas Press.

Schwarzschild, R. 1999. Givenness, Avoid-F and other constraints on the placement of accent. *Natural Language Semantics* 7: 141–77.

Seidl, A. 2001. Minimal indirect reference: a theory of the syntax-phonology interface. *Outstanding Dissertations in Linguistics*. New York: Routlege.

Selkirk, E. 1980a. Prosodic domains in phonology: Sanskrit revisited. In M. Aronof and M.-L. Kean, eds., *Juncture*. Saratoga, Cal.: Anma Libri, 107–29.

——— 1980b. The role of prosodic categories in English word stress. *Linguistic Inquiry* 11: 563–605.

——— 1981. On prosodic structure and its relation to syntactic structure. In T. Fretheim, ed., *Nordic Prosody II*. Trondheim: Tapir, 111–40.

——— 1984. *Phonology and Syntax: the Relation between Sound and Structure*. Cambridge, Mass.: MIT Press.

——— 1986. On derived domains in sentence phonology. *Phonology Yearbook* 3: 371–405.

——— 1995. Sentence prosody: intonation, stress and phrasing. In J. A. Goldsmith, ed., *The Handbook of Phonological Theory*. Oxford: Blackwell, 550–69.

——— 2002. Contrastive FOCUS vs. presentational focus: prosodic evidence from right node raising in English. Paper presented at Speech Prosody 2002, Aix-en-Provence, France.

Shlonsky, U. 2004. The form of Semitic nominals. *Lingua* 114(12): 1465–1526.

Sportiche, D. 2003. Reconstruction, binding and scope. Ms., UCLA.

Stechow, A. von and S. Uhmann. 1984. *On the Focus–Pitch Accent Relation*. Groninger Arbeiten zur germanistischen Linguistik 25: 223–263.

Stjepanović, S. 1999. What do second position cliticization, scrambling, and multiple wh-fronting have in common? Doctoral dissertation, University of Connecticut.

Stroik, T. 1990. Adverbs as V-sisters. *Linguistic Inquiry* 21: 654–61.

Stump, G. 1985. *The Semantic Variability of Absolute Construction*. Dordrecht: Reidel.

Suñer, M. 1982. *Syntax and Semantics of Spanish Presentational Sentence Types*. Washington, D.C.: Georgetown University Press.

——— 2000. Object-shift: comparing a Romance language to Germanic. *Probus* 12(2): 261–89.

Svenonius, P. 2001. Case and event structure. In N. Zhang, ed., *ZAS Working Papers* 26. Berlin: ZAS.

——— 2002. Case is uninterpretable aspect. Proceedings of the "Perspectives on Aspect" workshop, Utrecht.

Szendrői, K. 2003. A stress-based approach to the syntax of Hungarian focus. *The Linguistic Review* 20: 37–78.

Tamrazian, A. 1994. The syntax of Armenian: chains and the auxiliary. Doctoral dissertation, University College London.

Tancredi, C. D. 1992. Deletion, deaccenting, and presupposition. Doctoral dissertation, MIT.

Tenny, C. 1994. *Aspectual Roles and the Syntax-Semantics Interface*. Dordrecht: Kluwer.

Toman, J. 1986. A (word-)syntax for participles. *Linguistische Berichte* 105: 367–408.

Travis, L. 1988. The syntax of adverbs. *McGill Working Papers in Linguistics. Special issue on Comparative Germanic Syntax* 280–310.

——1991. Derived objects, inner aspect and the structure of VP. In *Proceedings of the North Eastern Linguistics Society* (NELS) 22. Amherst: University of Massachusetts, GLSA.

——1992. Inner aspect and the structure of vP. *Cahier Linguistique de UQAM* 1: 132–46.

Truckenbrodt, H. 1995. Phonological phrases: their relation to syntax, focus and prominence. Doctoral dissertation, MIT.

Tuller, L. 1992. The syntax of postverbal focus constructions in Chadic. *Natural Language and Linguistic Theory* 10: 303–34.

Uriagereka, J. 1999. Multiple spell-out. In S. D. Epstein and N. Hornstein, eds., *Working Minimalism*. Cambridge: MIT Press.

Vahedi-Langrudi, M.-M. 1999. Passive with *šod-an* in Persian: a lexical and syntactic analysis. Paper presented at the 26th annual meeting of the Linguistic Society of Canada and the United States (LACUS), Edmonton, Canada.

Välimaa-Blum, R. 1993. Intonation: a distinctive parameter in grammatical constructions. *Phonetica* 50: 124–37.

Vallduví, E. 1992. *The Informational Component*. New York: Garland Press.

——and E. Engdahl. 1996. The linguistic realisation of information packaging. *Linguistics* 34: 459–519.

Wagner, M. 2002. Configurational stress in derivatives, compounds and phrases. Ms., MIT.

——2003. Linear order and phonological domains. Paper presented at the "Phases and the EPP" workshop, MIT.

——2005. Prosody and recursion. Doctoral dissertation, MIT.

Watters, J. R. 1979. Focus in Aghem. *Southern California Occasional Papers in Linguistics* 7: 137–98.

Webelhuth, G. 1992. *Principles and Parameters of Syntactic Saturation*. Oxford: Oxford University Press.

Winkler, S. and E. Göbbel. 2002. Focus, p-movement, and the nuclear-stress rule: a view from Germanic and Romance (Review of Zubizarreta 1998). *Linguistics: An Interdisciplinary Journal of the Language Sciences* 40(6): 1185–1242.

Wurmbrand, S. 2003. Syntactic vs. post-syntactic movement. Paper presented at the Canadian Linguistic Association annual meeting, Halifax.

Xu, L. 2004. Manifestation of informational focus. *Lingua* 114(3): 277–99.

Zubizarreta, M. L. 1998. *Prosody, Focus, and Word Order*. Cambridge, Mass.: MIT Press.

Index

OXFORD STUDIES IN THEORETICAL LINGUISTICS

PUBLISHED